Successful Programs for Fitness and Health Clubs

101 Profitable Ideas

Sandy Coffman

Human Kinetics

Library of Congress Cataloging-in-Publication Data

Coffman, Sandy, 1942-
Successful programs for fitness and health clubs : 101 profitable ideas / Sandy Coffman.
   p. cm.
Includes index.
ISBN-13: 978-0-7360-5974-9 (soft cover)
ISBN-10: 0-7360-5974-1 (soft cover)
1. Physical fitness centers--Management. 2. Physical fitness centers--Marketing. I. Title.
GV428.5.C64 2007
796.06'8--dc22

                    2007000689

ISBN-10: 0-7360-5974-1
ISBN-13: 978-0-7360-5974-9

The Web addresses cited in this text were current as of April 2007, unless otherwise noted.

Acquisitions Editor: Michael S. Bahrke, PhD; **Developmental Editor:** Amanda S. Ewing; **Assistant Editors:** Maureen Eckstein and Carla Zych; **Copyeditor:** Julie Anderson; **Proofreader:** Erin Cler; **Indexer:** Betty Frizzéll; **Permission Manager:** Carly Breeding; **Graphic Designer:** Robert Reuther; **Graphic Artist:** Kathleen Boudreau-Fuoss; **Cover Designer:** Robert Reuther; **Photographer (cover):** Sandy Coffman; **Photo Asset Manager:** Laura Fitch; **Photo Office Assistant:** Jason Allen; **Art Manager:** Kelly Hendren; **Illustrator:** Al Wilborn; **Printer:** Versa Press

Printed in the United States of America   10   9   8   7   6   5   4   3   2   1

Human Kinetics
Web site: www.HumanKinetics.com

United States: Human Kinetics
P.O. Box 5076, Champaign, IL 61825-5076
800-747-4457
e-mail: humank@hkusa.com

Canada: Human Kinetics
475 Devonshire Road Unit 100, Windsor, ON N8Y 2L5
800-465-7301 (in Canada only)
e-mail: orders@hkcanada.com

Europe: Human Kinetics
107 Bradford Road, Stanningley, Leeds LS28 6AT, United Kingdom
+44 (0) 113 255 5665
e-mail: hk@hkeurope.com

Australia: Human Kinetics
57A Price Avenue, Lower Mitcham, South Australia 5062
08 8372 0999
e-mail: info@hkaustralia.com

New Zealand: Human Kinetics
Division of Sports Distributors NZ Ltd.
P.O. Box 300 226 Albany, North Shore City, Auckland
0064 9 448 1207
e-mail: info@humankinetics.co.nz

I dedicate this book to my husband, Bud,
who has encouraged me to teach others
what I love and do best.
He has been my biggest fan and best critic,
and his guidance and support are never ending.
I am so very thankful and appreciative
of him and my career.
It's been a wonderful journey.

Contents

PART I Programming Overview   1

1 Programming and Retention 3

What are the five steps to programming success? What about the 10 keys to retention? This chapter will answer these questions and show you the steps your members must go through to be fully retained.

2 Hiring and Training the Right People 15

Good employees need more than a degree and certification. They need to have a good personality and a willingness to improve their communication skills. This chapter shows you whom to hire and how to train them to improve their professional communication.

3 Program Director 35

Does your facility need a program director? You bet! This chapter shows you the role of the program director, looks at the four types of members the program director needs to know about, and shows you how to complete a program study analysis.

4 Promotions. 49

Your customers need to know about your programs—promotion is the key! This chapter looks at the internal and external promotions you can do to make sure everyone knows what's happening at your facility.

5 Niche Marketing. 57

Every member is different and looking for something unique out of his or her experience at your facility. This chapter identifies the different niche markets and how to tailor your programming to each market. It also looks at niche markets throughout the day and year.

PART II   Portfolio *Programs and Programming Ideas*   65

Program Finder

This program finder lists in alphabetical order all of the programs and programming ideas presented in this book. Use this finder to locate programs based on the type of program (court sport, fitness center, and so on) or type of member (new member, women only, children and youth, and so on).

While the programs in this book are presented for a particular group, that doesn't mean the programs can't be modified to work just as well with another group. Be creative! Check out the programs presented here and use them as a springboard for other ideas. With a little creativity, any program can be adapted to work with any group.

Program title	Court sport	Fitness center	Aquatics	Group exercise	New member	Introductory program	One-day event	Women only	Children and teens	Baby boomers	Specialty programs	Page
12 Days of Fitness					✓			✓			✓	178
20/20 Women's Life-Changing Club								✓			✓	187
Abs and Stretch		✓		✓	✓					✓		110
Aerobic Championships		✓		✓			✓				✓	124
Aqua Cardio Sculpt			✓									141
Aqua Circuit Training			✓									140
Aqua Kick			✓									141
Aquacize			✓			✓						140
Arthritis Foundation Aquatic Program			✓							✓		.141
Balance Your Fall		✓			✓							102
Birthday Parties							✓		✓			167
Bodyattack		✓		✓								137
Bodybalance		✓		✓								137
Bodycombat		✓		✓								138
Bodyjam		✓		✓								138
Bodypump		✓		✓								137
Bodystep		✓		✓								137
Bodyvive		✓		✓								138
Breathe and Stretch				✓	✓	✓				✓		111
Bronze-Level Youth Swimming			✓						✓			143
Children's and Junior Swim Programs			✓						✓			142
Circuit Training Classes		✓			✓							97
Congratulations!	✓	✓	✓	✓	✓	✓	✓	✓	✓	✓	✓	105
Core Cardio Programs		✓			✓	✓				✓		88
Corporate Membership Programs	✓	✓	✓	✓	✓	✓					✓	109
Cruisin' Campaign		✓			✓						✓	185
Dancing Like the Stars				✓						✓	✓	123

(continued)

(continued)

Items on CD-ROM

Foreword

This is a book about programming for health and athletic clubs. It is written by a person whom every veteran in the health and athletic club industry acknowledges to be the foremost expert on this subject. But I would go further than that. I would say that no one understands or can articulate the heart and soul (I use those words advisedly) of the health and athletic club industry better than the author of this book.

The reason for this is simple. For Sandy Coffman, successful programming is an art that serves a deeper and more profound function. For her, programming is a tool to turn "outsiders" into "insiders." For her, programming is an expression of hospitality. It is a means—and she would argue that it is the optimal means—of making health club members feel appreciated, recognized, accepted, and cared for. Above all, it is a means of bringing enjoyment and camaraderie into the experience of being a health club member.

The great philosopher of running, the late Dr. George Sheehan, said, "No one can continue for long to do anything, no matter how good it is for them, unless it is fun, unless it is enjoyable, unless it is social." This applies to running. It applies to exercise. It applies to membership in any health or athletic club. Unless the experience of being a health club member is fun, enjoyable, and social, no one will for long continue to be a member.

For Sandy Coffman, programming is fundamental to membership retention—and every experienced club owner would agree with her. It is fundamental to developing a happy, energized, and enthusiastic membership. Without outstanding programming, a so-called health club is merely a storehouse for fitness equipment.

But let me go one step further. For although this book is about programming, it is even more about *programmers*. It is about the men and women who provide the programming. On this subject, Sandy Coffman takes no prisoners. For her, if the people running the programs are not hospitable and welcoming, if they are not upbeat and enthusiastic, if they do not take the time to recognize and show their appreciation to every single person in their classes, then they are simply not fulfilling the function as it was meant to be fulfilled.

Truly great programmers are the pied pipers of their clubs. They breathe life and spirit into all that they do. People leave their classes feeling uplifted, encouraged, motivated, and inspired. Their entire message to every person in their programs is not only "you can do it" but also "this is fun."

I have watched Sandy Coffman instruct programmers on how to provide programs for eight-year-olds and for 80-year-olds. I have never left one of her sessions without feeling more joyful, more energetic, and more lighthearted.

Sandy Coffman is, in short, this industry's ultimate ambassador to all who would be fit and to all who would exercise if only it were fun. If Sandy Coffman's message is taken to heart, the health club industry in America would not be approaching 50 million members; it would be approaching 100 million members.

It is my privilege to recommend this book to you without reservation or qualification.

John McCarthy
Past executive director
for 25 years of IHRSA

Preface

If you aren't prepared to run a program 100 percent, don't run it at all!

In a short time, the fitness industry has become successful serving people across our planet. Our clubs, large or small, have something that can benefit every man, woman, and child in the world with a healthy environment and a quality lifestyle. And yet, at the writing of this book, there are said to be 90,000,000 inactive people in the United States, and nearly two-thirds of the population is overweight. For the first time in history, children are prone to diabetes and other related diseases attributable to inactivity and obesity; elderly people will live 20 to 30 years longer than anticipated and are in desperate need of physical activity to keep them active, vital, and healthy. There has never been a greater need for quality programming in our industry than now.

Professional, successful programming requires more than just elementary programming ideas. The requirements include teaching skills, communication skills, marketing techniques, and follow-up procedures. Every program must have a purpose, a goal, a plan, a budget, and a result that matches the goal. Every good program must have a checklist of foolproof things to consider that will guarantee success if completed. You must keep track of who is coming to your club, when they are using the club, and whether they stop using the club—so you can invite them back. This will keep them from becoming inactive and eventually dropping out of the club because they aren't using it. Our responsibility in running a professional program is to help members meet other members who have common interests, schedules, and abilities so that they develop a sense of belonging with other people like themselves, while experiencing a sense of commitment, achievement, and purpose. This book will provide you with all the tools you need to run successful programs.

Purpose

The purpose of this book is to present actual turnkey programs created for every department of your facility and for every market segment—adults, families, kids, older adults, women only, the fit, and the unfit. It includes programs in the fitness center, group exercise studios, pools, gyms, and classrooms. You will learn, for example, introductory programs in the fitness center that will get hundreds of new members involved immediately. Each of these programs is designed to make every participant a winner!

This book has instructional programs for beginning, intermediate, and advanced participants, and the menu of programs will cover all court sports as well as group exercise programs. The programs in this book include one-day events, five-day camps, eight-week sessions, seasonal leagues, and ongoing classes. You will also learn about the many educational programs you can offer. You will be able to run nutritional seminars, sport-specific sessions, and lifestyle enhancement programs such as smoking cessation clinics.

Yes, programming affects many facets of our business. Specific programs can fill downtime or non–prime time. Programs designed for specific times can be promoted toward members likely to fill that time. Some of the benefits of professional programming are

- increased participation,
- reduced attrition,
- greater retention,
- more referrals,
- less downtime, and
- improved staff productivity.

This book outlines specific programs for specific times such as holiday programs, summer programs, and spring flings. As you will see, the benefit of this comprehensive book of programming includes marketing, promotional, scheduling, and follow-up techniques as well as the programs themselves. In essence, you will be able to create, implement, and deliver successful programs—guaranteed!

Remember, ours is a service industry! The more service you can provide, the happier your members will be and the more participants you will enroll.

Your club's very existence may depend on how effective you are in developing successful programs for your organization. Good programs are adaptable within fitness clubs and recreation centers. Good programs can be worked, tweaked, and adjusted to fit small clubs, large clubs, independent clubs, chains, franchises, for-profit clubs, not-for-profit organizations, sports clubs, age-related facilities, hospital-based facilities, spas, corporate fitness centers, universities, or community centers. Each of these attracts a different clientele, but the programs are adaptable and the role of managing the programs and the programming staff is the same. The programs in this book have been tried and proven successful all over the world. You will find programs for every niche market, for any facility, and for all activity areas.

But the workout, the sport, the equipment, and the facility aren't the elements that make the business successful; rather, the programs drive the participation, and it's the programmers who create, develop, and implement the programs that generate participation. Retention, the ongoing participation in programs, ultimately improves people's lives physically, mentally, and emotionally. Retention of members builds the club's profitability.

This book is more than a programming manual. It is a tool for owners, managers, teachers, instructors, or anyone who is sincerely interested in helping others succeed.

Organization

A program is more than an idea, and part I is all about outlining what it takes to run successful programs in our clubs, because delivering programs to our members is what keeps us in business. Chapter 1 looks at how you can create successful programs that lead to retention. Programming is not successful unless you can keep your members coming back for more. This chapter shows you how to do that. Chapter 2 looks at the hiring and training processes. Without the right staff, even the best programs won't succeed. Chapter 3 addresses the specific needs of a program director. What is a program director? What is his or her role? Can your facility afford to *not* have a program director? Chapter 4 takes you into promotions: Now that you have the staff and the programs, how do you get your members to participate in those programs? Promotion is the answer, and promotion is related to chapter 5—niche marketing. Finding creative

ways to involve all of your members in your programs can be challenging; this chapter helps you meet the challenge.

Part II gives you the programs—lots of them—for every type of member and every activity department in a club. Chapter 6 introduces programs for court sports. Chapter 7 looks at programs you can conduct in and around your fitness center. Cardio programs, circuit training, and weight training are just a few of the programming areas outlined in this chapter. Chapter 8 moves on to group exercise, which is a great way to involve lots of members at one time and in one place. Chapter 9 takes a look at aquatics programs. Aquatics programs mean more than just lap swimming; this chapter introduces you to many ideas to help you use your aquatics facilities to their full potential. Chapter 10 takes a look at a specific type of member—the baby boomers. Have you fully tapped into this market in your facility? The programs presented in this chapter show you how to target this specific audience to make your facility inviting to members of all ages. Chapter 11 moves to the other end of the age spectrum and focuses on kids' programming. The programming ideas in this chapter will help you encourage lifelong fitness in your youngest customers. Chapter 12 wraps up part II with a focus on specialty programming. These are programs that are run annually, seasonally, or as one-time special events.

It may be tempting to immediately turn to the second half of the book, scan the list of programs that seem new or interesting or perhaps familiar, and start implementing some of the programs in your facility. The programs do work! But without the preparation outlined in the first half of this book, the programs themselves will not guarantee you success.

Remember: A program is more than an idea! If you aren't prepared to run a program 100 percent, don't run it at all!

CD-ROM

To help make your programs even more successful, we've included a CD-ROM with this book. The CD-ROM contains supplemental materials for many of the programs; these include 19 Word documents that you can manipulate to fit your facility, 37 PDF files of scorecards and checklists that you can print out and distribute to your participants, and 6 JPEG files of logos that you can use to create

T-shirts or other incentive prizes. Programs that have supplemental materials are identified with the ⊙ symbol.

Important Terms

Before embarking on putting the programs in place, you need to become familiar with some terms that are used throughout this book.

● **Vision.** Your vision will always be member retention. It's the big picture of your entire business. Our industry is able to serve every man, woman, and child in the whole world in some way, but our main objective is to get people to exercise regularly, safely, and with a positive attitude and a strong commitment. That's a tall order, because for most people exercise is not as much fun as they want it to be, and therefore they quit exercising altogether. Yes, they know it's good for them. Oftentimes a doctor has even recommended a regular exercise program to enhance the health and well-being of an individual, and yet that person will stop exercising within weeks simply because she isn't enjoying it! Some people think that a fitness program is a six-week project: Working out three times a week at a target heart rate should result in losing weight, getting in shape, getting back in shape, or qualifying as a regular exerciser. We know that isn't true. Exercise is definitely a lifestyle, a commitment to health and a quality of life. Fitness can't be stored up, and it is never finished. It must be nurtured, tested, and developed to such a degree that the mind anticipates and prepares for it, the body responds to it, and the spirit enjoys it.

● **Mission.** Our mission is to create program participation. Our mission is what we do daily to accomplish the vision. Creative, fun programming is the answer. People quit using equipment, people quit going to fitness facilities, but people don't quit friendships and fun experiences. Programs are created to turn fitness into fun and to keep members coming back regularly, eager to participate.

● **Tracking.** Tracking a member's activity is often overlooked, but it's a valuable aspect of programming. You must be able to identify all participants and track each individual in terms of attendance and performance. Keeping track of attendance and performance makes each participant feel important and encourages regular activity. It helps the shy, intimidated person to feel more accepted. It helps the new member to feel part of the group. It will help the underachiever to begin enjoying friendly competition and will provide that person with the most competitive venue in which to excel.

● **Retention.** Retention occurs when you have a variety of programs that offer many different experiences and challenges that will keep your members active, fresh, and excited month after month, year after year. Remember, your member will become bored with the same routine, so new experiences are necessary to spark new interests. But new experiences will also mean new challenges and therefore new programs. In essence, exercise is our product, and we package our product in various packages called programs. We must sell many different packages or programs over the course of a year to keep our members committed and returning to the club regularly. Retention means repeat business. Retention means repeat *sales*. Retention will come after a member experiences and enjoys several different programs. It will take approximately six to eight different programs in one year to get your member committed to your club and a lifestyle of health and fitness. It will take six to eight *sales* to give your member a retention program that has the probability of staying with him or her for a lifetime. The sale begins after the sale!

● **Promotion.** Promotion creates the initial interest. Your promotional expertise—what you say and how you deliver the message—may make or break a great campaign. Professional promotions create the initial interest that will drive the success of your marketing plan and will determine the degree of participation in any program you offer. Promotions are created to get an immediate and initial response from anybody who might be interested in that program. People will decide in seconds if they are interested in getting more information or if the idea is appealing or applicable to them. Promotions include bulletin boards, fliers, conversations, and announcements. Successful programs must be created for specific markets. Members will stay committed and retained if they are exercising with other people like themselves. No one joins a club or a program to be a sheep in a flock of 50 or 2,000. Members need to be categorized according to their wants, needs, abilities, and schedules. This is how relationships occur, friendships are formed, and camaraderie abounds. Programs created for target markets are most likely to result in retention.

• **Training.** You may be responsible for hiring and training people to promote and run your programs. This book provides guidelines for making sure that every program is run in a professional manner and achieves the result that is needed to increase sales and retention. Training clearly goes beyond the administration of programs. Employees must be trained in communication skills, sales techniques, promotional strategies, telephone skills, and scheduling techniques, as well as implementation of programs. No training is complete without outlining your expectations of the employee.

• **Accountability.** In the end, the program director, leader, or administrator is held accountable for the results. The more members you program, the more members you will retain. The more members you retain, the more members you will gain through referrals. The more new sales you gain, the better your bottom line.

My Background

I've been fortunate to have been part of the wonderful health and fitness industry for more than 30 years. I've devoted that time to understanding the industry and the people in it and have been committed to programming for participation and enjoyment. I was program director of three racquetball and fitness clubs in Wisconsin with approximately 2,000 members each (now the Wisconsin Athletic Clubs, Milwaukee). I developed introductory programs, instructional programs, one-day events, competitive events, and social programs, all designed around racquetball. These programs resulted in the largest racquetball program in the United States. Especially successful was the women's racquetball program in one location, in which several hundred women played in organized league programs every week and continued to do so for the 11 years I was there and for many years beyond. As the fitness industry grew, I successfully adapted these programs to all the fitness and exercise areas of a multipurpose facility.

I know that I have changed the lives of thousands of people by getting them active through the programs presented here. I wish success to those of you who read this book, and I am confident that this book will enable you to change the lives of millions more.

Acknowledgments

I am grateful to IHRSA, Club Industry, Athletic Business, Can-Fit-Pro, ICAA, USTA, and YMCAs throughout the United States for inviting me to speak at their conferences for more than 25 years. Their continuing support of my company, Programming for Profit, has enabled me to reach thousands of clubs and facilities throughout my career, and through them, I have been able to make a difference.

I thank the individuals and fitness organizations all over the world who have embraced my programs and allowed me to present them in many countries, to all nationalities, and in several languages. I have learned that in our industry, people across the planet share more similarities than differences.

To all those who have sent letters, notes, and e-mails telling me how I have motivated them to become better leaders in our industry—thank you!

I want to acknowledge the people who helped me get my start in the fitness industry, including the women of the West Allis Athletic Club, who first inspired me to create the programs that made fitness fun for them . . . and for me.

PART

I

Programming Overview

Are you tempted to flip immediately to part II—to look at all of the programming ideas and pick the ones you want to implement at your facility? There are a lot to choose from. Perhaps you think the Women on Weights (WOW!) program looks like a great fit for your needs. Maybe you even offer it . . . and it fails. Was it because it's not a good program? No; it's a great program! But it takes more to run a successful program than just offering your participants new activities. Without the proper understanding of what programming is and how it works, you will not be able to implement a successful program.

The information presented in part I is vital if you're going to run successful programs. Remember—a program is more than an idea. It takes careful planning and an understanding of how your facility, your staff, and your clients interact.

Very often we sell memberships or activities in terms of the type of equipment available or the amount of it. Initially, we sell and people buy in terms

of physical characteristics in a facility. Although physical characteristics are important, it is the personality of the club that will keep people coming back. Your active long-term member doesn't measure the value of your club or the value received for each dollar in terms of how much equipment you have. He or she measures it in terms of recognition, relationships, and camaraderie. These are the attributes of programming. You can provide state-of-the-art equipment, a fitness evaluation, and three workout sessions with a fitness instructor, but the majority of members won't commit to coming back on a regular basis. If you take that basic program and add some fun, in the form of contests and recognition for a variety of different achievements, your members will be motivated to exercise more often and with greater enjoyment.

For a program to be successful, you have to have people participate in that program . . . not just once, but repeatedly. Chapter 1 begins with how to create successful programming. You will learn the five steps to programming success, which will help you organize every program professionally and then evaluate each program's effectiveness. You will also become familiar with the 10 keys to developing a successful program. Chapter 1 then moves on to the goal of programming—retention. It introduces the wheel of logical progression, which is a tool that takes a member from his or her first day of membership to the completion of a year's experience of fun and fitness in programs at your club.

Another critical issue affecting the future of programming is, of course, the programmers themselves. Not enough club owners, directors, supervisors, and managers realize how crucial the talent and expertise of the staff are to the success of their programs. If you want to offer creative, high-caliber programs, then you need employees who are well trained and highly motivated. Our fitness programs will continue to be judged on the basis of leadership, recognition, and camaraderie as well as individual results. Group programming with unending service and a constant calendar of events is the answer. And the future success of our programs lies in the quality of the people we hire to develop and run those programs.

Chapter 2 gives you insight into the people who *do* the programming. You will have a better understanding of whom to hire, how to train them, and what to measure as you develop a career as a program director. High energy, enthusiasm, and passion are as important as qualifications, certifications, and skills. Learn how to identify and prioritize these characteristics for your business. Chapter 3 outlines the role and the job description of a program director. This chapter defines communication skills and organizational skills needed by the program director to integrate a new member into a lifestyle of fitness at your club. You will see the complete picture of how the program director brings your market and your business together successfully.

Chapter 4 looks at all the avenues of promotion, both internal and external. From flyers to bulletin boards to picture campaigns, promotions are ongoing responsibilities to ensure successful program participation. Chapter 5 defines all the niches of members in your clubs. Interests, skill levels, schedules, personalities, ages, and genders make up groups of people, or "niches," who find familiarity and enjoyment in one another when participating in programs together. You will find the niches that work best in specific programs and at certain times. These groups of people and the programs they participate in will become clubs within your club.

Together, these first five chapters outline the entire procedure of programming and will help you eliminate 10 of the major problems that all clubs experience:

- Prime-time overflow—This is when too many members use the club at one time.
- Poor attendance—This is when too few members use the club at a certain time of day, week, or year.
- No-shows—Nothing is more disappointing than no-shows. There is an answer!
- Frequent cancellations—Find out why (the real reasons).
- Downtime during the day—Programming can solve this.
- Downtime during the year—Programming can solve this.
- Lack of new participants—You should always be seeing new faces.
- Lack of program growth—Always use one program to promote another.
- Poor profitability—This book is about programming for profit!
- Lack of responsibility or accountability—The leader is you!

Programming and Retention

Customer service and programming are the two key elements in running a successful business in the health, sports, and fitness industry. Programming is our business—big business—because programming is the key to retaining members by keeping them active and committed. In addition, programming provides you with new business. It is common knowledge in the industry that 60 to 80 percent of your new business comes from referrals and word of mouth. Up to 80 percent of your new business can come from the quality of your programs, because people like to go where the action is. So you want to have everyone in your community talking about how much fun they're having at your club and about all the new people they've met through club programs.

Before you can work on retaining your members, you first need to identify and address the needs of various markets. Niche markets and populations are many and varied. Your participants will join your programs and stay active in them if they are participating with other people like themselves, with similar interests, skill levels, schedules, personalities, ages, genders, and lifestyles. Among these subdivisions, all members must be placed in four main groups of people for programming:

- New members
- Active, existing members
- Inactive members
- Potential members

Programs virtually become clubs within clubs, where people develop relationships and commitments to one another as well as to the activities themselves. Once you've identified the needs of your markets, you can start to implement programming ideas. Formulas and systems are available for successful programming that will work for every fitness or recreational activity in our industry.

This chapter begins by looking at the five steps of programming success. If you follow these five steps in setting up your programs, no program should fail. After we look at programming, we take a close look at the main goal of programming—retention. We'll look at the wheel of logical progression, which is a tool that will keep people coming back for more as you move them through a series of programs, beginning with an introduction or orientation phase, continuing with an acceptance phase, and finally moving into a commitment phase. The 10 keys to retention provide a final check to ensure that the program is complete and will lead to retention and growth.

Five Steps of Programming Success

There is no reason for any program to fail. That is a very bold statement to make, but it is true. Some programs may be better than others, of course, but none need to be cancelled or to fail completely.

For nearly every program I have seen that has been considered unsuccessful, failure was not attributable to the program at all. In fact, I think just the opposite—most programs have merit and potential. It's all a matter of how they are presented to the member. After a program was dubbed a failure, I would hear excuses like "The members didn't like it." "The members didn't want it." "No one showed up." "No one signed up." After asking some probing questions about the promotions, marketing efforts, and follow-up procedures, however, I invariably would find that the failure was directly caused by a lack of effort and poor follow-up by the programming staff. Any club that thinks a program need only be presented with a sign-up sheet or an announcement in a newsletter will get very good at finding excuses to explain program failure.

Many club managers and program directors don't really understand how to put together a successful program. For many of them, the programming scenario has sounded something like this: (1) get an idea, (2) put out a sign-up sheet, (3) announce the program in the club newsletter, (4) talk it up, and (5) sit back and hope it flies. Programs that are great ideas will fail with that system. Instead, let's start using a more professional approach, an approach I call the five steps of programming success. The steps to achieve a program that will attract a high level of participation and have a positive effect on your club's retention rate are the following:

1. Define a purpose.
2. Set a goal.
3. Develop a promotional plan.
4. Measure the result.
5. Promote a follow-up program.

Let's take a closer look at each of these steps.

Define a Purpose

Before putting out the sign-up sheet, you must define the purpose of the program. How will it benefit the member? How will it benefit the club (business)? For whom is the program designed? The purpose of a program may be to get new members committed to an eight-week cardio circuit program. They will meet other new members like themselves and will gain stamina, endurance, and satisfaction by completing the program. A staff member will be assigned to track participation, give recognition for performance, and promote the next program. The member will have enjoyed her involvement and gained a sense of belonging, a degree of personal achievement, and confidence to take on a new challenge.

Set a Goal

A program is a club project that directly affects the bottom line, and a smart businessperson doesn't undertake a project without a clear goal .The success of a program will be measured first by the number of participants. What is a realistic number to expect if the program is clearly beneficial to the club and to a specific group of members?

Let's look at a new member cardio circuit program. If a club is selling an average of 50 new memberships per month, it is very reasonable to think that 20 to 30 percent of those members would be good candidates for a cardio circuit program. Conservatively, 20 percent or 10 new members in the last month would enjoy the program and benefit from it. If you consider that new members are *new* for the first three months of membership, new members from the previous two months would be good candidates for this program as well. That would give another 20 potential participants or 30 total for our new member cardio circuit program.

You should always set an attainable goal—one that is easy to reach and possible to surpass. The goal, however, must be reached. In this example, we will set our total goal at 20.

Develop a Promotional Plan

Up until now, the sign-up sheet was the major promotional tool for a program such as our new member cardio circuit program. There are two things to remember about sign-up sheets: They are absolutely necessary and absolutely worthless! A sign-up sheet may be absolutely necessary because it is a good promotional tool—it will create an initial interest in a program. That's good, but it is unlikely to encourage the type of member for whom the program is designed to sign up, and it will not likely entice the number of members needed, as defined in your goals, to make the program a success. The program promotional plan must resemble a marketing plan for new prospects. First, all programmers, trainers, and instructors for the program must be able to verbalize the positives of the program—its features, benefits, and purpose. Second, they must be able to overcome objections such as "I'm too busy," "The program costs too much," and "I don't want to make a commitment right now." Third, a good salesperson must ask for the sale three to five times. Asking may consist of a postcard, an e-mail, and, most important, up to three phone calls delivering a personal invitation to the member. How often do your programmers ask a member to participate in any given program? The sales team is trained to ask a potential member for the sale at least three to five times before closing the sale, and your programmers must do the same thing when asking a member to participate in a program. In this way, the sale begins after the sale.

Measure the Result

If you follow a system of programming by defining a purpose, setting a goal, and developing a promotional plan, you will be able to decisively measure the result. In our new member cardio circuit program, we have now established that the program is good for the member and is designed for a specific member, in this case the new member. We've set our goal and followed our marketing plan. Now we must measure whether the result is good for the club's bottom line:

- 50 new members per month
- 10 of those new members (20%) involved in a new member program such as cardio circuit
- $40 dues per month per member
- 120 new members (10 per month) paying $40 per month for 12 months—$57,600 in annual revenues

Isn't that the result we are all looking for? Yes, of course, but it happens only if all participants com-

plete the program. That again will be the result of constant communication, promotion, and recognition by the programming staff.

The program is only as good as the way it is managed. Active, happy new members in their first year of membership are most likely to bring in 60 to 80 percent of your new business by word-of-mouth referrals. A professionally trained programming staff with a well-planned program calendar should be able to run six to eight different programs, six to eight times per year. Well-managed programs will keep hundreds more members enjoying themselves and using your club regularly.

Promote a Follow-Up Program

Retention doesn't occur automatically after the first six- to eight-week program. If you want your new members to become active club users, then timely, well-designed follow-up programs are crucial. The programming calendar must include activities for everyone—men, women, juniors, seniors, first-time exercisers, and competitive athletes. Professional programming involves leagues, lessons, clinics, contests, classes, seminars, and tournaments—all carefully targeted to different groups of members sharing similar interests that will bond them together in a congenial atmosphere. And each of these programs must be delivered as a new challenge or a new beginning. Always use one program to promote another to keep the retention ball rolling. Diversification in programming will keep members interested.

You should have special events to lure back inactive and former members, recognition programs to keep new members active, competitive programs to keep the dedicated exerciser interested, social programs to get the members involved, and educational programs for those who are misinformed or confused about health and fitness issues. All of this should be done in an environment that's fun and comfortable and should be orchestrated by a leader with good communication skills. Increasingly, the really successful clubs are those that have professional programming—programming with a purpose, a goal, a promotional plan, a result, and a system for continued success and growth.

The true sale begins after the sale of the membership. For example, a variety of entertaining programs can make your club a fun place to be—and fun keeps members coming back. An innovative program calendar will include enough variety to keep every member active in several types of programs throughout the year. The calendar would include the following:

- Introductory programs
- Intermediate and advanced programs
- Programs for all ages, genders, and abilities
- Programs in all activity areas
- Programs in all the time frames of a day, week, or year

Exercise can get boring, and bored people quit exercising. Programs keep exercise fun, interesting, and challenging. Your responsibility is to encourage your members to experience several types of programs in a year that keep their exercise schedule fresh. You must constantly sell them new programs to keep them active.

Retention

Now that you know the steps to successful programming, you can focus on what it takes to retain your members. Whether you are a for-profit or not-for-profit facility, to achieve success you must retain your members, because it costs four to six times more to get a new member than it does to keep an existing one. You will have a higher financial return per member if members are committed to one or more programs; therefore, you must provide as many options (programs) as you can for each participant, member, or prospective member.

A program for retention is a step-by-step plan to take every member in your club from orientation to involvement to commitment. Many clubs scramble to sell enough memberships every month to replace the number of people who are leaving. While that is happening, an equal number of members who joined a few months earlier have already stopped using the club on a regular basis, which is the step before actually quitting. This cycle has been repeated over and over and will continue unless action is taken.

Clearly, the goal of our clubs is to provide opportunity, education, and leadership in a club atmosphere that ensures an ongoing program of activity resulting in fitness, exercise, and health. The operative word is *ongoing*. Unfortunately, working out regularly for three months will not provide the lifetime of fitness that our members need or that we offer. Yet that's the scenario for the majority of the people who joined with the idea of a lifetime commitment to exercise. Most people don't join a club or begin using a facility with the intention of working out alone for years on end. If they had such single-minded dedication, they would have bought a home gym or an exercise bike, and you'd never see them at all. The reality is that most people do own one or more pieces of home equipment already and don't use it! They joined your club or facility because they wanted some ambiance; they are looking for friendships and they need direction, encouragement, and leadership. Buying the membership begins that process and the commitment to programs follows. Each program becomes a club within a club. For example, people will like to meet the same people regularly when they come to the club to exercise. They will tend to talk before or after their workout and will more than likely join other programs together. They will become comfortable with one another and committed to each other as much as to the instructor or activity or class.

Let's look at how we can set up our programming business so that we retain members rather than lose them.

Wheel of Logical Progression

First of all, you must accept that it takes a full year of programming to consider a member to be a retained member. During that year of programming all of the following must occur:

- A member should use your club at least one or two times per week.
- A member should participate in a scheduled program every week.
- A member should participate in a group program with people of similar interests, skill levels, schedules, personalities, ages, and genders. In other words, a member is more likely to become a retained member if he or she forms relationships and friendships along the way.
- A member should use the club or facility on the same day, at the same hour, with the same people, and with an instructor every week.
- A member should feel a commitment or loyalty to one or more of your staff. An instructor, trainer, supervisor, or receptionist who welcomes a member as a returning friend creates loyalty, trust, and a comfortable familiarity—all things that contribute to retention.

• A member should experience more than one and perhaps six to eight programs within the year. After a full year of enjoying the club and its programs regularly, members will have put your facility into their daily or weekly schedule. Exercising in your club will be part of their weekly routine, and they will become retained members of exercise as well as retained members of your club.

How can we track whether a member has reached retention? We can use the wheel of logical progression. The wheel of logical progression is best illustrated by imagining a wheel (see figure 1.1). When people join a club or any exercise program, they will go through three stages of retention within the first year:

1. The integration stage
2. The acceptance stage
3. The commitment stage

As you can see in figure 1.1, these three stages form the outside of the wheel.

The inside of the wheel contains six programming spokes—six levels that lead to retention:

• Introduction
• Instruction
• Involvement
• Achievement
• Improvement
• Fun

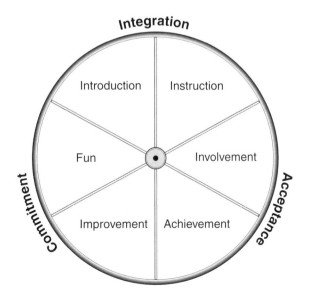

Figure 1.1 Wheel of logical progression.

The three stages of retention and the six programming spokes in the wheel of logical progression fit together like this:

1. Integration stage
   • Introduction
   • Instruction
2. Acceptance stage
   • Involvement
   • Achievement
3. Commitment stage
   • Improvement
   • Fun

This whole system is completely adaptable to any facility, any recreational activity, any fitness program, and participants of any ability or skill level. For example, a person who is new to exercise or sport can begin participation on the wheel of logical progression and continue on. A person who is very experienced, active, and fit, and with an already high level of achievement will find that the wheel offers the exact level of experience necessary for beginning a new type of activity or sport and will move through the progression as slowly or quickly as needed.

You need to actively sell your members at every stage and phase. By structuring your programs and advising your members in accordance with the wheel of logical progression, you gradually elevate your members from one comfort zone to the next.

The wheel is an excellent tool for every program in your club, be it fitness center programs, group exercise classes, or court sports. It will help you complete a program calendar for every activity department and will keep your members active, challenged, comfortable, and constantly moving forward. You always use one program to promote another, and the result is having fun in a club environment—which leads to retention.

Let's take a closer look at the six programming spokes in the wheel of logical progression.

Six Programming Spokes

Members should complete the six programming spokes during their first year of membership or participation to reach full retention. Chances are that you are already doing some of these programming activities. The key is to identify any gaps in your programming system that might cause a member to drop out. You will see where you can fill those gaps with the appropriate programs.

The concept of a gap is important. One of the major mistakes made in the industry is skipping programming spokes, because this will cause lack of achievement, poor performance, or just plain frustration. It's important, for instance, to begin at step one, not step four, and not to skip any steps. The majority of people who drop out of a program or club quit before they ever get started. By that I mean that they don't get started in a program that automatically leads to another level or program, and then another, and so on.

Every program should be designed to promote, encourage, and inspire participation in a follow-up program. This is more likely to occur, of course, if the programs are enjoyable, achievable, and successful.

No doubt, you are beginning to see how the sale begins after the sale. Our definition of *retention* indicates that each programming spoke must be promoted and sold to the participant or member after he or she has bought the membership. Note here how important the role of the program director, instructor, trainer, or leader will be. The program director or leader must be held accountable for selling the idea of progressing through the wheel of logical progression. The program director must be held accountable for keeping the member or participant involved in a program or series of programs throughout the year.

Retention Stage 1: Integration

The integration stage is often called orientation, and basically it gives members a beginning experience, but it must be designed to encourage further participation. Most clubs will have a program or system to introduce members to a new activity or program, but then members are expected to be comfortable being on their own and to call on the leaders when improvement is wanted.

Realizing that the majority of members quit using a club within the first 90 days, most clubs make an effort to set up a system through computers or programs to track member participation for the first three months of membership. But setting up individual workout programs for members does not particularly create a club atmosphere, and it surely doesn't provide enough guidance and encouragement from the leaders or others to continue. New members receive their initial orientation and have a goal-setting session, and then they are essentially thrown into the club and left to fend for themselves. The problem is that these members won't use the facilities very frequently, and eventually they drop their membership. To prevent this, you need to give your members a variety of reasons to keep coming to the club and using it regularly. The integration stage begins that process.

There are two spokes in the integration stage: Introduction and Instruction.

Introduction

The introduction spoke is the most important of all six spokes and usually the most poorly implemented. The biggest mistake made in the introduction program is that instructors typically try to give too much information! Think of the words that are important here—integration, orientation, introduction, a new beginning. They all mean getting new information: learning or trying something for the first time. Do not try to teach too much too soon. There are three objectives for the participant within the introduction phase.

* Develop a new interest—learn something new.
* Have fun—be encouraged and complimented by the leader.
* Experience some degree of success.

The introduction spoke might consist of a one-on-one orientation, an introductory class, a new member party, a beginners' clinic, or some combination of these types of activities. The best advice here is to remember the KISS method—"Keep it simple, Simon." This is definitely not the time to show off, try to impress anyone with an enormous amount of knowledge or expertise, or rattle on with unfamiliar or technical terms. The participant already has your attention and appreciates your knowledge. The goal of the introduction spoke is to create an environment that makes the participant eager to come back and learn more.

The member should feel confident, educated, and accomplished. An introduction program must leave the participants feeling at least somewhat successful. Don't confuse them, don't overwhelm them, but do compliment them and find a reason to applaud their efforts.

Instruction

The instruction spoke introduces the member to goal setting and gets him or her to start using the club, playing the sport, or doing regular exercise. During this spoke you want to establish a specific workout schedule and begin the education process including terminology, safety, correct form, and general dos and don'ts. The two objectives for the participant in the instruction spoke are to learn more and to get better.

The instruction spoke should be more than a one-time clinic, because what we are trying to do is gain retention. We need members to commit to a series of lessons so they will keep coming back to learn more. Four to eight lessons in a series are ideal. Fewer than four doesn't give enough momentum to the series to reach a certain level, and more than eight weeks become redundant and boring. You will find that the dropout rate increases dramatically after eight weeks.

Another great reason for the series of lessons is that in six to eight weeks, the participants feel a sense of belonging that encourages commitment. For instance, if the program is in a group setting, some of the participants will develop relationships or form friendships, which are keys to retention.

At this point we have to consider evaluating the instructor's teaching expertise. The all-important introductory and instruction phases will fail if the instructor does not have rapport with beginners. Instructors must have empathy for beginners and a sincere understanding of their frustrations and fears. The biggest fear, of course, is failure, and this is not the time to let the participant fail or even have the perception of failure.

For example, take an introductory racquetball clinic or a beginning racquetball lesson. The instructor must realize that most members will never progress beyond an intermediate level of achievement. If the instructor happens to be the local or state champion, fine, but being the best player has little to do with being the best teacher. The best player often doesn't have the empathy or the desire to really teach and promote the sport as fun and enjoyable exercise. When encouraged to try to be a superstar, many new participants become disappointed and drop out.

Retention Stage 2: Acceptance

The acceptance stage of the members' year of retention is the second of the three stages. Members have gone through the introduction phase; become familiar with the activity, sport, or exercise; met other people like themselves; gained respect for the instructor; gained a little self-confidence; and moved on to learn more and get better.

If you have been tracking their attendance and encouraging their performance, they probably have developed a real sense of belonging and are eager to continue their efforts. The acceptance stage is when the member gets involved in an ongoing program and subsequently can receive formal recognition, participate in a competition event, and even win an award for personal achievement.

There are two spokes within the acceptance stage: involvement and achievement.

Involvement

Now it's time for the member to start using the club or participating in a program regularly. At this point, retention is really starting to occur. An involvement program means that your member will make a commitment to participate in a specific program on a specific day of the week and a specific hour of the day. It also means committing to a certain number of weeks. An example of an involvement program is any type of a league or a series of classes, meetings, or clinics.

A league program is a good example of a program that follows the instruction spoke of the wheel. Once participants learn something new and get better at it, they will want to continue the activity. As an example, introductory clinics or lessons in racquetball, tennis, or volleyball will encourage a player to join a league whereby the player will meet with other players every week and compete for a prize at the end of a specific period of activity. Leagues are fun, social, and competitive. Participation in a league enables the member to put your club or program into his lifetime schedule of events.

For example, a racquetball or tennis league will meet at the same time on the same day every week with the same people playing each other. The players look forward to seeing familiar people, competing with them, and talking about the game afterward. This sort of experience is eagerly anticipated and will be made a priority by the player. You see why the involvement program is so critical to achieving retention. It truly offers the participant a sense of belonging.

Another form of involvement programming is offering sessions or a series of classes such as group exercise sessions or circuit training classes. Again, the group exercise program will consist of a variety of classes and types of exercises. Each class will have its own time slot every week with the same instructor. The majority of participants in that class choose to come to the same class every week. They will set that time aside in their schedule and hold it as a priority.

The quality of the program and the skill of the instructor will, of course, be the deciding factors in whether the participants continue, but we'll cover that later. The point here is to understand the significance of the regularly scheduled activity as an involvement program in the acceptance spoke of the wheel of logical progression and its influence on retention.

Points to consider in the involvement program include these:

- The program should be offered on the same day and at the same time every week.
- The program should have the same instructor or supervisor directing the activity during each class or session.
- The majority of participants in a given class should be "regulars" so they will have an opportunity to create rapport and develop relationships or friendships.

Achievement

The introductory program has created an initial interest, and members have had fun participating. The instruction program has been successful if the participants were eager to learn, had fun, and truly believed that they improved in their sport or activity. The logical progression of programming is under way, and everyone gets involved in leagues, sessions, classes, or clinics on a regular weekly schedule. Now it's time to give recognition for performance or achievement.

The achievement program will probably be the pivotal program within the wheel of logical progression. The participants at this point are feeling good about themselves and their new experience, but they need encouragement and recognition from the leaders, program directors, or instructors. The objective of this phase is to encourage a desire for more activity. As a result, you raise the members' self-esteem and comfort level. Essentially, you take time to recognize the accomplishment your members have made in the involvement phase.

The achievement spoke is often eliminated because (1) clubs have a tendency to rest on their laurels and assume that if the members get involved they will remain involved and (2) awards and recognition events take time and money, and club operators believe that they can't afford either. Not only can you afford to give out awards—you can't afford *not* to give out awards. Everyone needs and wants recognition for something, and nothing makes a person feel more important than getting recognition for personal achievement by the leader and in front of peers.

The best achievement programs will be in the form of awards ceremonies or, at the very least, visible and memorable presentations. Personal achievement needs to be recognized by the leader and demonstrated in front of peers for maximum

© Human Kinetics

Inexpensive ribbons make great awards!

impact. The good news is that all awards need not be huge, expensive items. Awards or prizes such as ribbons, small trophies, or T-shirts are as appreciated as more costly items.

Recognition for achievement can be as simple as giving out ribbons, posting names on recognition boards, featuring members' names or pictures in your newsletter, or even giving an enthusiastic handshake and asking for applause from the other participants.

Awards need not be given strictly for the biggest, best, fastest, fittest, or first-place winners. Competition does not have to be the only criterion for giving recognition. Indeed, very often giving recognition on a competitive basis may actually leave out the participants who want and need the experience most. For example, presenting an award based on attendance rather than performance will provide a wonderful experience to someone who may not ever receive an award for achievement based on performance alone. The bottom line is to be creative and find ways to recognize everyone for something. It's the ultimate goal in the achievement phase.

The objectives of the achievement program are these:

* Recognition for participation or competition
* Awards presentations by the leader in front of peers

Retention Stage 3: Commitment

We know now that retention will occur only when the member becomes committed to the program, the lifestyle, and the club. We've learned, too, that it takes a series of programs and activities to achieve that commitment. Without setting up the cycle of programming described here, many clubs scramble to sell enough memberships every month to replace the number of people who leave. While that is happening, an equal number of members who joined a few months earlier have already stopped using the club regularly, which is the step before actually quitting.

The object of the commitment stage is to enhance the member's commitment to the club by creating a deeper level of socialization and bonding between members and staff. During this stage, you get the member involved in a club-wide event, such as a holiday party, a competition, a tournament, a seminar, or some other type of social function or health education.

There are two spokes within the commitment stage: improvement and fun.

Improvement

Members should aim for a higher level of achievement as they progress in their exercise routines or sport activity. Very important is creating the members' desire to improve. That desire will be evident if all of the objectives were met in the introduction, instruction, involvement, and achievement spokes. You'll want to help members establish new goals and diversify activities. The beauty of getting to this phase successfully is that it provides you with another opportunity to recognize achievements and build a sense of belonging.

When people are comfortable and confident in their ability levels, even if it is a beginning level, and feel good about themselves, they are ready to learn more and accept new challenges. Improvement programs add new dimensions to the prior programs. As participants gain confidence they also get a heightened competitive edge. Even those who declared themselves to be noncompetitive will enter the improvement phase of programming comparing themselves with others in the program. The quest to improve or advance to a higher level of fitness is exciting and will solidify the member's commitment to activity even further.

There's a psychology behind the improvement spoke. The club member has experienced a good deal of success by this time. If he had not been through the first four stages of programs, the club may have left him feeling inadequate, unfit, unfamiliar, uncoordinated, unknowledgeable, and uninspired. It's exciting to see a member willing to take on a new challenge with confidence and a positive attitude. At this point you know you've done your job. You've traveled yet another mile down the road to retention.

Improvement programs include these:

* Competition events
* Education, seminars, and clinics
* Diversification—new programs or activities
* More advanced level of play or exercise programs

Fun

The last spoke of the wheel of logical progression is fun—the social events and other special events. At the end of the day, it's all about enjoying what you are doing, feeling comfortable, and having fun. Making fitness fun has been a mantra for the health and fitness industry for nearly 10 years, and it has been the most difficult part of the business to accomplish.

When you run an all-club event such as a holiday party or a member appreciation party, more than 90 percent of the attendees are members who have been active in the club for more than a year, are using the facility regularly, and have made friends with other members or even the staff. Even though a club party or special event is designed to be social, friendly, and fun, your most important members, the newest members, will not participate if they have not felt needed, wanted, or appreciated. They will not participate if they have not been introduced to others like themselves, participated in a regularly scheduled activity, been rewarded for their achievements, and acquired confidence and familiarity along the way. You can't just announce that you are having a party or a special event and expect new people to participate without having had a friendly, fun experience in the club.

If the members who have joined the club within the last three to six months have experienced an introductory clinic with other new members and have been participating in a regularly scheduled program every week, they will likely feel comfortable enough to attend an all-club event. In such a case you would know that your programming efforts were working with the members who would normally be the most likely to quit and certainly be the least likely to attend an all-club function. You would have nurtured their experiences with a systematic calendar of programs that include physical activity, recognition, education, productivity, and camaraderie, all of which led to a sense of belonging. Your members will be committed to your club and their new lifestyle.

Ten Keys to Retention

The objective of every program is to get members to use the club, enjoy the club, and therefore come closer to becoming a retained member. But members do leave our clubs. Why? These are the excuses we've heard for years and still hear today: "I'm not using the club enough," or "I don't have time." Members are not exactly lying with these excuses, but the reality is that they are not using the club and can't find the time to exercise because the experience they have while at the club is not of value to them. Most members who are left to

fend for themselves and work out alone with little or no direction or leadership do not realize a club experience. The value of a club membership is in sociability, camaraderie, friendships, relationships, leadership, and group experiences. Those are things that programs provide.

When members make friends in the club and work out with others like themselves, they have a much more enjoyable experience than when exercising alone. If we provide programs that bring people together to exercise in a fun, social environment, the number of referrals increases significantly, retention increases, and attrition decreases. Thus, our programs must be developed with systems that guarantee these experiences.

The wheel of logical progression is a great tool to measure your customer retention. But there is more that you as a programmer can do to ensure even better retention. Use the following 10 keys to guide you as you develop your successful programs, and then use them as a checklist to ensure that the programs will result in retention as well as excellent participation.

1. Communication

You must personally contact every new member who joins your club, at the very least within the first week of membership. It has been proven time and time again that most new members quit before they ever really start using the club regularly. Even for people with the best intentions, it is difficult for a new member, certainly an inexperienced one, to enter a club alone and feel perfectly comfortable walking into a group exercise class or getting on a piece of equipment. A personal invitation to a specific event at a specific time will be the most effective form of communication you can use. You can send a reminder postcard or an e-mail, but a sincere phone call is the best. Members who are intimidated or inexperienced will probably not come to the club without it. For your script, see the 10 magic words in chapter 2.

2. Responsibility

Just because you called and invited the member to a program or event, don't think your work is done. Professional communication includes following up on your invitation or promise. If you don't receive a response from your member, call again, perhaps up to three times, especially if the member indicates that she is not sure about participating.

Even after the invitation is accepted, a confirmation call 12 to 24 hours in advance of the program is absolutely necessary to ensure participation and avoid a no-show. The follow-up phone calls show that you are taking responsibility for helping the member achieve her goals.

3. Recognition

You must give personal recognition to every new member who participates in a program or activity. People need to feel important. You can give an award, a ribbon, or a trophy for excellent performance, but recognition can be given for many other reasons that are far more important to the new member or beginner. Giving a compliment, taking a picture, or extending a sincere handshake can be just as effective. Something as simple as keeping track of a member's attendance gives you an opportunity to recognize participation. You can always find a way to make people feel important. The most important thing is that recognition must be given by the leader and in front of the member's peers.

4. Sociability

When people join a club they want to be with other people like themselves. If people are in a group situation or a group program, they are more likely to enjoy themselves, have more fun, meet others like themselves, and form friendships. Most members join clubs for fitness, but they stay for fun. Sociability, camaraderie, and friendships are all key ingredients to a club experience. Group programs provide a sociability factor, and sociability is a major key to retention.

5. Commitment

Certainly the member must be committed to the program, to exercise, and to a new lifestyle, but other commitments must be established before that happens. Some say a member's commitment is to the activity itself, or the leader, or to the other members of the group. These are all good commitments, and if they occur the member is sure to feel the sense of belonging that will keep him coming back. The commitment that will be the key to retention, however, is a commitment to a specific schedule or time frame. Retention occurs when the members put your club into their lifestyle—coming to the club on the same day, at the same time, every week.

6. Diversification

A huge factor regarding retention is providing diversification for the member. People get bored doing the same routine over and over, so new challenges, goals, and experiences will keep them interested or renew their interest in exercising. Cross-training is another reason why diversified programming is so important. We know that cross-training will give better fitness results, so diversified programming is good mentally, emotionally, and physically. Diversification also can come in the form of a higher level of achievement in the same program, such as moving through beginning, intermediate, or advanced levels of performance. Diversified programming is key for existing, already active members. It will keep them coming back, and that's the goal of programming.

7. Progression

Progressing through a series of programs is the objective of the wheel of logical progression. It ensures retention through a year of diversified programming. New members begin their membership tenure with an introductory program and progress to instructional opportunities that prepare them for the regular involvement in programs such as sports leagues, fitness clinics, circuit sessions, or group exercise classes. Participating in progressive programming is absolutely essential to keeping members active, interested, goal driven, and successful. The wheel of logical progression provides an ongoing check on every phase of programming for every member. Always use one program to promote another, and the progression will continue. The objective for members is to become integrated in the club through introductory programs, become familiar and comfortable with activities, and, finally, commit to a schedule that puts your club in their weekly routine.

8. Promotion

A member is not considered a retained member until he is using your club every week consistently for a full year. Professional promotion starts with a calendar of events that is posted at the beginning of the year and offers a variety of activities and programs that will remain consistent throughout the year. The promotions of these and other programs must include posters, notices posted on bulletin boards, and fliers promoting the onset of the programs, and those promotions must be completed and available no less than three weeks in advance of a program. In addition to the readable promotions, telephone campaigns inviting members to a specific event at a specific time are productive if done no less than three weeks in advance and followed up with confirmation calls 12 to 24 hours in advance of the program.

Most programs need to be promoted verbally throughout the club as well. For example, the front desk has the opportunity to promote a program to every person who walks in the door, the group exercise instructors can promote programs in their classes, and fitness trainers should promote programs to their clients for the purpose of cross-training. All promotions must be scheduled and monitored as much as the programs themselves, and a full staff effort must be organized and managed to make sure all promotions are put in place on schedule.

9. Reliability

Reliability is a key issue that is most often misunderstood or ignored altogether. Reliability means that you must set a precedent whereby the programming schedule is not only reasonable to get started with but, more important, easy to progress with. For example, a programming schedule that offers a beginning-level program on a Tuesday and an intermediate level of the same program on a Thursday should remain constant with that schedule for at least six months and preferably a year or more. Members and prospective members need to plan ahead, and your club must remain consistent in some of its core program offerings to allow people to make room in their weekly routines for your club and its programs. If you constantly change the same program to a different time and different day, you eliminate the members who spend weeks preparing their schedules to make room for a 9 a.m. Tuesday class only to find out that it has been changed to Wednesday!

Keep a number of core programs on a consistent calendar of events to set a reliable precedent for members and potential members.

10. Accountability

Every program must have a leader who is held accountable for all 10 keys to retention—from communication to diversification, progression, and promotion. Programming for your club is worthy of a program director's position. If it is not feasible to hire a program director, you must assign a leader to each program who is capable, responsible, and held accountable for taking every program through all 10 keys of program development. At the end of the day, the success or failure of a program will be linked to how well the 10 keys presented here were implemented in the program's structure and development. A program cannot run successfully without accountability, not only for its presentation but for growth and retention as well. Professional programming is the heart of membership growth and retention

Never run a program unless you run it 100 percent!

2

Hiring and Training the Right People

High-quality, successful programming is necessary to run a growing and profitable business. As we saw in chapter 1, you can take specific steps to create successful programs and retain your members. But before you can even look at programming, you need to make sure you've hired and trained the right people. We have a unique business that is absolutely dependent on its leaders, and contrary to old opinions, the primary personal quality to look for when hiring is an engaging personality. The fitness industry has come a long way from thinking that a fit body, a degree, a certification, or exceptional expertise in a physical sport is all that a fitness leader needs. In fact, to become an effective leader in the fitness industry today, you must be willing and able to develop a professional personality and learn how to manage it.

Let's face it—most people hate exercise. If they truly enjoyed exercising, they wouldn't bother coming to our clubs. They would be working out regularly on their own. Yet they do come in, hoping to find an experience that will inspire them to continue their quest for fitness. The instructor makes or breaks that experience. The first people our clients respond to are our leaders—the instructors, trainers, and all the personnel who promote and implement our programs.

Leadership starts at the top, so if you are an owner or manager or a prospective owner or manger, everything that we will discuss about hiring and training the right personnel pertains to you, too. If you are evaluating yourself, your business, and your staff at this point, let me ask you, have you hired happy people? Yes, this is very subjective criterion, but necessary, nevertheless. Success in every phase of our business lies in ourselves and our staff.

IHRSA, the International Health and Racquet Sport Association, outlines seven characteristics that should be found in a leader in our clubs:

1. Interpersonal skills
2. Self-confidence

3. Aggressive friendliness
4. Sense of teamwork
5. Flexibility
6. Love of the industry
7. Qualifications

Items 2 through 6 are either there or not there. They are part of a person's basic character. Items 1 and 7 are either learned or acquired. Qualifications, for example, are certainly important and can easily be measured in terms of degrees and certifications guaranteeing academic knowledge of fitness or physiology. As important as this knowledge is, however, it will be 100 percent ineffective if it isn't communicated in a professional, sincere, personal manner using learned, practiced, polished, systematic, and proactive interpersonal skills. Interpersonal skills should be number one, but they are often neglected or excluded from an employee training session.

In this chapter we'll look at whom to hire—the qualities and characteristics you should look for in your staff. Then, we'll look at what you can do to train your staff in professional communication, making sure they give good first impressions to your clients as well as create an inviting, friendly environment. As the fitness industry continues to grow so do the professional opportunities, but there will be more demands for professionals who have a variety of communication skills. It follows then that it is our responsibility to hire the right people in the first place and then provide the proper training so they can develop their professionalism. Finally, we'll look at ways you can evaluate your staff—how you can tell whether your staff needs a refresher in professional communication.

Characteristics of a Good Hire

It's obviously important that the leaders in your facility be well versed in the science of exercise and training. Certification from ACSM, NATA, ACE, AFFA, NASM, USWFA, or NETA gives your staff the professional qualifications to teach and instruct your clientele. But certification alone doesn't create a good hire. The staff at your facility need to possess personality traits that enable them to work effectively, energetically, and in an upbeat way with every person who enters your

facility. Specifically, you want people to work at your facility who can do the following:

• **Be happy.** In our industry, the majority of staff should have an upbeat, high-energy, enthusiastic, happy personality. These are the words that describe the environment we try to create in our clubs and in our programs. We need to get positive enthusiastic responses from our members, so we obviously must hire people with those attributes. It's been said that 20 percent of the people we hire are in either the wrong position or the wrong industry. Twenty percent of our employees are probably not successful leaders for our business or our programs. This doesn't make them bad people or wrong in their thinking; it simply indicates that they may be better suited for a different vocation, may have been hired for the wrong reasons, or may not have had a good training program.

• **Accept new ideas.** Every person on staff must have an open mind and a willingness to accept training in communication skills, marketing techniques, sales, and service.

• **Be success oriented.** Yes, there should be an obvious, recognizable commitment to excellence. All personnel must use their skills to ensure that all programs are successful, showing high usage, retention, and growth. Everyone who works at a club must understand and acknowledge that the goal of programming is retention, that people will respond positively to positive people, and that leaders will be evaluated on how well they manage their personality to achieve that end result. In a nutshell, we must hire success-oriented people who are willing to develop professional personalities and consistently strive to manage them productively.

Everyone wishing to work in our clubs—front-line staff, program directors, and instructors— should demonstrate, within the first few minutes of an interview, that they either already are or have the potential to be happy, accepting of new ideas, and success oriented. Be very aware of that indication. The first impression that the applicant makes on you is the same first impression that person makes when meeting a new member or prospective member.

Here are a few things to look for during the interview:

• Does the person look happy?
• During an interview, does she smile (a) most of the time, (b) some of the time, or (c) seldom? A smile can often tell more about a

person than a two-hour questionnaire, but a smile isn't any good if it isn't aimed at somebody!

• Does the candidate look at you and make eye contact during the conversation? Or do you see him looking down, off to the side, or at another object, glancing your way only periodically?

If the answers to these questions are positive, chances are your first impression is that of a happy, upbeat personality. (Why not try this out on your existing staff? You will probably be surprised to find out how inconsistent the personalities are. Consider how significant this could be to retention.)

An interview can surely reveal a generally positive attitude or an energetic, upbeat, friendly personality. First, take specific note as to how the applicant introduced himself to you. You may even want to ask him to candidly introduce himself to some other members of the club. Yes, this may seem awkward or uncomfortable, but isn't this exactly what is expected of every employee every day? Our clubs will always have people we don't know—new members, guests, prospective members, even existing members whom we haven't met. Every professional in our industry must be eager to meet new people, to approach strangers, to recognize the opportunity to establish a new relationship, and to develop a rapport with someone immediately. If, like most clubs, you are open 17 hours a day, seven days a week, you must be ready, willing, and able to smile and greet people professionally, consistently, and energetically at all times . . . even if you don't feel like it. This is not easy, but it is necessary.

An interview could include an evaluation of the following list of characteristics. Ask applicants to rate themselves on a scale of 1 to 10. Include a brief explanation of each answer:

• Appearance
• Conversation skills
• Organizational skills
• Ability to take direction
• Self-motivation
• Ability to get along with others
• Personal characteristics
• Understanding of the nature of the job
• General type of personality
• Stamina

Ken Blanchard, author and speaker, addressed an IHRSA convention in a keynote speech several years ago and stated brilliantly, "I've visited your clubs across the country and I have one thing to say to all of you, 'The condition of your face is not optional!'"

Professional Communication Skills

Once you've identified someone who has a happy personality and is willing to accept new ideas and strive for success, you can then help her shape her professional personality. Surely we need leaders with technical knowledge of exercise to educate and help our members, but we must first develop professional personalities that allow staff to develop a rapport and build relationships of trust, respect, and friendliness with members.

If our leaders fail to develop rapport and relationships with people, they will miss opportunities to fill our programs. In fact, 60 to 80 percent of our members—those who want us and need us most—are the least likely to ask us questions or seek our direction. We must be able to read those members, perceive the correct actions, and ask the right questions. The members who make up that 60 to 80 percent are intimidated, misinformed, unknowledgeable, inexperienced, or deconditioned. They may be new to the club, new to fitness, or new to the industry. A survey published in the early 1980s attributed 68 percent of lost business to poor staff communication skills. In fact, the unsatisfied customers faulted management for failing to provide proper communication training to their staff. They said, "The staff must talk to me at my level, in my terms, at my age." In addition, it was noted that only four percent of dissatisfied customers bother to tell anyone why they leave a business; the rest just quietly leave.

We must learn how to ask the correct questions at the right time in the proper manner to get new members, keep members, and get them involved in programs.

Knowing how to greet people professionally and create an immediate rapport pays off. The previously mentioned survey also reported that most of the people who left a club or a program would have stayed if someone on staff had talked to them directly. Seventy percent would have come back if they were called and invited back. The customers said that staff must make them feel important. Staff

Asking the Right Questions

A boy named Johnny worked in a pharmacy. One day, mid-afternoon, with few customers in the store, Johnny asked his boss if he could use the phone. He spoke to a lady on the other end named Mrs. Smith. Johnny asked Mrs. Smith if he could have the gardening job she had offered. Mrs. Smith informed Johnny that she had already filled the position. Johnny proceeded to ask whether the new hire was doing a good job, whether he arrived at her home on time, whether he was neat, respectful, knowledgeable, and timely. After hearing yes to all the questions, Johnny thanked Mrs. Smith and said he would check with her again in a couple of weeks. After hanging up, Johnny's boss said, "Johnny, I thought you were Mrs. Smith's gardener." Johnny replied, "I am. I just wanted to know how I was doing!"

must approach people professionally, positively, and consistently.

The survey also said that the people who received a positive experience from the staff told 8 to 12 others about it. Those who had a negative experience or a noncommunicative experience (apathetic) shared that with 15 to 20 others. These are significant numbers; negative advertising obviously has a greater impact than positive advertising, so can we afford to not give professional communication training to our staff?

Let's look at some tools you can use to train your staff in this very important area of professional communication.

Seven–Eleven Principle

If you find yourself in a group of people whom you've never met before, you make an immediate judgment about someone in a few seconds. You tend to immediately react positively or negatively, often before any conversation even takes place! You may actually think, *Gee, I think I'd like to get to know that person better. That person seems really friendly,* or you may think, *Wow, is that person a jerk!* We are so judgmental and quick to make decisions about others. Smiles, eye contacts, and body language tell a great deal about a person's makeup.

I have found that the ultimate first impression may be made within the first seven seconds of meeting someone. In fact, people might make up to 11 decisions about someone within those first seven seconds. I call this the seven–eleven principle. Some decisions people make in the first seven seconds of meeting someone include the following:

- Do I like you?
- Do you like me?
- Do you care about me personally?
- Are you willing to spend time with me?
- Are you listening to me?
- Do you hear what I'm saying?
- Are you honest?
- Are you sincere?
- Are you knowledgeable?
- Are you friendly?
- Can I trust you?

Learning how to create a positive experience in the first seven seconds is crucial to becoming a professional communicator. It is crucial to creating the ultimate first impression. It is actually the first step in developing a professional personality and learning how to manage it. There are five things that people react to immediately at an initial meeting or encounter with someone:

- Appearance
- Body language
- Personality
- Greeting
- Knowledge

Professional Communication Starts at the Top

I cannot talk about professional communication training without making a point about the importance of this skill in owners and managers. If professional communication is part of a customer service program, we must identify the two major groups of customers—internal customers and external customers. We all tend to focus our attention on the external customer—the members, prospective members, or guests who either join or visit our facilities. Obviously, our business depends on the external customer, but the internal customer drives the service and communication that sell our product. The internal customer is your staff—the owners, managers, and all employees who work together. Every one of the communication skills that we work on and train ourselves to deliver to the external customer must be practiced among ourselves, the internal customer, first. If we don't treat each other with respect, friendliness, enthusiasm, and professionalism, how can we expect to deliver these things to our members?

It bears repeating! Customer service and professional communication must begin with the owners and managers treating their employees the way they would like to have their employees treat their customers.

What you are ultimately doing is creating a happy work environment to set the overall service culture of your club and customer experience. You can't just tell your staff what to do, and your staff can't just tell your members what to do. You must lead by example. It is much like the manner in which children are taught right and wrong from their parents. Telling a child not to smoke doesn't cut it when a parent lights up a cigarette. Telling children not to lie, cheat, or steal doesn't work when they hear and see mom or dad do just that in everyday life.

The question is not, what can we do to improve our service? No, the big question is, what can we do to make a better workplace so that we set the stage for excellent service to take place?

Here's an example. In nearly every club I visit that has between 50 and 150 employees, the owner or manager will admit that she has not even met some of the newest employees. Yet we tell our staff how important it is to introduce themselves with a professional greeting to new members and prospects who come through our doors. When was the last time you saw an owner or manager walk into a club and shake hands with the employees at the front desk, dish out a specific compliment, and tell them what a great job they are doing? Have you seen an owner or manager walk up to a new employee, shake hands, acknowledge that they hadn't been formally introduced, and welcome him on board? Would this make a new employee feel important? Of course! Isn't that what we expect of our staff? By the way, remember that 60 to 80 percent of your new business comes from quality word of mouth. Well, 60 to 80 percent of terrific employees can come from word of mouth, too. If your staff is proud and happy to work for you, the training process will certainly be more productive, and you will probably attract the right personalities to hire in the first place. Professional communication must be an ongoing practice within the internal organization. It starts at the top. It starts with you.

Let's take a closer look at each of these and how they affect the seven–eleven principle.

Appearance

In the first seven seconds, a first impression will always begin with a reaction to the person's physical appearance. We know that the first thing noted will be "teeth and eyes"—a smile and eye contact. Neatness and cleanliness are, of course, a given, but there's more. Every staff member should always wear a uniform with the club logo and a name tag (identification badge).

A uniform gives a professional appearance, creates a consistent look, and immediately identifies the people in charge. It identifies someone as a leader, a professional, a valued employee, an informed employee, a knowledgeable employee, a trainer, a program director. The club logo printed or embroidered on the uniform adds to the identification of the employee, but it also shows a sense of belonging and a team spirit among the staff. It's comforting for the member to see and feel a team spirit among the staff. Your member will then identify himself with your club and have a sense of belonging to what he sees.

The name tag is too often unappreciated. A name tag enables members to know staff members' names. A member will read your name, use it, and remember it. For this reason it may be more important for your members to know your name than it is for you to know theirs because the more your members use your name, the easier it will be for you to remember theirs. When your members call you by your name, they subconsciously experience that sense of belonging they need. This is exactly what you are trying to achieve, so wear your name tag! And wear it proudly. Your name tag says, "I'm proud of who I am, I'm proud of the club I'm in, and I'm proud of the industry I represent." It is truly a part of professional communication. Here are some tips for success with name tags:

- The name tag should be big enough to notice. A small, obscure metal piece with a name etched in it that is nearly unreadable is ineffective.
- The name tag should include the club's name and logo.
- The name tag should have your first name printed in big, black, bold letters. Other information clutters the name tag and makes it difficult to read. You should be able to read a name tag from three to five feet away.

- Extra name tags should be available for misplaced or forgotten ones. It is part of the uniform and must be worn as consistently. Choosing not to wear a name tag gives a message totally contrary to everything we have talked about.
- The location of the name tag is very important. It should be worn on the right side just below the shoulder and opposite the logo, which is printed on the left side of a shirt or jacket. Why? When you shake hands with people their eyes will automatically be looking at your right side; also people begin reading from your right side with their eyes moving from your right to your left. Keep the name tag from hiding under hair, a collar, or a jacket. A name tag is ineffective if it isn't readable. This would further suggest that name tags hung on lanyards are quite useless. Make it easy for your member or prospective member to use your name.

Body Language

Body language speaks volumes without words. In fact, 55 percent of communication is in body language, 38 percent in voice inflection, and 7 percent in words. Body language indicates a person's interest, personality, confidence, pride, and energy level. Trainers, instructors, and program directors express their enthusiasm with good posture, smiles, and eye contact when talking to people, and even before approaching them. Your posture and positioning tell how visible and accessible you are. For example, do you spend too much time behind a desk in the fitness center? Do you teach a group exercise class with your back to the group, or do you face them directly, allowing them to mirror your personality as well as your movements? Does a lifeguard sit in a chair quietly and unresponsively instead of greeting people when they arrive in the pool and encouraging the lap swimmers? What I'm asking is, do you appear interested, enthusiastic, and confident? Or uninterested, bored, or shy? Generally speaking, bored people are boring, and disinterested people are uninteresting. Which one is on your staff? Body language is definitely worth evaluating when you are considering whom to hire and is almost always a necessary part of developing professional personalities and learning how to manage them.

Personality

You know that a happy, energetic personality is important in our industry. Are you letting your clientele see that personality? Your appearance and your body language will begin to describe a personality immediately.

The Greeting

Let's say that a member or prospective member has come through the door of our club. The person immediately looks around to find someone in charge—a leader or representative of the business. He sees someone in a uniform. If the staff person is aloof, appearing too busy with other things or not interested in a meeting, that member will probably not pursue him. That member may look around to find another person in uniform and check out his face as well. Should this person look up and smile at the member—actually aim a smile at him—the member will likely smile back and look at the name tag to either use the name or, at the very least, take note of it. The professionally trained staff person will at this point greet the member with energy, sincerity, and enthusiasm—enough for the member to respond with a greeting as well. The professional greeting will develop a rapport that provides the opportunity to engage in conversation.

Knowledge

In the future the fitness industry will demand more knowledgeable and skilled staff than ever before. The industry itself will become more scientific, specialized, and diversified than ever before. There will be more organizations and advanced certifications than ever before. Clubs will have to raise the bar on the level of professional personalities and communication skills needed to implement programs, grow the programs, and retain members to ensure a healthy lifestyle. The industry and universities are rapidly advancing the technical and physical requirements needed for program specialists, but it may be up to the clubs themselves to take on the challenge of applying that knowledge to achieve results. Many education programs, for example, are great at teaching fitness trainers to not let their clients hyperextend their knees on a leg extension machine, but they spend little or no time teaching them how to basically say hello to someone. In essence, the technical, physical knowledge of a trainer or programmer, although essential, will only be as beneficial as the appearance, body language, personality, and greeting.

The number of fitness facilities will continue to increase, and the competition for new members will be fierce. Consumers are becoming much more educated about their needs and fitness opportunities. They are better informed and have greater expectations than ever before. Technology will become commonplace.

The difference between the best and the rest will be measured in how the member or prospective member is handled. When hiring a new employee for your club, you need to hire people with pride, confidence, and an eagerness to excel.

Professional Greeting

We do not have an option as to how we present ourselves and the programs we promote—not if we want to get a positive, lasting response from our participants. To create a good first impression—to succeed at the seven–eleven principle—you need to have a good professional greeting. There are five steps to the professional greeting:

* Smile
* Aim your smile
* Introduce yourself
* Shake hands
* Engage in conversation

Smile

We know that smiling is important, but the smile must be visible, memorable, and exaggerated. It immediately establishes a rapport, begins to build a relationship, and says that you are a friend or, at the very least, friendly. Friendship is one of the most meaningful parts of life for everyone, and we have the opportunity and the responsibility to build friendship into the club experience. When you smile broadly and sincerely at someone, chances are they will smile back at you. You may be thinking, No. First, a smile is a friendly gesture, and it will be accepted as such almost all of the time. Second, the more you practice smiling at people, the more sincere you get! Why? Because you will experience an absolute revelation as you discover the joy of smiling at people. You will realize that the need for friendliness is overwhelming. People immediately appear happier when you smile at them, and you can't help but feel good about that.

The positive response you will experience from people will convince you that this is not only the right thing to do but the only thing that will set the scene for inviting members into your programs. So, even if you can't be 100 percent sincere 100 percent of the time, keep smiling. Your sincerity will become real in no time. Practice makes perfect.

Aim Your Smile

Eye contact is the most difficult body language to perfect but probably the most important. The good news is that you can train yourself, just by practicing to aim your eyes directly at someone else's eyes while speaking. You will find that you will get a positive response. Think about it—if you smile but don't direct it at someone the smile may not be returned, but if you look the person straight in the eye when smiling, you will get a smile in return 99 percent of the time. Direct eye contact helps you focus on whom you are speaking to and dispels preoccupation with other people or other activities in the area. Aiming your smile will make your introduction a positive one and your conversation more productive. Emotionally, direct eye contact gives energy to both parties and forces concentration and interest. Physically, when two sets of eyes meet, both of you will experience an increase in heart rate, body temperature, and blood circulation. Aiming your smile is a simple concept, but it's not easy to implement. Practice!

We really can't talk about professional communication and eye contact without mentioning listening skills. Well, eye contact is key to honing your listening skills. As a matter of fact, I believe that you hear with your ears, but you listen with your eyes! See "How Well Do You Listen?" (page 23) to test yourself. You'll find it very helpful.

Introduce Yourself

Don't wait for members to introduce themselves to you—introduce yourself to them first! In the world of business this is called being proactive. Your members, guests, or first-time participants will not likely approach an instructor, trainer, or any other employee and introduce themselves. In the meantime, they may be feeling uncomfortable, insecure, or almost embarrassed as they watch the activity of the club. They see existing members busy at their workouts and staff bustling around talking with club members or one another. Many new people entering a club or group program will often just walk out and not return because they feel uncomfortable. Introducing yourself first not only puts your participant at ease, but it demonstrates pride, enthusiasm, and self-confidence. You and your fitness professionals must practice approaching people you don't know and introducing yourselves first. You will find that people will automatically respond with their own names, and the conversation is under way. In the survey, we found that 68 percent of people leave because no one talks to them.

Many fitness professionals with whom I talk tell me that they understand how important communication is, and when I ask them what they think they need most in a training program, they say they want to know how they can be more approachable. My first reaction is to tell them that they must learn to approach people first, rather than wait to be approached or even seem approachable. This may seem like a matter of semantics, but it's an important concept to understand and accept. Our clubs are filled with people who are intimidated, misinformed, or unknowledgeable.

They are often too embarrassed to ask a question or perhaps don't even know where to start or what question to ask, for that matter. If you wait to be approached, no matter how approachable you may seem, it may never happen. Practice introducing yourself—first.

Shake Hands

A good firm handshake is always appreciated, respected, and accepted as a gesture of professionalism in every business and walk of life. Shake hands as though you mean it. I must admit that in the hundreds of clubs I've worked in as a consultant and trainer, getting staff members to shake hands at all, let alone correctly, has been the biggest struggle. Teach your staff how to shake hands correctly.

Extend your hand (also using your smile and eyes), lock your thumb with the other person's, let the palms touch, and embrace her hand firmly but gently. You don't need to pump up and down as though you are looking for water or to shake hands for an interminable period of time, and you don't have to try to impress anyone with a knuckle-breaking grip.

Another tip—don't be duped into thinking that women need a fingertip handshake. In the real world, men expect a good handshake and respect a good handshake. Women often don't expect a good handshake but they will always respect one. Not only must you practice the handshake, but it must become a part of the communication culture of your club and an ongoing part of your training program.

Without advanced warning, shake hands with all your existing staff. You will be surprised at the experience. You may find very few genuine, professional, confident, appropriate handshakes. Regularly shake hands with your instructors and trainers, and make the handshake a fundamental part of greeting customers.

How Well Do You Listen?

 Go to **How Well Do You Listen?** on the **CD-ROM** for a printable version of this exercise.

Read each question and assign a number ranking.
The rankings are as follows:

5 = Always   **4** = Usually   **3** = Sometimes   **2** = Seldom   **1** = Never

_____ I allow speakers to complete their own thoughts and sentences.

_____ I make sure I've understood the other person's point of view before I answer.

_____ I listen for the important points and the speaker's feelings.

_____ I listen without interrupting.

_____ I am in control, relaxed, calm.

_____ I selectively listen, filtering out those messages that are not important to the situation.

_____ I use positive listening noises and gestures whenever possible, such as saying "yes" or "I understand" and nodding my head affirmatively.

_____ I keep my emotions from getting the better of me.

_____ I keep my mind from wandering. Instead of thinking what I'm going to say next, I really listen to what the speaker is saying.

_____ I listen even if the speaker or subject is uninteresting to me.

_____

Total Score

44 – 50	Excellent
34 – 43	Good
24 – 33	Average
< 24	Uh-Oh!

From S. Coffman, 2007, *Successful programs for fitness and health clubs* (Champaign, IL: Human Kinetics).

Make the First Move

While traveling to Boston to present a customer service seminar to an IHRSA group, I decided to visit the IHRSA offices in downtown Boston. I went to the taxi stand at the airport and met a woman who was also traveling on business, and we decided to share a cab. I introduced myself to her, Marilyn, and asked what business she was in. "The digital equipment business," she answered. "What a coincidence," I said. "I'm in the health club industry and much of our fitness equipment has digital programming." I asked her if she belonged to a club. She got very embarrassed and defensive as she explained that she used to belong to one but didn't use it very often, and because she was often away on business she believed the membership wasn't valuable enough to keep. I assured Marilyn that I heard many other people express the same concerns. She expressed that she was considering joining the club again when she returned from this trip. She continued to tell me that she had gained some weight since she stopped exercising and would like to get back in shape. I assured her that many other people shared her concerns and felt the same way.

She then was eager to tell me that she had a treadmill in her home (which, of course would solve the problem), but when I asked her if she used it, her reply was much the same as her previous reply. She said she used it when she first got it but found that she was either too busy or too tired most of the time, and she hadn't used it for quite a while. I tried to set her mind at ease by telling her that most people have experienced the same thing with home equipment. She proceeded on a more positive note, sharing with me that her mother, who has arthritis, visits Marilyn and uses her treadmill quite often. She said her mother claims that she has less pain and more flexibility when she uses the treadmill. Of course, I immediately endorsed that statement, exclaiming the virtues of exercise for people with arthritis. Marilyn, however, quickly rebutted, "That may be true, but do you want to know the real reason my mother uses my treadmill?" "Yes, of course," I said. "It's because it gives her an excuse to come over and talk to me!"

Wow! It was as though I was hit with a bolt of lightning! Aren't Marilyn and her mother much like our members and prospective members? They used to exercise, they know they should exercise, they wish they would exercise, they plan to exercise, and they would like to exercise . . . if someone would just come over and talk to them.

Engage in Conversation

The object of the professional greeting is to set the scene for a productive conversation. For the most part we are striving to gain respect and trust so that our members will follow our lead when we invite them to join our programs. We're also trying to establish a relationship and develop a rapport with that person. To further the effort, and make the conversation effective, use the person's name at least once and up to three times while talking with him. In the survey, members told us that they need the staff to make them feel important. There is very little that will make people feel more important than when you use their names while talking with them. Now you are ready to proceed with the conversation. A conversation with members and clients should always include a compliment, a suggestion, and a promotion.

Compliment.   A compliment is well received by almost everyone, and few people will complain because they get too many of them. It's actually common courtesy. Think of yourself as a host or hostess of a club and your members as special guests, much the same as if you were hosting a party at your home. As you greet your guests, you probably would say something such as "You look great in that color," or "It's so nice to see you again." In a club, a compliment is given on only two things: appearance and performance. You can compliment a member's T-shirt, jewelry, tan, new shoes, or attractive haircut. It's an easy, effective way to get a positive response. You can also compliment a member for good attendance, good form, good posture, or an obvious extra effort during an exercise routine.

Here is a great training tip. Have the staff list 25 generic compliments on appearance and 25 generic compliments on performance. Practice these compliments with each other during staff meetings. Then use the compliments on your members whenever appropriate. You and your staff will have compliments on the tip of your tongue whenever you need them.

Suggestion.   A suggestion coming from a leader is a powerful form of communication. Many people are unaware of doing things incorrectly or may be too embarrassed to ask for help. They likely will not approach you, so you must go to them in a confident, friendly, nonthreatening manner. The professional greeting has set you up perfectly for this opportunity. Inform, direct, and educate before members need to ask. Some suggestions or corrections may include (a) raising or lowering the seat on a machine or exercise bike, (b) keeping knees slightly bent during some stretch routines, (c) breathing rather than holding one's breath when exercising, (d) making a slight change in the hands when gripping a racquetball or tennis racket, and (e) keeping arm movements smooth and slow rather than jerky when lifting weights. Seize the opportunity to promote appropriate programs. Your members will thank you.

Promotion.   Offering a suggestion or making a correction is a perfect lead-in to a promotion. You will find that the opportunity to promote programs is everywhere you are and in everything you do.

For example, if you offer a suggestion on technique while someone is on the treadmill, promote one of your cardio programs. Or, if the member is lifting weights, promote one of your strength programs. While a member is taking a break at your snack bar, promote an upcoming program on nutrition. Whether you are discussing specific club events, various workout opportunities, or other new programs, the promotional part of an instructor's conversation may hold the key to member retention. Remember, our goal is to keep a member committed for a full year. Use the wheel of logical progression in chapter 1 for ideas on how to promote one program with another.

The Good-Bye

The professional greeting would not be complete without talking about saying good-bye. The greeting, of course, is part of your ultimate first impression and sets the tone, the scene, and the atmosphere of an entire visit. The last impression, however, may stay with a member or prospect the longest. Your members will take mental snapshots of your club and their experiences throughout their visits at your club. The snapshots will be positive, negative, or ho-hum, but they will surely surface when members consider a return visit or discuss the club experience with other people. So when practicing the professional greeting, remember to say good-bye the same way you said hello. It's giving a second chance at the seven–eleven principle; you'll be delivering the ultimate last impression as well.

"Creating the Ultimate First Impression" on page 26 is an exercise that will enhance your training program. This exercise is a great tool to use in training new employees, but it's also a good reinforcement exercise for all staff to repeat on a regular basis. See how you do.

10 Magic Words

There is more to programming than creating a program . . . you have to get people to commit to participate in that program. Remember, we're trying to get our members to be committed, retained members, and we must learn to "sell" the commitment. Programmers often say, "I don't want to be a salesperson. I just want to teach people and train clients. Leave the selling up to the sales department." In our business, the sales department

Creating the Ultimate First Impression

 Go to Creating the Ultimate First Impression on the CD-ROM for a printable version of this quiz.

After reading this book, especially the sections on the characteristics of a good hire and professional communication skills, you should be able to fill out the following quiz for creating the ultimate first impression. The suggested answers are listed at the bottom of this quiz. You may think of others that would apply.

Creating Customer Service Excellence

1. Hire a _____ personality.

2. Manage the _____ professionally.

3. A _____ isn't any good if you don't _____ it at someone.

4. Make sure the member knows _____.

5. Practice your _____.

6. A professional conversation includes (1) _____, (2) _____, and (3) _____.

7. Be 100% _____ 100% of the time.

8. Create a positive experience. Avoid _____.

9. Policies are guidelines. Be flexible and fair. _____, don't _____.

10. Your members are _____ _____.
    You are a _____ or _____.

11. Don't hesitate to _____.

12. _____ your member.

13. _____ the correct action.

14. Look for ways to say _____.

15. Speak _____.

16. Seek out _____ _____ opportunities.
    (Otherwise known as _____.)

17. Cater to the _____.

18. Encourage the _____.

19. Promotion is in _____ you do and in _____ you go.

20. Say _____ the same way you said hello.

Creating Customer Service Excellence

(1) happy or professional (2) greeting or communication (3) smile, aim (4) your name (5) handshake (6) compliment, suggestion, promotion (7) sincere (8) negativity or apathy (9) bend, break (10) special guests, host; hostess (11) apologize (12) read (13) perceive (14) yes (15) kindly, sincerely (16) problem solving, complaints (17) inexperienced (18) underachiever (19) everything, everywhere (20) good-bye

From S. Coffman, 2007, *Successful programs for fitness and health clubs* (Champaign, IL: Human Kinetics).

must promote programs when selling memberships, and the program department must sell programs after the member has joined. In fact, everyone on staff is expected to promote programs. Everyone on staff sells retention. If you clearly outline these goals and expectations when hiring your staff, you'll have a better chance of hiring the right people in the first place. Then outline the training techniques that will help them meet those expectations. One excellent training tool is offering an effective vocabulary when trying to get a member to participate in a program. The 10 magic words presented here are a great tool to enhance your staff's vocabulary to sell the commitment and help retain members:

- Invite
- Join
- Enjoy
- Fun
- Other people
- Want
- Need
- Help
- Terrific
- Guarantee

These 10 magic words, when included in your promotions, will enable you to sell programs. What makes these words magic? They are simply words that people consistently respond to favorably. They are simple words, but people need to hear them said to them. Say them out loud. Don't they make you feel good?

For example, a trainer can personally *invite* members to *join* a *group of others* to try a new program, and he or she can *guarantee* a *fun* and *enjoyable* time. If a trainer is sincere, confident, and enthusiastic, the member will probably respond favorably and join. It's sort of like being in show business, where you would be handed a script to rehearse. The script has been designed by professional writers who know what message the audience will respond to. Your job as a performer is to deliver that script with passion and professionalism. Following is a script for your "performers" (programmers) to use on their "audience" (members). Use this script to rehearse the 10 magic words, but feel free to put them in your own context as you promote your programs. It's a terrific training tool that will help grow your programs—guaranteed!

Magic Words at Work on page 28 is a training tool you can use to implement these words with both new hires and existing staff. The words do not have to be used in order, but the words in context are powerful.

These are magic words, but every good salesperson knows that he must be ready to overcome objection. Keep in mind that objections are often a subconscious effort to get more positive feedback about the event. People need to be convinced that the experience will be worthwhile and comfortable. They need to be reinforced.

Here are three more words to lead you into the 10 magic words: For example, "I know exactly how you feel. I've felt (or others have felt) just like you before. But I found (or they have found) that the experience was terrific and they were very happy they participated. The exercise titled Using the 10 Magic Words to Counter Objections on page 29 gives you and your staff more opportunities to practice using the 10 magic words. As you fill in the blanks to all the objections, take special note of the last objection regarding money ("I can't afford it"). The answer may be "I know exactly how you feel. Many other people felt the same way, but after participating, they found it was a great experience. That's why I'm personally inviting you to join us. In fact, I guarantee that you'll have fun, enjoy

Script of the 10 Magic Words

I would like to personally **invite** you *(gives a special, personal feeling)* to **join** us *(gives a sense of belonging)*. You will **enjoy** yourself *(people don't say no to enjoyment)* and have **fun** *(exercise can be fun; fun brings a smile to everyone)*. Many **other people** like you will be there *(feel part of the "in" crowd)*. I **want** you to experience the fun we have *(everyone needs to be wanted)*. I **need** you to attend *(everyone wants to be needed)*. Would you **help** me make this event a success *(everyone wants to be important)?* That would be **terrific** *(you are sincerely happy and genuinely pleased)*. I **guarantee** you will **enjoy** yourself, have **fun,** and meet **other people**.

Magic Words at Work

Go to Magic Words at Work on the CD-ROM for a printable version of this exercise.

"Hello _____, my name is _____. I am *personally inviting* you to *join* us at our member appreciation party on _____. It's a special event we are having at our facility on _____. You'll really have *fun* and *enjoy* yourself. It's for everyone, of course, but it's especially for *new members just like you*. Please be sure to come. I really *want* you to be at this particular event because it's special to everyone, and we only hold it one time a year. Check your schedule. You being there will *help* make it a success.

That would be *great!* I *guarantee* you'll *enjoy* yourself, have *fun*, and meet a lot of *other people* just like you. I'll look forward to seeing you!

From S. Coffman, 2007, *Successful programs for fitness and health clubs* (Champaign, IL: Human Kinetics).

yourself, and meet other people or . . . I'll give you your money back!" Yes, this is a strong statement, but think of what you guaranteed: They will have fun, enjoy themselves, and meet other people. If you can't guarantee this, you are not ready to run the program. If you can guarantee this, your performance will get a standing ovation!

How Successful Is Your Staff?

Now that you know whom you should be hiring and how you and your staff should be behaving, perhaps it's time to evaluate your club and your staff or even time to set up your first training program agenda. The Checklist of Professional Communication Training on page 30 highlights desirable staff skills.

Imagine potential members standing outside your fitness center and asking members as they leave, "How would you describe the experience you just had?" Our members look for and need education, social interaction, direction, motivation, a personal challenge, a feeling of accomplishment, and yes, an experience that is satisfying emotionally as well as physically. Because few members

really get emotionally involved with a piece of equipment, their response would be apathetic at best unless they had some form of interaction from the floor trainers or instructors. To impart knowledge or engage in any conversation at all, the leaders must be visible and accessible.

Let's look at your fitness center at 6 a.m. on a Monday. You probably have a large number of members working out on the equipment. This should be a wonderful opportunity for your trainers to introduce themselves to members, introduce members to other members, ask questions, answer questions, promote programs, give compliments, make corrections, and offer suggestions. Does your scene look like this?

- You can't find the trainers.
- One or two trainers may be behind a fitness desk, and one trainer is in front of the fitness desk, leaning on it.
- Two or more trainers may be on the periphery of the fitness center. They are engaged in conversation with each other. One of them is bouncing a basketball.
- One trainer is sitting on a piece of equipment talking to a member—his or her workout partner.
- One member is obviously confused about programming a treadmill, but the only trainer

Using the 10 Magic Words to Counter Objections

 Go to Using the 10 Magic Words to Counter Objections on the CD-ROM for a printable version of this exercise. You'll also find a filled-in version to help guide you in how to respond to each objection.

Here are some objections that we hear constantly. They can be overcome by using the 10 magic words. Fill in the blanks with the answers to the objection at the left. Begin with *feel, felt,* or *found,* and continue using the 10 magic words in your sentences.

Objection	*Answers*
"I'm not sure if I'll be able to come. I've been so busy."	_____ _____ _____
"I'm supposed to be doing something else that day. I'll think about it and let you know."	_____ _____ _____
"I don't think so. I won't know anyone there."	_____ _____ _____
"I'm not sure I'm ready for that. I haven't been to the club in a while."	_____ _____ _____
"I really don't like competition."	_____ _____ _____
"I can't afford it."	_____ _____ _____

From S. Coffman, 2007, *Successful programs for fitness and health clubs* (Champaign, IL: Human Kinetics).

Checklist of Professional Communication Training

 Go to Checklist of Professional Communication Training on the CD-ROM for a printable version of this exercise.

How successful is your professional communication training? Ask new hires and existing staff if they can do the following:

Deliver the professional greeting.

Give a compliment.

Make a correction.

Promote a new program.

Use the 10 magic words that get a positive response.

Give recognition for personal achievement.

Create a social environment.

Encourage camaraderie.

Get a laugh or give a laugh.

Effectively communicate with all ages, interests, abilities, and personalities.

Make fitness fun.

Inform, teach, and demonstrate, not dictate, mandate, or intimidate.

Make people feel important.

Turn complaints into problem-solving opportunities.

Use body language positively.

Be spontaneous.

Listen effectively.

Dress professionally and appropriately.

Create a happy environment—(hire happy people).

Train customer service from the inside out.

From S. Coffman, 2007, *Successful programs for fitness and health clubs* (Champaign, IL: Human Kinetics).

on the floor is a personal trainer and he or she is totally engrossed in his or her client. The trainer is neither aware of nor interested in anyone else.

- None of the trainers are smiling or laughing— except the one bouncing the basketball.

- None of the members are smiling or laughing.
- One or more trainers are standing against a wall, almost at attention, arms folded across their chests, ready to answer any questions that a member has—if only a member would dare to come up and ask one. You recognize

them. They are the "fitness center sentries" of a club—fully knowledgeable and qualified.

Or, does your scene look like this?

- The trainers are interspersed throughout the fitness area.
- Each trainer is actively engaged in conversation with one or more members.
- One trainer is giving hands-on attention to members by making corrections in their posture or technique.
- One trainer is shaking hands with members.
- Some trainers are distributing fliers that promote programs and giving information on the programs.
- One trainer is introducing a member to another member or to another trainer or employee.
- One trainer is taking a picture of one or more members.
- One or more trainers are smiling or laughing with members about something.
- Each trainer (except personal trainers) moves to other members after a reasonable period of time, making sure that everyone is connected with at least a greeting.
- Personal trainers, although focused on one client, are aware of other members and gesture, smile, and greet others when possible.

I hope you are doing a quick evaluation of your staff right now or at least visualizing how you would like to see your fitness center in action. Which scene would produce the most positive reports from your members when you ask them how they would describe the experience they just had? Which scene has the type of professional personalities that are most likely to grow your programs?

Let's visualize the leadership in another activity—a group exercise program. You may have a large number of members standing next to a step waiting for class to begin. This should be a wonderful opportunity for your instructors to introduce themselves to members they don't know, introduce members to other members, ask questions, answer questions, promote programs, give compliments, and make suggestions. Does your scene look like this?

- Everyone is standing and looking straight ahead. The only people talking to each other are those in the front row.

- The instructor arrives and immediately fixes the music.
- The instructor says hi to the front row, asks if anyone is there for the first time, and cautions people to work at their own pace.
- The instructor periodically tells the class they are looking great, asks how they are doing, and encourages them to do eight more.
- The instructor shows amazing stamina, endurance, and coordination.
- The instructor gets on the floor and does abdominal work with the first three rows. The last three rows take a nap.
- The instructor thanks the class, gathers the music, and talks with the people in the front row or the next instructor.

Or does your scene look like this?

- Everyone is standing and looking straight ahead. The only people talking to each other are those in the front row.
- The instructor arrives early and enters the room with gusto. The instructor makes an entrance with confidence, a friendly attitude, and an obvious love of teaching.
- She quickly walks around the room shaking hands and greeting members.
- The instructor introduces herself and the name of the class and makes announcements about other programs in the club. (Always use one program to promote another.)
- The instructor begins the warm-up, facing the class and smiling, aiming the smile at everyone, and allowing the initial movements to go on long enough until everyone in the class is moving comfortably.
- During a routine, the instructor walks through the class, saying hi to latecomers and to new members or guests. She has no problem getting back to the head of the class to begin the next routine.
- If you check out the scene after 20 minutes, the instructor is teaching from a different side of the room, having the opportunity to address a "new" front row.
- Perhaps 20 minutes later, the class is doing floor work and the instructor is walking throughout the area making corrections and giving compliments. She is concentrating on those in the back of the room, the sides, and the corners.

• At the end of the class, the instructor is at the doorway, thanking everyone for coming, possibly handing out fliers for other program opportunities. Everyone is smiling, including the instructor.

These are just two areas in the club that we have visualized. But remember our original question: "How would you describe the experience you just had?" What if we were able to evaluate a prospect's or member's experience at every point of contact during a visit at the club? The front desk, the lobby, the locker rooms, the child care area, the pool?

Could we recognize opportunities to promote programs, sell participation in programs, or even sell memberships? With our visualization exercise, can we see many missed opportunities as well? Does our staff consist mostly of professional communicators or sentries waiting to be approached? Use the Test Your Professional Personality exercise on pages 33-34 to help your staff improve.

Test Your Professional Personality

Go to Test Your Professional Personality on the CD-ROM for a printable version of this quiz.

Imagine a person standing at the exit from the fitness center or group exercise room asking every current member, "How would you describe the workout experience you just had?" Their responses would probably directly reflect how well you, as a fitness professional, communicated with them. Use this quick quiz to check your communication skills. Then develop your professional personality with the accompanying suggestions.

1. Are you able to recognize people who need or appreciate attention?
   ___ Yes ___ No

Look for red flags, such as someone standing alone or reading directions on the wall, a woman who is pregnant, or a person with poor form.

2. Do you introduce yourself to people who appear to need help?
   ___ Yes ___ No

If you don't know the person, greet him or her with a smile, an introduction, a handshake, and conversation. If you've seen the member around the club, open with, "Do you remember me? My name is _____." Offer information about the activity or a safety tip. Offer options for performing moves at various degrees of difficulty. Explain appropriate attire for safety and comfort. Suggest what materials are comfortable for working out, or mention a local store that has a good selection of workout gear.

3. Do you notice individuals who are not talking with other people?
   ___ Yes ___ No

If you see a person who doesn't appear to know anyone, introduce yourself first and then introduce another member in the class or training area. Position yourself between the two people, for example, between their two treadmills or their two steps.

4. Do you wait for clients to ask a question instead of initiating conversation yourself?
   ___ Yes ___ No

Encourage questions at first by giving a compliment or a suggestion. For example, "It's good to see you again," or "You've been in several times this week, haven't you? That's great. Are you working toward something special?"

5. When individuals make eye contact with you, do you aim a smile at them?
   ___ Yes ___ No

If clients make contact first, follow up with a smile, an introduction, or a suggestion. Otherwise, initiate the contact yourself. To get a member's attention, aim your smile and hold eye contact as you approach. Use the member's name if you know it, or introduce yourself. Offer a compliment on his or her performance, and then make a suggestion about the workout, such as "How's your seat adjustment? Let's try putting the seat up a notch."

(continued)

Test Your Professional Personality *(continued)*

6. Do you introduce yourself by name?
   ___ Yes ___ No

Use your first name only. Pointing to your name tag also helps clients remember your name. Shake hands whenever possible.

7. Do you remember your clients' names?
   ___ Yes ___ No

If you remember members' names, use them as you say hi. If you don't remember, remind clients of your name, tell them you've forgotten theirs, and ask again. People don't mind if you forget; they mind if you're uninterested. Try to use a person's name at least two times in a conversation.

8. Do you shake hands when you meet people for the first time?
   ___ Yes ___ No

To shake hands, extend your hand and move forward slightly. If you don't offer your hand, why not?

9. When greeting people, do you give them time to respond to you or ask you a question?
   ___ Yes ___ No

Give clients time to make a comment by aiming your smile and pausing. When you wrap up a conversation, add a little humor, offer an anecdote about yourself, give a compliment, or recognize an accomplishment.

10. Do you offer specific suggestions to further engage members in an activity?
    ___ Yes ___ No

Examples of suggestions that make clients' workouts a positive experience include fitness tips ("Let me show you how to increase your range of motion") or breathing techniques.

Program Director

I s a program director necessary for your business? Many club owners and managers debate this issue, but a look at the numbers should convince you that a program director will increase retention and decrease attrition. The real question may be whether you can afford *not* to have a program director in your club.

A club director has many responsibilities, some of which include the following:

- Integrate new members into the club. Every new member must be contacted, interviewed, and invited to a program that offers immediate and easy entry.
- Set up a calendar of events and programs for a full year following the logical progression of programming.
- Schedule programs to accommodate all the time frames of a club during the day as outlined in chapter 5.
- Create promotional pieces and marketing plans for all programs.
- Help existing members diversify their workouts.
- Reactivate inactive members.
- Provide programs to meet the needs of all the niches of the club.
- Track participation of members in the programs.
- Meet programming budgets.
- Be accountable for the growth and profit structure for all programs and program leaders—measuring the percentage of enrollment in programs.

In this chapter we'll take a closer look at the varied roles of a program director and discuss what you should look for in a program director. We'll also look closely at the four groups of members whom a program director must consider to help establish quality programming that leads to retention. We'll look specifically at two tasks a program director must complete—telephone communication and program analysis. Finally, we'll take a close look at our market and why a program director must know what our clients know and want.

Role of a Program Director

The role of a program director is to keep the programming calendar full, the members active, the promotions moving through the club, and all the instructors and trainers productive. A program director may teach a class, run a league, give a lesson, or work one-on-one with a client, but business is measured in terms of results, not just activities. For example, a program director will measure the percentage of enrollment of every program, class, or session and help the instructors organize and grow the programs by activating new members, reactivating inactive members, diversifying existing members, and motivating potential members to buy memberships. A program director must have a genuine appreciation for every program and every member.

The qualities of a program director include leadership capabilities and communication skills on a management level as well as the ability to relate to all your members on a service level. Telephone skills, teaching skills, and selling skills are important.

The program director must be success oriented, even sales driven. In fact, the program director can be called an internal salesperson and be compared to a sales manager. A sales manager manages the sales team, sets goals, holds each salesperson accountable, and brings teamwork into the sales department. The program director does the same thing for the programming department, but the responsibility is even greater for the program director. When a salesperson sells a membership, he or she is virtually finished with the sale. For the program director, the sale begins after the sale! As explained in the logical progression of programming, members may need to experience six to eight different programs in a year before becoming retained members; therefore, the program director will be responsible for seeing that all new members "buy" a program six to eight times after they've bought the membership. The program director is ultimately held accountable for retention.

Successful program directors know how to balance the needs of a variety of people, including club members and staff, while setting aside time to work on long-term projects and program goals. The skills include developing budgets, making program reports, and creating marketing plans. The real talent, however, is being able to create an environment of positive and engaging energy . . . of fun. Many people don't stay with

Credo of the Program Director

You believe in yourself and are excited about your job.

You sincerely enjoy helping people.

You are flexible, tolerant, convincing, and fair.

You have high energy levels and are enthusiastic.

You organize your time wisely and efficiently.

You focus your attention on selling recreational hours and enjoyment.

You are the host or hostess of the club, being everywhere and seeing everyone.

You give personal attention to individuals and specific groups as well.

You are a promoter and a programmer.

You are unselfish and have a genuine interest in people and their choice for a happier, healthier lifestyle.

You are the hub of the club's activity.

You are a program director.

exercise long enough to see any results, and if they aren't enjoying the journey, they will never arrive at the destination. In our industry, we've spent 30 years developing state-of-the-art equipment and training personnel to tell people what to do and how to do it. It's time to step back and look at our business from a different perspective. Creating a fun and happy setting for your members through programming contributes to your bottom line. If you offer your members great service in the form of fun and laughter in addition to great classes, top-notch equipment, and qualified instructors, they will stay around. People like to be where there is laughter and fun because it simply feels better to be in a happy place. It feels good to laugh and it's good for you to laugh—or at least smile. Providing this type of service today will determine your sales in the weeks and months to come.

The role of the program director is indeed complex and diverse. The job requires a balance between the energetic, happy promoter and the goal-minded, responsible businessperson. Enthusiasm, passion, a sincere appreciation of the industry, and an understanding of people's needs best describe a successful program director.

How to Find a Program Director

If I were to interview someone who was interested in assuming the role of a program director, I would ask the following questions. "Have you been working in the industry as an instructor or trainer and been considering a move into management? Are you ready to take on the additional responsibilities inherent to being a manager? Are you genuinely interested in the growth and development of the members as well as the club?"

The program director must be able to handle several projects simultaneously and must have excellent interpersonal skills, a passion for the industry, and boundless energy and enthusiasm. She or he must understand every program and sincerely care that every member join a program that will be fun and inspiring.

So how do you find a program director? What words would describe the type of individual who would apply for the program director's position? A typical ad looking for a program director is shown in figure 3.1.

Wanted!
Program director for fitness club. High energy leader with organizational, teaching, telephone, and interpersonal communication skills. Duties include promotion, marketing, administration, documentation, and follow-up of programs.

Position Description & Qualifications
This position will oversee member participation and retention with the main purpose of creating a positive impact through improved member retention. Skills required include outstanding written and verbal communication skills, high level of energy, outgoing personality, and the ability to be a team leader and a team player. Must be able to work flexible hours including evenings, weekends, and holidays. Specific core activities include:
- Plan and implement member retention and participation efforts for new members (first three months), existing members (three plus months), inactive members (zero visits in three months), and potential members (prospects and guests).
- Develop and maintain a customer-oriented culture and provide and continue to seek new ways to provide outstanding customer service and exciting program opportunities.
- Work with appropriate staff to implement programming to improve member-to-member connection (e.g., clubs, leagues, fitness classes, social programs).
- Provide members and prospective members with an experience that is more than just a membership or workout visit.
- Continuously increase knowledge of member retention strategies and tactics, programming ideas, customer service, and changes in the fitness industry. Use this knowledge to provide the necessary training and skill development to hire and train all programming staff.

Figure 3.1 Hypothetical want ad advertising for a program director.

Leadership Qualities: How Do You Rate?

Go to Leadership Qualities: How Do You Rate? on the CD-ROM for a printable version of this exercise.

Evaluate yourself on the 10 leadership qualities by circling a number from 1 to 10, where 1 is low and 10 is high.

Vision: A sense of what could and should be

    1   2   3   4   5   6   7   8   9   10

Ability: Job knowledge and expertise

    1   2   3   4   5   6   7   8   9   10

Enthusiasm: Ability to motivate others and to bring out their best

    1   2   3   4   5   6   7   8   9   10

Stability: Emotional adjustment and objectivity

    1   2   3   4   5   6   7   8   9   10

Concern for others: Loyalty to employees and an interest in their welfare

    1   2   3   4   5   6   7   8   9   10

Self-confidence: Inner strength that generates employee trust

    1   2   3   4   5   6   7   8   9   10

Persistence: Ability to see tough tasks through to completion

    1   2   3   4   5   6   7   8   9   10

Vitality: Physical and emotional strength

    1   2   3   4   5   6   7   8   9   10

Charisma: Magnetic ability to invigorate people and lead them without controlling them

    1   2   3   4   5   6   7   8   9   10

Sense of humor: Ability to have fun and make fun

    1   2   3   4   5   6   7   8   9   10

_____

Rating

    100 – 90   Excellent, exceptional

    89 – 70   High, very good

    69 – 50   Average, needs improvement

    49 – below Low, much work needed

From S. Coffman, 2007, *Successful programs for fitness and health clubs* (Champaign, IL: Human Kinetics).

The evaluation of leadership qualities on page 38 is an appropriate self-evaluation for anyone pursuing the position of a program director. The role of the program director will be demanding for sure, but the reward of making a difference in people's lives makes a program director appreciative and appreciated.

Four Groups of Members

A goal of every program director is to integrate a specific number of new members into programs every month, and that number is determined by the number of new memberships sold each month. The program director is also responsible for reactivating inactive members, increasing the activities of existing members, and inspiring potential members to buy memberships. Every person—member or prospective member—falls into one of the following four categories.

Active, Existing Members

Active, existing members usually get the most attention. They are easy to program for because they are already using the club regularly, they are familiar with activities, and they have already put exercise into their lifestyles. Most programs are created for the active member, but these members would probably work out with their own routines two or three times a week and use only one or two organized programs. Many clubs give the most attention to this group of members, when actually they need it the least.

Inactive Members

Inactive members are important because unless we get that group active in the club, they will probably drop their membership altogether. But inactive members have already had a bad experience or no experience at all, and it will be very difficult to change their negative feelings. Although they are important, they are the least productive group to work with. A major objective is to prevent members from becoming inactive in the first place.

Potential Members

Potential members are important, of course, because we are in the business of selling memberships and growing the business. Potential members mostly consist of guests and trial members. Whether a program is a one-time special event or

a few experiences during a trial period, it should turn potential members into new members.

New Members

The most important member to get into a program is the new member, because studies have shown that the majority of members who quit the club or quit using the club are new members who never got started. They are members who were never involved in a program, so they never realized the club experience that they expected when they joined. New members need to feel a sense of belonging. They need their exercise time scheduled for them—a specific time and day every week—so they can immediately put exercise into their lifestyle. They also need to meet other people like themselves, with similar interests, skill levels, schedules, personalities, ages, and genders. Developing relationships in the club will provide a social, friendly, comfortable club experience. These members need a program! And they need to get involved in a program within the first week or two of their membership so they don't drop out. Most of the attrition in our business could be avoided if we got new members committed to a program at the point of sale or within the first week. Once involved, new members will retain their memberships and bring their friends into the club. We know, in fact, that 60 to 80 percent of your new business will come from word of mouth or referrals, and the majority of referrals will come from new members who are involved in the club through new member programs and activities. The most important member to the program director, therefore, is the new member, and integrating new members into programs is the number one priority.

Here is a typical club example of how new members affect your bottom line.

- Monthly membership rate is $40 per month, or $480 per year per member.
- Getting 10 new members per month involved in a program versus 10 new members who do not get into a program and will likely become inactive and drop out will result in an additional $57,600 per year.
- New members who are active and happy in the club—involved in regularly scheduled programs—will refer 60 to 80 percent of your new business.

Although the new member is obviously the most important member for the program director to work with, some challenges are involved. One common mistake is assuming that a member who just joined the club is ready, willing, and eager to get involved. In many cases, good intentions are overcome by intimidation, lack of confidence, inexperience, or fear of not fitting in. The member finds that getting committed to an exercise routine is not as much fun as she thought and takes a lot more effort than she imagined. Don't assume that the "new member packet" given at the point of sale with a list of all the programs and schedules is enough to motivate the member to begin using the club immediately and regularly. Remember that for the programmer, the sale begins after the sale.

New Member Profile

After joining the club, new members must be contacted and interviewed to assess their interests, skill levels, schedules, and personalities. The personal contact will establish a relationship between the member and the club. Ideally, this could be done by the sales department, but it is more productive coming from the program department. That's not to say that the salesperson should not contact the new member. That's just good business. But real participation will be a result of communication from the program department.

The information gathered at the point of sale must be documented so that there will be an ongoing follow-up and tracking procedure ensuring the activity and retention of the member. Your best chance of getting a new member to become a retained member begins now! The member's information is best kept in the form of an interest profile. It is a tracking procedure designed to ensure regular activity, enjoyment, recognition, and new experiences. The programming department, overseen by the program director, becomes accountable for keeping new members active and interested in the club for the first full year.

The information on the interest profile is really very simple but is powerful to use when promoting a program or special event. The profile must include the following:

- The name of the member
- Phone numbers, including home, work, and cell phone
- E-mail address
- The member's join date
- One or two basic initial interests
- Availability to use the club
- The answer to the question "Do you like to have fun?"

- Space for notes including
    experience,
    special needs or physical limitations,
    specific goals,
    age and birthday, and
    other pertinent information.

The interest profile on a new member must be used and periodically reviewed for a full year. It will be filed according to the member's joining date. Let's say the member joined the club October 1, 2006. The interest profile will be filed in *October 2006* along with all of the members who joined the club in October of that year. The month is divided into two sections—(a) Active and (b) Inactive. If the member gets involved in a program, the interest profile is filed in the Active section, and if not, then it is filed in the Inactive section—the goal, of course, is to have the Active section filled. The program director empowers other programmers in the club to oversee the interest profiles pertaining to their specific departments, but in the end, the program director is accountable for the activity and program participation of every new member in the club.

We know from experience that any member who is active in a program and uses the club regularly for a full year is a retained member; thus, when members are active in programs, retention increases. Keep the interest profiles in the join date (month) section of your files for a full year. If the member who joined in October 2006 remains in the active section of October until 2007, you know that he or she is a retained, happy member who has probably brought in friends, relatives, or coworkers as guests and referrals over the course of the year.

An example of a new member interest profile is shown on page 41. You may add the activities and programs that are in your club, but the basic information will apply to all situations.

New Member Introductory Program

The journey of one thousand miles begins with a single step. We have all heard that phrase. Just getting started is the most difficult part of accomplishing whatever task we are about to pursue, and you need to have empathy for the new members who join your club. They are taking the first step down the long road toward a new lifestyle and a behavioral change. The introductory program that we give them is our first step down the long road toward retention, so for the members and for our

New Member Interest Profile

Go to **New Member Interest Profile** on the CD-ROM for a printable version of this profile.

Date joined _____   Membership type _____

Name _____   Birthday _____

Home phone _____   Cell phone _____   E-mail _____

Availability or preference for exercise

_____ Early bird   _____ Weekday mornings   _____ Noon hour

_____ Afternoons   _____ Evenings   _____ Saturdays   _____ Sundays

Notes:

Areas of Interest

_____ Fitness center   _____ Group exercise   _____ Health and lifestyle

_____ Personal training   _____ Aquatics   _____ Nutrition

_____ Court sports   _____ Dancing   _____ Spa therapy

_____ Cycling classes   _____ Running or walking   _____ Social

_____ Children's programs   _____ Older adults   _____ Young adults

Which areas of the club are you not familiar with but would be interested in learning about at a later date?

_____

_____

_____

_____

_____

Do you like to have fun?   _____ Yes   _____ No

Notes: Skill level _____   Experience _____

Special needs _____   Other _____

From S. Coffman, 2007, *Successful programs for fitness and health clubs* (Champaign, IL: Human Kinetics).

business we must make that first step a positive one. Here are 10 points to consider as you develop and deliver the introductory program that will lead to a successful journey or retention.

- **Choose programs of one hour or less:** The introductory program should be one hour or less. Long-term commitments are often the first objections cited by new members. A single-session, one-hour experience will more likely be successful than a longer workout. In this one hour, your members must experience a club atmosphere, education, a social experience, enjoyment, a feeling of achievement, and, most of all, the desire to return for more!

- **Enroll the new member in a group activity:** Commitment to a group of people may well be the key to a member returning to the club, and a return visit is the first step to retention.

- **Teach, don't just perform:** Demonstrations and directives by an accomplished, busy instructor become intimidating and confusing. An effective teacher takes the time to help members feel an exercise or movement. If necessary, the teacher will physically move the member's body through a range of motion. There is nothing more discouraging to a new member than watching an instructor go through seat and weight stack adjustment, hopping on a piece of equipment, whipping out 10 or 12 repetitions, and moving on—assuming the member got it all.

- **Teach vocabulary and terminology.** We use terms from anatomy and physiology in our daily conversations and throw out names of pieces of equipment that are totally foreign to many new members. A good teacher knows that if an exerciser can talk about a subject comfortably, he will develop a greater understanding of it and gain confidence. For example, point to your thigh and ask the member to repeat the word *quadriceps*. By saying the terms out loud, a student is more likely to remember them.

- **Promote camaraderie and sociability:** The essence of a club environment and a group activity is sociability. Many clubs consider a one-on-one meeting with an instructor as an introductory program for a new member. It may be valuable time spent, but it does not create a clublike or social atmosphere. Conversations among several people breed questions, answers, and a friendly environment. Most people find exercise a very lonely activity, which is why they are seeking out a club environment. Provide an opportunity to cultivate friendships, and you will provide members an opportunity to exercise together on a regular basis.

- **Recognize individual achievements:** Everyone needs praise and recognition, and you can never give too much of it. From early on, children respond favorably to any kind of recognition from either their parents or their teachers. Adults respond in the same manner. Recognition makes people feel important, and they will always come back for more.

- **Qualify skill levels and abilities:** Skill levels can be defined as experienced or inexperienced, beginner or advanced. A professional leader knows how to qualify people's skills and abilities and use this information to provide the best atmosphere for learning. Understanding people's skills and abilities is the groundwork for determining the program that will best suit the new member or participant.

- **Categorize personalities:** Your members' strongest commitment to your club may be in the way they relate to each other and enjoy making new friendships. Putting compatible personalities together may be the core of your retention program.

- **Impose no additional cost:** Since the first step is the most difficult but the most important, leave no unnecessary barriers to success, including cost. The experience that the member gets in the introductory program should set the scene for the next several years of activity. The introduction, when properly administered, will clearly define the credibility of the membership, define the value of your programs, and provide the basis for ongoing participation.

- **Promote involvement:** Your role in retaining your members is to constantly promote participation. By putting people together in groups, recognizing individual achievements, and helping them reach small goals, you are encouraging them to be involved in activities that promote health, fitness, and a more enjoyable lifestyle. Since retention is our goal, promotion is an ongoing quest. The introductory program is the springboard to promoting a new activity. Always use one program to promote another.

Effective Telephone Communication

The program director must be an expert in communication and must pass these skills on to her staff. Professional communication will always be a key to successful programming, and using the interest profile information effectively and productively is a prime example of that. Asking the right questions, using the 10 magic words (see chapter 2), and developing a sincere rapport in an ongoing relationship will surely result in a more enthusiastic member who is eager to become involved in a club activity. The initial interview can be done in person or by e-mail but will more likely be done by telephone. Telephone contact is more personal than e-mail contact and less intimidating than face-to-face contact. Telephone communication is the most effective way of communicating with your members.

The script on page 44 is an example of an effective telephone interview from a program director to a new member. Note that each question or statement has a purpose and that the conversation is not muddled with unnecessary rhetoric. Make your time productive and accomplish your goal. Do the following:

1. Use the 10 magic words.
2. Introduce yourself and use the member's name.
3. Extend the invitation, in which you invite the member to a specific program on a specific day and time.
4. Set the member up for ongoing communication.
5. Gather specific information for follow-up.
6. Prepare the member for a confirmation call.

The telephone call has several objectives:

- Get a reservation or a commitment to a specific program at a specific time.
- Set the member up to expect a follow-up call. Be sure to tell him when you will make that follow-up call. Then make it! It may take two or three follow-up phone calls to get the "fence sitters" involved.
- If the member commits to the program, tell him to expect a confirmation call confirming the reservation. Then make it!

Make a confirmation call 12 to 24 hours before the program begins. A confirmation call will eliminate the majority of no-shows, possibly up to 80 percent of them. The confirmation call could make or break your program.

When you're talking on the phone, keep these tips in mind:

- Smile when talking. Your body language is "seen" over the phone as much as in person. Be happy!
- Sit tall with your head up. Sit in front of a mirror as a reminder.
- Find an area in which you do not feel any inhibitions or need to be quiet. Energy is the word of the day.
- Be aware of your mood or attitude. Your mood will dictate how well your sincerity comes across, and sincerity is the key to success.
- Be persistent. Ask every question possible and use the 10 magic words.
- Be sure your member knows your name. This is as important as your using his name. You are developing a relationship.
- Let your own personality come through the conversation, but always have your script in front of you for reference and use it as a checklist. You are managing your professional personality.

Making telephone calls to fill your programs must be one of the daily tasks of the program director and the instructors and trainers whom you train and empower to take charge of their own telephone campaigns.

Set a personal goal to complete 5 to 10 calls per day four days a week (Monday through Thursday). This means 5 to 10 conversations—not messages! It will usually take 20 to 25 calls to achieve 5 to 10 conversations and will require one to one and a half hours of uninterrupted time. The uninterrupted time is crucial.

Making the calls in one time slot will give you a rhythm and a continuing thought process. It will be much more productive than if you try to make calls sporadically during the day. You will have to experiment with various times to find your most effective and productive time. Don't waste your time. What may be a good time for you may not be good for the members, so time management will be important.

Each conversation should take five to six minutes. You must ask the right questions, get the needed information, and set up the next phone call. A good telephone campaign will result in three to five commitments per day from the 25 calls. In one week, calling Monday through Thursday, you will get 12 to 20 commitments to programs. The telephone campaign is productive.

To summarize:

- Make calls Monday through Friday (four days per week, minimum).
- Schedule one to one and a half hours of uninterrupted calling each day.
- Make 25 calls during this time.
- Complete 10 conversations from the list of 25 calls within the alloted time.
- Rehearse, use a script, and limit each call to approximately six minutes.

- Get three to five commitments within the 10 conversations.
- Get 12 to 20 commitments to programs per week.
- Make a confirmation call for every commitment.

The program director will need to call all four groups of people from time to time to fill the various programs on the wheel of logical progression—new members, active existing members, inactive members, and potential members—but the

Effective Telephone Script for a New Member

"Hello, _____ (new member's name). This is _____ (your name) from the Five Star Athletic Club." **Introduction**

"Welcome to the club. You've made a great choice!" **Reinforcement**

"Tell me, what made you join our club?"

"What areas of the club interest you most?"

"What areas are you least familiar with?" **Let's talk about you**

"Would you be interested in learning about those areas at a future time? Perhaps after you've been here a while?" **Follow-up**

"Have you been to the club since you joined?" **An opening**

"When (how) are you using the club now?" **A conversation**

"Great!" **Enthusiasm and sincerity**

"I need to know what days are best for you. Could you help me by telling me your work schedule?" **Scheduling**

"I'd like to personally invite you to join us at _____" (schedule a specific appointment, activity, or class here). **Invitation**

"Many other members who joined the club for the same reasons (or with the same schedule) as yours will be there too." **Sense of belonging**

"I guarantee that you will have fun and enjoy yourself. I'll look forward to meeting you then, and I'll call you to remind you of the date because I really want you to be there. You will really help make it a success." **An immediate friend**

"Thank you, _____ (member's name). Again, my name is _____. It was nice talking with you, and I'll look forward to meeting you in person. By the way, _____ (member's name), you do like to have fun, don't you?" **A little humor!**

"Thanks. Good-bye."

most important calls are to new members. The new member is most likely to need two to three calls before making a commitment and will definitely need the confirmation call.

Program Study Analysis

After programs are implemented, program directors must evaluate the value of the programs to the members and the effectiveness of the programs to the business, because a successful program must serve both the member and the business. A

program study analysis will help you define your purpose, set an attainable goal, and then proceed with a marketing plan to achieve the result you need. Before plunging into promoting new programs, you must acquire accurate information on what is happening daily at the club. The program study analysis helps you develop the growth and profit structure on every program in the club.

For example, you may decide to design a program and a marketing plan to increase the usage by the inactive membership by 10 percent or to add three introductory classes to the group exercise program. You may need to add two more players to a racquetball league or four new members to a

---

Program Study Analysis of Group Exercise

▷ Analysis: To determine the percentage of occupancy in the group exercise program. The program runs Monday through Friday, 9 to 11 a.m. and 1 to 3 p.m. The group exercise studio holds 35 participants at full capacity.

▷ The goal at full capacity:

35 participants × 4 hours per day = 140 participants per day

140 participants per day × 5 days per week = 700 participants

▷ The actual participation during the day is 20 participants in 2 hours of classes.

20 participants × 2 hours per day = 40 participants per day

40 participants per day × 5 days per week = 200 participants

▷ To determine the existing percentage of occupancy for the four hours per day, five days per week, divide the actual number by the goal number:

Actual 200 ÷ Goal 700 = 28.6% occupancy

Your new goal may be to increase the percentage of occupancy to 40%.

▷ What type of programs or classes would be most successful in this time frame?

▷ What group or niche would best fill those classes?

▷ How many classes are offered during the four hours? How many participants are in each class?

▷ Do you need to add more participants to each class, add more classes, or both?

▷ Are the leaders, instructors, and trainers delivering the programs professionally?

circuit class. You may need to add new programs during specific time frames of the day or simply to increase your percentage of occupancy in some existing programs at certain times of the day.

Thus far, I have set the foundation and built the leadership structure with a very concise outline of whom to hire, how to train, and what leadership skills to measure. These guidelines are imperative to developing consistency among programmers and creating a team spirit that encourages promotion of all programs and activities from all departments within the club. Clearly the message is that everyone on staff must be a leader, and all club leaders should have boundless energy, enthusiasm, and professional communication skills. The team of programmers must constantly promote their own programs, but they must also cross-promote programs from one department to the next, not only for the good of the business but for the member as well. Cross-training and cross-promoting of programs will keep members active and increase retention.

As our clubs get bigger, however, the programmers get busier, the number of programs increases, and communication between departments breaks down. Trainers, instructors, and programmers tend to stay in their own comfort areas, so the club becomes very departmentalized. For example, the court sports director rarely gets involved with the group exercise department, the fitness trainers never leave the fitness center, no one on staff seems to care about the aquatics program, and the front desk doesn't even know about half the programs on the calendar. The crossover constantly decreases. The members are uninformed, get bored, and become inactive, so the business suffers! It's vital to keep the programming team working together, the programs moving forward, and the members served, which is why your club needs a program director.

Understanding Our Market

Members and prospective members are more educated than ever before. The medical and scientific communities, and the emphasis placed on fitness by the media, are making people more aware of the health benefits of exercise. The industry is faced with a responsibility to provide more programs to an informed and diverse public. Clubs will differentiate themselves from other clubs by the number of specialized programs offered such as weight management, personal training, sport-specific classes, nutrition programs, age-related programs, strength training, conditioning programs, flexibility classes, and recreational sports programs. The trend over the years has grown from an emphasis on aerobic (cardiorespiratory) exercise to a more holistic approach to exercise including yoga, Pilates, tai chi, and meditative exercises, all of which are moving toward a mix of programming for mind, body, and spirit.

I'm describing a "whole," or total approach, to fitness, now referred to as "wellness." Fitness professionals need to be more knowledgeable, skilled, energized, and enthusiastic than ever, and it will certainly be more difficult for programmers to stay up to date on the science of exercise and the specialized programming it demands. A program director is the leader of leaders, the manager of programs, and the link between your members and your business.

Members are getting more demanding too. We have found over the years that people want more than a general workout routine from their club membership. They want leadership—someone to tell them what to do, how to do it, and when to do it and then to tell them that they did a good job. They want results, but they want their exercise experience to be fun too! A profile of today's members may look like this.

They

- need health and fitness,
- want a sense of belonging,
- expect state-of-the-art equipment,
- react to service and attention, and
- respond to leadership.

Programming is the answer. Just think: Most clubs are open 17 hours a day, seven days a week and are available for members to drop in and work out whenever they have the time or the inclination. Some may think that people joined the club because they like to exercise and that this open schedule is a convenience to the member. In reality, however, most people dislike exercising, so they don't find the time and they usually don't have the inclination.

The number one excuse in the industry for not using the club is "I don't have time." Most people will never find time to do something that they dislike, even if it's good for them. We also know that people who exercise with friends or other people like themselves are more likely to exercise regularly and make it part of their lifestyle. People who dislike exercise will certainly not be very inclined to do it by themselves. Just opening the doors and providing opportunities won't help retention one bit! In fact, taking only those steps contributes to attrition. People respond to leadership, encouragement, and a social atmosphere. They need programming. Members who join specific exercise programs use the club on the same days every week, at the same hour, with the same people. They look forward to going to the club and putting their exercise time into their daily or weekly schedule. They are the happiest, healthiest, most retained members of your club.

Promotions

The most creative programs won't be successful unless you know how to promote them and get people to participate in them. The power of professional promotions creates the initial interest that will drive the success of your marketing plan and will determine the degree of participation in any program that you offer.

Promotions experts tell us that most businesses do not tell the story of their products to their customers in their promotions. Your promotional expertise—what you do, what you say, and how you deliver the message—may make or break a great campaign, a major program, a special event, a tournament, an open house, a pro shop sale, or whatever is happening or about to happen in your facility.

In this chapter, we'll look at how promotions are essential to growing our industry and how we can make them effective.

Customer Responses to Promotions

Fitness professionals should understand that they are promoting more than just exercise. People participate in fitness activities for many different reasons—health, fun, diversion, weight control, mental well-being, socialization—so people will react to promotions in several different ways and for several different reasons. Some people respond to visible advertisements, whereas others react more quickly to verbal promotions. Here are five ways that people respond to promotions. Keep them in mind when considering what attracts your customers and what makes them take action.

- **See it.** People will see an advertisement, such as a billboard, bulletin board, flyer, or newspaper article. In two seconds, people will decide if they want to read further to find out more about the promotion. The two-second reaction is usually dependent on a picture, a clever title, the use of color, or a few words in very large print. Something must catch the eye in two seconds.

- **Read it.** In two seconds, people will decide whether they want to know more about the promotion or the program. If they read on, they will subconsciously be asking themselves, *Does this apply to me personally? Am I interested in this? Does it meet my comfort level? Do I need it?* The promotion will create the initial interest, but it must then target that interest and zero in on the exact type of person it will appeal to, such as specific age groups, genders, interests, skill levels, or personalities.

• **Hear it.** Many people respond quicker to hearing a real person explain a promotion. Sometimes a verbal promotion carries more credibility or seems more real. A radio advertisement will often be repeated over and over and will therefore have a lasting effect on someone. A real live person making a promotion face to face with someone has the added advantage of creating a relationship with a customer. If it's a positive relationship, the promotion will be much more effective because people will usually respond to people more quickly and more confidently.

• **Experience it.** One of the best promotions is the free trial. Give your member the opportunity of experiencing your program or product. You may be trying to sell a membership, a time commitment, or a six- or eight-week program. You may be offering a new activity. You may be charging what is perceived as a great deal of money for a program that is unfamiliar to your member or prospective market. In our industry, most prospective customers, new members, beginners, or inexperienced people are intimidated, misinformed, or unknowledgeable about us and exercise programs in general. Getting a commitment with that mind-set is difficult. If a promotion initially caught your eye, if it appealed to you personally, the opportunity of experiencing the promise is difficult to pass up. A free introductory experience makes for an easy entry into a program and an ideal response to a promotion. Hitting a racquetball, doing jumping jacks to some great music, or lifting a few barbells for the first time will almost always be exciting.

• **Tell it to others.** Sixty to eighty percent of your new business comes from word of mouth. People talk to other people about their experiences, and there is no better way to increase participation in programs than letting your members do your ongoing promoting and marketing for you. People share their positive experiences and—bingo!—you have a referral.

Let's review. The promotion started with a two-second "grabber," something that created the initial interest immediately. That interest was followed with information that targeted the interest. You appealed to a specific niche or population categorized in terms of interest, skill level, schedule, personality, age, or gender. Now you've got a participant. Your member experienced the program and will, at the very least, continue in this program or another version of it. It will likely result in a referral, as the member tells others about it.

Sell the Promotion

Although our industry is nearly 30 years old, the number of individuals who regularly engage in physical activity has a disappointing rate of growth. Even worse is the number of beginning exercisers joining our clubs or our programs. We originally thought, *If we build it, they will come.* We found that that was not the case. Clubs need to increase marketing efforts to attract new members, and program directors need to engage in more promotions to grow the programs. Fitness-related programs and activities in themselves are not fun to the average individual. We need to do more than put up sign-up sheets for program participation. Gaining participants requires an expenditure of time, energy, and skill. Your promotion techniques must clearly articulate how your program will benefit the individual and why your program or product is different from all others. You must establish a unique selling proposition that your customer will understand, appreciate, and react to positively.

Example 1

You might be trying to market a beginning racquetball program in your club. Your target market would be new members or prospective members who do not play racquetball. Your promotion could read as follows:

> Beginning Racquetball Lessons at the ABC Club
> Five Lessons—$25
> Call now for more information.

or

> WANTED! Beginning Racquetball Players!
> Where . . . The ABC Club
> When . . . Wednesday mornings or Wednesday evenings
> What . . . 5 Lessons—5 Weeks—$25
> GUARANTEE . . . You will have fun, meet other beginning players like you, and be comfortable playing racquetball anywhere . . . or YOUR MONEY BACK! Call now: (phone number)

Which promotion would you most likely respond to? The guarantee is certainly a unique selling proposition. It definitely differentiates the two programs and will be very appealing to the beginning player, who is the target market for both clubs. Even if you eliminated the $25 fee in the first promotion, it probably wouldn't be as effective as the second.

Example 2

Most clubs need to promote the free weight area of the club to women, especially to women who are new to the club or new to exercising. One promotion might read as follows:

> Beginning Weight Training for Women
>
> Learn the benefits of strength training for the beginner.
>
> Six-Week Sessions, $45

Another promotion might read

> WOW! Women On Weights! Join Us Now!
>
> Six-Week Sessions, $45
>
> Come to a FREE INTRODUCTORY CLASS on _____.
>
> GUARANTEE—You will meet other women in a comfortable environment with a common interest and have fun exercising.
>
> EXTRA! A FREE pair of weightlifting GLOVES to all first-time participants in the six-week session!

Which promotion do you think would be more successful? Do you recognize the unique selling propositions in the second example? The title is exciting, a free introductory class is enticing, and a pair of gloves gives greater value for the $45 fee.

Deliver the Promise

The program must deliver what the promotion promises and what the customers expect. You can't afford to run programs without promotions but you also can't afford to promote something that could cause a bad experience. The fact that a good program experience can bring in 60 to 80 percent of new business also means that it can turn away that potential market as well. Word of mouth is powerful, and negative word of mouth can do an exponential amount of damage to your business. It's a quirk of human nature that people love to find something to complain about and then tell it to others. One survey company estimated that people who have a positive experience tell 8 to 12 others about it, and people who have a negative experience tell 15 to 20 others about it. Just as in the logical progression of programming, always

use one program to promote another. The promotion promotes the program, which promotes the referral that results in growth and retention. One of the best strategies for successful promotion is simply called "Follow up! Follow up! Follow up!" Deliver what you promise.

Effective Promotion Tools

You use visible and verbal communication tools in internal and external promotional opportunities. Regardless of the medium you use, the end result will tell people about the personality of your club, so you want to choose your promotions and presentations with that in mind. Some of the words that should define the personality of a successful health and fitness club are *energy, excitement, fun, friends, friendly, enthusiasm,* and *empathy.* Choosing the right words and presenting them visibly and verbally are important, but think of the subconscious words that a picture can give. A picture says a thousand words, so we'll first look at the power of using pictures—a visual communication tool. Then, we'll look at the two most visible (printed) internal promotions that are used in all clubs—bulletin boards and fliers. Several dos and don'ts apply to both, and following some guidelines will ensure that these promotions will convey the right message, the full message, and a message that encourages a positive response. Finally, we'll look at unique things you can do with buttons and T-shirts.

Pictures

Pictures portray images that become a club's identity or personality. The better the image, the greater the trust in the club's programs. The more believable the image, the greater potential for participation in the program. If the image relates personally to the onlooker, the response will be quicker and more positive. The best way to secure the right image in your promotion is to include pictures of people participating in an event. Using pictures of people is the most productive and the easiest means of promoting programs.

Most often, however, pictures aren't used effectively. Billboards, bulletin boards, fliers, newsletters—you name it—often use pictures of models, beautiful people, perfect bodies, people without names, identities, or connections to the club. If you want people to respond to your promotions, then use pictures of real people participating in your programs. You want to show the club's personality, and what better way is there to do this than to put your club's personalities in your promotions? Show people the actual type of members you want to attract for a specific program. If you're targeting a specific population segment, include pictures of people specifically of that age, gender, and activity or skill level. If an event is not targeted to a special audience, include pictures of people of all ages, genders, and body types. Above all, make sure the people in the picture are having fun! Are they smiling, laughing, talking, gesturing, or doing something, rather than just posing? Here are some points to consider when choosing the people to put in your promotions.

Within two seconds, prospective participants will decide if that activity interests them. Now to target that market. Let's say you are promoting a senior program—definitely geared to an aging population. Use a picture of people between the ages of 55 and 70 who are doing something active, and you will attract more of the same. If you are a women-only club, or are promoting a women's weight training class, use pictures of women working out with free weights and spotting one another; this will highlight the socialization factor in your promotion and thus will add to the appeal for the female market. One picture conveys a huge message.

How does this work? I'd like you to visualize a bulletin board in your club. The board has valuable information regarding the latest news on the effects of exercise and nutrition on diabetes, arthritis, and obesity. It also has a list of programs available at your club pertinent to the information. How many people stop to peruse the bulletin board, take time to read the material, ponder the programs, and discuss them with others ? Probably very few, certainly not many, and, more important, not enough. Take the same bulletin board and put pictures, even snapshots, around the perimeter of the printed information. The pictures are of actual members of the club: men, women, older, younger, some slim, some heavy. How do you think your members would react to that bulletin board? Members, guests, even people on a tour would stop at the promotion and look at the pictures. The first thing they would look for is to see if they are in the pictures. Second, they would look to see if they recognize anyone in the pictures. Third, they would visualize themselves in the pictures and look for people who remind them of themselves. A tip: Make sure that the people in the pictures are smiling.

Anyone looking at scenes that depict fun, sociability, camaraderie, and a comfortable environment would like to be part of a scene like that. Prospective members will actually feel part of the club and get a sense of belonging by visualizing themselves in the pictures. After customers see the pictures, of course, then you move their attention from the people to the educational material and the programs that are available. The use of pictures is a powerful promotional tool.

Bulletin Boards

Bulletin boards are great for constant and consistent internally visible promotions. There are 10 points to consider to ensure that your bulletin boards are effective.

• **Strategic locations.** Every activity department should have a place that promotes the programs of that area, and it should be readily available for everyone to check often. If you don't have wall space for a bulletin board, you can put it on an easel and place it at the entrance of the fitness center, group exercise room, or pool area. If the programs are for women only or men only, the boards could be placed outside of the locker rooms. Bulletin boards must be visible and accessible to be effective.

• **Current information.** Almost every club that I visit has a bulletin board with outdated material on it. A bulletin board that contains outdated promotional material, pertaining to a program or event that has come and gone, will cause the member to lose interest and possibly miss other, more valuable information.

• **A title.** Remember the two-second rule. A visible promotion should catch your eye or get your attention within two seconds. Large, readable lettering of a title or subject of the main information on the bulletin board tells everyone what the program is about. Within two seconds, customers will know whether they are interested in knowing more. Do not put superfluous information on a bulletin board that does not pertain to the title.

• **Colored backgrounds.** Use different colored paper or cloth backgrounds to change the look of bulletin boards. Changing the background color of a bulletin board may even be relevant to the two-second rule. A bright green background, for example, is sure to catch the eye of a member who has walked past a cork-colored bulletin board for several weeks or months.

Courtesy of Sandy Coffman

An effective bulletin board, like this one for WOW! Women on Weights, has a visible title, a colored background, and decorations; is placed in a strategic location; and contains graphics, photos of participants, schedules, and registration information.

• **Window dressings and decorations.** Along with colored backgrounds, borders and other decorations can enhance bulletin boards. One example is to use various background colors to coordinate with the four seasons—yellow for summer, orange for autumn, white for winter, green for spring. Seasonal decorations such as flowers, leaves, and snowflakes work well too. Decorations or borders can enhance the promotion of certain programs and activities. For example, a string of bicycles or silhouettes of runners, swimmers, dancers, or weightlifters will make the first two seconds come alive with interest to everyone interested in a particular activity.

• **A single-subject message—or one of many.** Ideally you want each bulletin board to promote one type of fitness activity or program to get the most advertising out of your space, but that is not always possible. Several programs or subjects can be promoted on one board with the simple use of colored backgrounds. One board, for instance, can be divided into two or three sections, each with a different color background. Each section can have its own title and information below it.

• **Neat and orderly.** Bulletin boards are notoriously messy! All too often they are cluttered with outdated information, or too many subjects may be crammed onto one board. Papers, fliers, or even pictures are put up with one thumbtack in a corner, and the papers and fliers are often torn or have writing on them. Every promotional item tells a story of the personality and professionalism of your business.

• **Legible names.** Often bulletin boards are used to announce winners of contests, participants in programs, or introductions of members for various reasons. Displaying names of members can be an excellent promotional tool, but only if the names are displayed with care, pride, and professionalism. Just as people like to hear their name used in conversation, they like to see their name used in print. Be sure to treat a name with respect. Make it legible.

• **Pictures.** Pictures will always add to the impact of written material. A bulletin board is an excellent tool to showcase your members and the activities of your club. If members or prospective members can visualize themselves as part of your club's membership, your participation numbers are sure to grow and your retention rate is sure to increase. Pictures are a promotional tool that can be used very effectively on your bulletin boards.

• **Frequent changes.** Every quarter or every season, the bulletin boards should get a new look. Backgrounds, decorations, and window dressings give a new beginning to your promotions and programs. If you have several programs or leagues, for example, that run in 6-, 8-, or 10-week blocks, the programs, names, and pictures must be changed in a timely manner to make the promotions productive. Bulletin boards that announce birthdays, anniversaries, births, awards, or unique announcements pertaining to your members will need new information at least monthly. I guarantee that members will consistently check to see if their name or picture is on the board. Here's a tip: A bulletin board with the preceding information could be placed near the front entrance and titled "Now You Know" or "Did You Know?" or "What's Happening?" Bulletin boards can offer many types of promotional opportunities and have many different marketing advantages.

Fliers

Fliers are very versatile in that they are mini take-away bulletin boards, and they can be used as traveling information tools. (See the CD-ROM for examples of several well-designed flyers for many of the programs listed in part II.)

- **Logos—identification.** One of the biggest mistakes I see in fliers is that they are printed on plain paper, by which I mean paper without identification. Every flyer should be printed on club letterhead or at least contain the club name and logo.

- **Title subject.** Remember, a flyer is a promotion! It must grab you in two seconds, so the title of the program or subject of the promotional information must be visible and clear. The club name and program title may be the only things that will catch or hold people's attention.

- **Large print and white space.** Too much printed material on one page will turn readers away before they look at the information. Small print immediately sends the message that the information must be studied or will take too much time and effort to read. A flyer must get people's attention, pique their interest, and give enough information to keep their interest.

- **Varied letter size.** Two or three pieces of information are all people need or want when looking at a flyer. Where is it from? What's it about? Whom is it for? If you answer these questions in three different sections of the flyer with two or three different size fonts or styles, you'll get the job done. The eye must be able to flow freely and quickly from one area to the next.

- **Clip art and borders.** Fliers obviously don't have as much room as bulletin boards, but clip art can usually take the place of photos of people. A picture, sketch, or design can pull a message together without the use of printed words and will get and hold your audience's attention.

- **Color-coded activity identification.** Promotion is often accomplished by creating familiarity. The simple use of color coding can promote your programs to the right market throughout your club. For example, if you are promoting a group exercise program and use a yellow background on your group exercise bulletin board, use yellow paper for your group exercise schedules. If you keep this color consistent in your promotions, you will educate your members that yellow identifies group exercise promotions, and whether people see a bulletin board in the back of the club or a flyer at the front of the club, they will learn to immediately identify yellow with a group exercise message.

- **W-W-W-W-$$$.** Because fliers are limited in space and are looked at, put away, taken away, and looked at later, they must have all the important information and no unimportant information to clutter or confuse the message. The main questions to address in every program flier are what is the program, whom is it for, where will it be, when will it happen, and how much will it cost?

- **Registration.** Where do I sign up? If you don't help your member to respond, react, and commit, you can't expect participation. Every program flyer must give registration information.

- **Phone number.** If you expect your members to respond to a promotion quickly, you must make it easy for them. Whether they want to register for participation or find out more information, they need to have a phone number at their fingertips.

- **Name.** Every promotion should have a contact person. People want to talk to a real person concerning a program that looks and sounds like fun because it is designed around their needs, interests, and enjoyment. This will make it comfortable and easy for them to join!

Buttons and T-Shirts

The name of the game in promotion is to be visible, memorable, and exaggerated. It has been said that people only remember 12 percent of what they see or hear, so if a promotion doesn't get the attention of customers and make some kind of an impact on them it just won't be effective, and an ineffective promotion costs a lot of money! If you are promoting a program to a specific group of people or a special population, the need for a lasting impression is even greater. If you think the power of pictures is great, just think how effective your promotions are when they are displayed on real people. Your staff can be walking billboards! The simple use of promotional buttons and T-shirts not only will announce a new program but will automatically make the program seem exciting.

The WOW! program—Women on Weights—is sure to be successful with the help of the staff. Buttons are inexpensive and can be made right in your club for all kinds of promotional opportunities. The buttons are easy to put on and can immediately be worn by every staff member. The button can simply say, "Ask About WOW! Join Us Now!" An even bigger promotion of WOW! is to put your promotional slogan, "Ask About WOW! Join Us Now!" on T-shirts and have your staff wear the T-shirts as the uniform. Can you visualize how dynamic the WOW! program will seem with the entire staff wearing T-shirts with the WOW! slogan?

You are sure to get opportunities to verbally promote the WOW! program (using the 10 magic words, of course) because most women will ask about the program. Or, you can open the conversation and verbally promote the program by referring to the button, or you may have the luxury of using the PA system in your club to jump-start the conversation.

How would members respond if an announcement came through the club saying, "Ask about WOW! Join us now! Does everyone see the buttons (or T-shirts) on our staff? Be sure to ask them about our new program, WOW!"

The use of people as walking billboards can go one step further. Let's use the participants in the WOW! program itself to promote the program. The slogan—"WOW! I Did It!"—obviously announces pride in participating in the program. It is placed on a T-shirt and given to all women who complete the six-week session.

You now not only have a walking billboard; you have a walking picture. If you take the same slogan, "WOW!" I Did It!" and put it beneath snapshots of the participants on your bulletin board, the promotion becomes consistent and familiar, more professional, powerful, and productive.

External Promotions

Bulletin boards, fliers, pictures, promotional buttons, T-shirts, and PA announcements are wonderful, but they are internal promotions directed to members. These tools used internally will promote participation and retention from members, but when they are adapted for use outside the club they become excellent opportunities to get new members as well. Following are some examples of external promotions:

• Send newsletters, brochures, or postcards to past members and guests of the club who have not yet joined. These are people who are already familiar with your club and who have shown interest in membership at some time for some reason. A specific program offered at your club may be just the thing that will encourage a prospective member to join. Your unique programs will set your club apart from the rest. A good program that

is promoted correctly will lead people to join your club for fun and fitness, a social environment, and a sense of belonging.

• Give demonstrations of a program wherever and whenever possible. For example, the WOW! program can be demonstrated in a parking lot, in a mall, or at a service club meeting, school, church, synagogue, corporate office building, or any organization that has public traffic or holds informational meetings. There are many opportunities to demonstrate the WOW! program and to give a promotional talk about it too. Of course, you will want to distribute the fliers to everyone interested. Your programs will sell your club.

• A good program, such as the WOW! program, if promoted properly, can attract media attention as well. Let's say you promoted a free introductory WOW! program to members and nonmembers alike who were interested in the benefits of weight-bearing exercises for women. In addition to the class and demonstrations, your club would provide two or three medical experts on osteoarthritis and osteoporosis to support the program. You could personally invite many of the female reporters and newscasters in your area to attend. Your program would become a community health resource and would very probably gain free public exposure. I once invited a local newscaster to my club to take beginning racquetball lessons. I was surprised when she arrived with a camera crew! Her lessons were taped and broadcast over the noon news for the entire week. That was a real wow!

A program that has created the initial interest and has established a desirable image through its enormous visibility will become memorable. Some programs are offered only at specific times of the year, or even annually. So each year when the promotion is presented, the members remember it, join again, and encourage others to join with them. The WOW! program, for example, may be offered in six-week sessions three or four times a year, but the introductory WOW! class may be offered only one time per year. Any promotion should begin no less than three weeks before the event to allow enough time for the promotions to work.

Remember, consistency makes the promotion memorable. Do it right the first time. Plan ahead, and be sure to keep the message simple.

When the whole promotion is put together, take a picture and document all the procedures and components. The next time you run the program, make sure you use the same name, location, color scheme, logo, and artwork. Make it easy for your members to recognize the program at a glance. If a program is worth doing once, it's worth doing again.

Of course, the programs must be run successfully and professionally to make the promotions credible, but the promotions themselves set the stage. If the visibility of the promotion is huge, then the participation in the program is huge. The total approach to promotion is what will make the program a successful venture. Whether internal or external, visible or verbal, promotion can be everywhere you are and in everything you do. Professional promotions will enable a fitness facility to effectively reach customers, better serve members, and ultimately find that they are programming for profit!

The Ultimate Promotion— A Party!

Okay, how do we take something as serious as health and fitness and make it fun? Throw a party! There are many reasons to throw a party at your club: holidays, national events such as the Super Bowl, and recognition for personal achievements at the end of a league or any six- or eight-week program in the fitness center. A few basic elements of a successful club party will spark conversation and excitement. Begin with pictures, decorations, and promotions on bulletin boards and fliers throughout the club. During the week of Halloween, the staff could wear costumes, wigs, or crazy glasses. It would surely get a laugh from everyone who came into the club.

No party would be a success without food and drink. The menu could be consistent with the theme, for example, corned beef and cabbage on St. Patrick's Day. Depending on the type of clientele you have, you could ask members to make a small contribution, such as an ingredient for a salad bar; this will get every member involved in the success of the party and lower your costs too. People like to be part of a party's success, and they like to take an active role in participating.

Key to a successful party is giving out awards and prizes. Giving recognition to your members for individual achievements is a sure way to increase attendance at the next event, but there is a secret to making the recognition program a success. Give out as many awards as possible—best attendance, most improved, most persistent, most determined,

best attitude. This can even be accomplished with something as small as ribbons with the sayings on them. Ribbons are also tangible, so they can be taken out of the club and the compliment will be remembered for a long time—probably talked about with other people.

Always have the program director give an award to someone in front of their peers. Take their pictures and put them on the bulletin board! Recognition is fun for everyone because everyone takes part whether they are receiving or applauding. The party will make everyone excited about their next league match, exercise session, or group exercise class.

Parties are great occasions for programmers to sign up members for other club activities or events. (Always use one program to promote another.) It is easy for a programmer to arouse enthusiasm in a large group of people in a fun, social environment. The program director actually becomes a social director and uses a party atmosphere to deliver exciting promotions that will save time and effort when introducing a new event. The program director is the host or hostess of every party, making sure that it will be a success for the business as well as for the member. All your staff should be involved in social programming. Members get involved and stay involved through social events. Members don't quit your club if they are having fun and making friends.

Have members' birthdays show up on the computer screen at check-in. Make it a point to surprise members who check in at the front desk on their birthday with a cupcake or a muffin with a little birthday candle. The treat along with a smile and an enthusiastic "Happy birthday!" greeting will go a long way. Announcing "Happy birthday to _____ (member's name)!" over the PA system will bring a smile to everyone in the club, and many members will immediately turn to the birthday celebrity with an enthusiastic "Happy birthday!" This small birthday program is huge to the members. Every member will anticipate the recognition and appreciate it. Do you think it would also contribute to retention? You bet.

You can give a small carnation to women on Mother's Day or a tiny flag on Independence Day, and on Valentine's Day be sure that all members and guests get a kiss as they leave the club. Yes, the kiss is wrapped in foil!

The essence of our business is fitness. Program directors take seriously the business of making fitness fun.

5

Niche Marketing

Niche marketing means programming by putting people together. Michael LeBoeuf, in his book *How to Win Customers and Keep Them for Life,* stated it so well when he said, "A business that tries to be all things to all people runs the high risk of becoming nothing to everyone" (p. 54). The group concept is the first step in niche marketing, and it works!

Every program is not for every person, but instead, a program is created for a specific group of people who share a common interest in the activity. That group is called a niche. Each niche can also be defined as a smaller club, thereby making our programs clubs within clubs. Niche programming is exactly what allowed our business to come so far so soon.

Our industry started out with recreational activities such as racquetball and tennis with lessons and leagues. The leagues were groups of people with similar interests, skill levels, and schedules who met weekly to share an active experience that included exercise, camaraderie, sociability, and recognition for participation and performance. Members formed relationships and friendships, received recognition at awards banquets at the end of the league season, and found sociability and fun. The leagues became clubs within clubs, solidifying the sense of belonging that comes with joining a club. Even today, any club offering a league program in any activity will report that league members are the most retained members of the club. Can we or should we be creating more programs that offer the league concept, say, in the fitness center? At this point in the fitness center we offer several lines of state-of-the-art equipment—cardiorespiratory equipment, weight machines, and free weights—and we tend to focus on individual programming with one-on-one consultations and individual workout cards. Members are encouraged to come to the club and work out on their own, probably by themselves, three times a week, working to reach their fitness goals.

We sell 80 percent of new memberships in our fitness centers and see most of our attrition come from the same area. We are selling more memberships, but we sometimes find that we are selling about the same amount as we need to replace those who leave or quit using our clubs every month. Admittedly, some people need, want, or are content with an individualized program. They are a niche as well. But statistics have shown that they are not the majority of people, and we must expand our programming efforts to serve those who are looking for a more clublike experience in their exercise routines and those who need to bond with and feel comfortable with others like themselves. They are the people who will remain members longer and refer more friends, relatives, and coworkers to the club. Niche programming is all about structuring our programs around a group concept that will result in retention. For example, the stationary bike used to be offered in a fitness center to any one person to use for an undetermined amount of time. Many bikes stood unused. Group cycling classes changed all that and became much like cycling leagues. More members are cycling now than ever before: They meet at the same time on the same day every week with the same instructor and enjoy each other's company as much as the workout itself.

In this chapter we'll take a close look at the different niche market segments you have in your facility. We'll also identify those who are most likely to use your facility at different times of the day and how their needs and wants differ. Finally, we'll look at how you can use holidays and seasons throughout the year to appeal to your many niche market segments.

Niche Marketing Segments

Let's examine all the different niches that should direct our programming efforts and see how niche marketing ties the ribbon on the complete programming package. A summary of niche marketing segments is provided on page 59 for your reference.

Interests

The first obvious niche is formed out of an interest in a particular activity. A person's interests are discussed during one of the first conversations held at the point of sale and are one of the main pieces of information gathered on the interest profile. A person's interest in a given area immediately ties her into a group of people, a niche, within your club.

Skill Levels

People with similar abilities are less intimidated than those mixed together with various skill levels. People are easily grouped in terms of beginning, intermediate, or advanced level of expertise. It is not unusual for beginners to feel inadequate with advanced people in the same group or for advanced people to feel bored and unchallenged when exercising with beginners. Inexperienced members will be less likely to stay involved if they are forced to be in a situation that caters to the more experienced exerciser or sport participant. People like to learn together, to advance together, and to compete with one another. That makes for a great experience and a great program.

Schedules

Our clubs are typically open approximately 17 hours a day, seven days a week. We know through experience that most people will not just find time during the day to go to the club to work out. Those who try to use their membership with that in mind fail—quite quickly. Programmers and program directors are responsible for discerning the time that each member is available to use the club regularly. (This information is also noted on the interest profile.) The responsibility goes far beyond that, however. We must offer programs that match the interests of the member at the times that the member is available. The program then must be marketed to other members with the same interests and availability. This is another example of how the sale begins after the sale. Promotional pieces such as fliers and posters will deliver the program information, but specific telephone campaigns will be key to filling the programs with members who will relate to one another as well as use the club regularly. Program scheduling must be coordinated between the members' schedules and that of the club.

Personalities

Personalities or personal characteristics often dictate whether people are comfortable with one another. In our business, where retention of members is so important, personality niches must be taken into consideration. For example, certain programs are more conducive to aggressive, competitive, experienced, or advanced members, rather than more passive, quiet, inexperienced, or beginning individuals. Although it is not always possible or easy to match personalities, it is important to consider them. People will stay together longer if they share similar personalities.

There is a pitfall to talk about here as well. The experienced, advanced, aggressive, and competi-

Summary of Niche Marketing Segments

Members

- Interests
- Skill levels
- Schedules
- Personalities
- Ages
- Genders

Personalities

- Aggressive or passive
- Quiet or social
- Competitive or noncompetitive
- Experienced or inexperienced

Ages and Genders

- Juniors
- Seniors
- Men
- Women

Skill Levels

- Beginning
- Intermediate
- Advanced

Four Major Groups

- New members
- Inactive members
- Active members
- Potential members

tive members make up about 20 percent of your membership. Visualize, if you will, a group exercise class. If there are 35 participants in the class in five rows, the first row (about 20 percent) will be the very fit, experienced participants. They will always be in the front row! Instructors, as other staff members in the club, tend to spend most of their time (about 80 percent) conversing with and teaching to that 20 percent. These members need the least attention and get the most attention because they are the easiest people to teach to, and they are confident and knowledgeable. The new members, the beginners, the inexperienced, the guests, or the sporadic users will be at the back of the class, in the corners, and on the perimeters. They are the majority of the members who need the majority of our attention and our best effort at programming. We have focused on the importance

of the new member throughout this book. You must identify the people who want and need the most help; they require your sincere, enthusiastic effort and 80 percent of your time and talent. They are the people who need to find friends, a sense of belonging, and the best club experience you can provide. Identify and categorize personalities as you build your programs, and you will increase retention and build your business.

Ages

Age groups form niches among your membership. One of the largest niches in our industry today is the aging market. It is probably the most diverse niche as well, because older people have varying degrees of experience, functionality, physical limitations, education, and desire. Seniors who have exercised regularly in a club for years will make it easy for us to create programs according to availability and interest, but the majority of people older than 55 years have not been members of a club in the past and are not comfortable in what seems like a business that caters to the young. Ironically, the baby boomers and beyond who have not exercised regularly are the people who want us and need us most, so our marketing efforts must be increased dramatically to accommodate this fast-growing older-adult population.

In addition to being one of the largest niches of our industry today, and one of the most important, the senior niche is also the most complex because of the varying degrees of abilities, experience, and aging issues brought to the table. The older adult market will need programming to accommodate these niches within the niche. Qualified fitness professionals as well as specialized programming will be needed to attract and then keep these people active so they can have a good quality of life for the rest of their lives. Fitness or wellness for the older adult takes on several dimensions of living.

Programs for the older adult will vary greatly within the physical and emotional planes of life depending on experience and general health status, but social, psychological, and spiritual well-being is as important to the older adult as physical fitness. A positive attitude, self-esteem, and friendships will play the biggest role in the amount of effort seniors will put into their exercise routines. The older-adult population is a very diverse niche and will probably become the largest market in our industry in the coming years. We have a responsibility to develop programs that will meet seniors' needs at all levels of fitness.

Children make up the other extreme of niche marketing according to age. Because schools are eliminating recreational time for activity and because child obesity is rapidly increasing, our clubs must seriously develop programs that promote healthy lifestyles for the young. Age groups such as 3 to 5 years, 6 to 10, and 11 to 15 need programs that are specific to them. Some need more variety than others, some need more competition, some need more encouragement, and they all need laughter and fun.

Both the aging market and children's market indicate the need to program with a social group in mind. Ironically, you will see lots of similarities in programming to the older adult and to the younger population. Specialized programming and niche marketing are the answers to serving

both markets and achieving success in your business as well.

Genders

The gender niche in our industry with the most potential for expansion is obviously the women's market. This niche needs a sense of belonging, leadership, direction, comfort, familiarity, a less intimidating environment, and socialization. These things are so important for women that entire clubs catering to women only have become not only the largest segment of growth in our industry, but also the largest business franchise opportunity in the world! Women-only programs and women-only clubs illustrate how niche marketing rules our business. The women-only drive in our industry speaks volumes to the need for socialization, self-esteem, a more clublike environment, a stronger sense of belonging, and a less intimidating atmosphere in our industry. We can accomplish it all with more professional leadership and programs of better quality.

Four Major Groups

We have already talked about how every person falls into one of four major groups of people in our clubs. The four groups are new members, active members, inactive members, and potential members and are all considered niches in themselves.

We need to use specific marketing techniques and programs to attract new members and get them integrated into the club. Introductory programs, beginning programs, and social programs are good examples of how to integrate a new member regardless of his interest, skill level, schedule, personality, age, or gender. Again, this is like having a niche within a niche. I define a new member as anyone who has joined your club within the last three months. A member is considered a new member for the first three months of membership whether she is active or not. Even experienced exercisers need to be introduced to new lines of equipment or new group exercise classes, and they most definitely need to be introduced to other members like themselves and to have an opportunity to make friends and get to know your staff. The programs that get your new members integrated into your club make up the first phase of the wheel of logical progression and will be key to turning new members into active members.

An active member is one who has been a member for more than three months and is using your club regularly. Active members ideally get involved in a scheduled activity and put your club into their weekly schedule or routine. They will use your club on the same day and the same time with the same group of people every week. Members who remain active in programs for a full year, experiencing all three phases of the wheel of logical progression, are your retained members—your most valuable members. Your objective is to get every member to become an active member. Your more important goal and first priority is to get every new member to become an active member.

The inactive member is often called a dropout. Inactive members are those who have joined your club but have not gotten involved in programs. They use your club sporadically at best, hardly ever, or perhaps not at all. The extreme inactive member is one who has not been in the club at all for more than three months.

As we have previously discussed, these members are critical because their activity, or rather inactivity, occurs right before they quit the club. Although it is critical that you activate them, they are the most difficult members to get active because they probably have already had a negative experience at the club or they would not be inactive or would not have dropped out in the first place. The best marketing technique for reactivating inactive members is to treat them the same as your new members. You must personally invite them—or reinvite them—into programs at the integration stage or introductory phase of the programming wheel. They need a new beginning, and they need to get into a structured program, ideally with other members like themselves and with new members who share the same interests, skill levels, schedules, and personalities. Putting the inactive member or dropout on a guilt trip by reminding her that she hasn't been exercising will seldom do any good. Members who do not get involved in regularly scheduled programs will more than likely become inactive members or dropouts. It's best to do it right the first time when they are new members, but you may have a second chance to reinvolve inactive members and move them along to become active members.

Potential members make up the fourth group. Anyone in your community who has not become a member of your club falls into this category, and most important for your immediate business, all the guests and people who toured your facility and did not join are potential members. One-day events and special events will be very productive in turning potential members into new members.

Open houses, grand openings and reopenings, charity programs, health fairs, and special days in the year—Administrative Professionals' Day, Boss' Day, Seniors' Day—are examples of some of the program opportunities that will be good for potential members. Your goal for potential members follows the same pattern as previously discussed: Turn potential members into new members and then into active members. Each group, however, is its own niche and needs special programming.

Daily Niche Marketing Time Slots

Niche marketing goes beyond typecasting members. For example, you can pinpoint six different time slots in a business day during which you will see some niches more than others.

Early Bird Hours: 5 to 9 a.m.

The majority of members who use your club at this time are businesspeople, type A personalities, regular exercisers, and those on tight schedules. Being on time is very important to these members because they are usually leaving your club to get on with a busy day. Personnel must be efficient, upbeat, organized, and cheery. Members who use the club at this time automatically form a social bond that creates friendships, relationships, and an appreciation for everyone being morning people. Clubs that offer on-time openings, a friendly smile, tons of energy, fresh coffee, and an occasional bagel will score high marks with the early birds.

Daytime: 9 to 11:00 a.m. and 1 to 3 p.m.

The majority of these daytime hours will bring in your female and senior membership. Child care will be key to young mothers, as will flexibility of schedules. The social environment for moms, if nurtured professionally, can create a women-only type of club within a coed environment. Your staff must be patient, caring, helpful, and understanding because unusual and unexpected situations occur with young moms trying to balance family time, exercise, and a social life within their club membership.

Older adults will also find these hours conducive to their lifestyle and schedules. The newly retired person or part-time retiree will enjoy a less hectic environment and a quieter time to exercise in the daytime. These clients will be very reliable in their attendance because they will most often specifically set their club time in stone each week and plan their exercise time as seriously as their dinner time. The older adults will need a special place in the club to socialize with one another, but they will also need a friendly accommodating staff who greet them professionally and use their names in a friendly, sincere manner. The ambiance, the music selection, and the friendly staff are key to creating an inviting, comfortable, and educational atmosphere. Our clubs will have the responsibility of hiring and training the right personnel to create programs that are specifically designed for older adults during the daytime hours. Your efforts will make a difference in their lives as well as in your business.

Noon Hour: 11 a.m. to 1 p.m.

The noon hour is often busier than the hours around it. The noon-hour exerciser is usually taking this time for a quick workout during the day or is even using your club to take the place of a long, high-calorie lunch. Thirty- to 45-minute classes usually work well here, and, again, starting class or a workout on time may be crucial to whether the noon-hour exerciser can stay with a program.

Late Afternoon: 3 to 5 p.m.

The late afternoon is often considered a downtime in clubs, but niche marketing means that if you identify the people who are available to use your club at a specific time, you can create programs that cater to those niches. Program directors are accountable for creating programs that fill downtimes as well as prime times. Teachers, nurses, and shift workers are examples of people who could use your club regularly at this time. After-school programs for kids—sport-specific and recreational—are excellent ways to use your club in the late afternoons.

Prime Time: 5 to 8 p.m.

Prime time is called that because it is generally considered the time that most people want to use the club. It actually is often a problem time, because too many members want to use the club during prime time. We call it "prime-time overflow," because we can only accommodate so many people in one area and often we have to turn people away from courts or group exercise classes just because we can't accommodate them all at the same time. The tragedy of this scenario is that the members who are turned away are usually the new members, the intimidated, the potential members, or the inexperienced—exactly the niches that should be given first priority.

The reality of prime time, however, is that people like to go where the action is, and most people who say they are only available after 5 p.m., especially new members, actually want to use the club when everyone else is because it gives them a feeling of being with the "in" crowd. Professional programming eliminates prime-time overflow by marketing to and creating programs for the niches that can fill hours around prime time. You will do your members a favor and develop your business as well.

Night Owl Hours: 8 to 10 p.m.

Late-night exercisers are usually younger adults who will work out before they socialize. Some clubs that have the physical design to attract late-night socializers will also attract late-night exercisers. This information is gathered in the interest profile, and a program director is able to identify late-night exercisers, provide the programs for them, and invite them to use the club when they will be most comfortable.

Weekends: Saturdays and Sundays

Weekends will most often find a combination of all the niches at one time or another. This can be good news or bad news. Some clubs tend to leave weekends as free-for-alls and run the risk of creating more negative experiences with members than positive ones. Families who take out family memberships will want to use the club in several activity areas and without specific programming agendas. This can cause problems if the staff is not trained to deal with all the nuances of various niches, such as lap swimmers wanting to use the pool during family swim hours. Weekends are also the time to run special events, open houses, parties, or tournaments. Weekends need managers, program directors, and organized activities for all the niches and programs.

You can see how important it is to be aware of the type of members, or niches, who use your club at different times. Your club actually takes on the personality of members during these times. Let's now look at how you can use niche marketing throughout the year.

Yearly Niche Marketing Schedules

The program director and programmers are always working at least six months in advance preparing for a programming season, an annual event, or special program. Each new season in a year should be a programming highlight in your club. For example, on the first day of spring you might hold an annual health fair titled "Spring for a Healthy Life," or on the first day of autumn you may hold a member or nonmember fitness event titled "Balance Your Fall." The first day of winter is a wonderful time to sponsor a 5K walk at your club for all four major groups of people—it's "The Big Chill." June 21, the first day of summer, could be an annual event—a day of swimming relays with tubes and noodles and a cookout.

This seasonal program will entice everyone to come to your club, join the fun, enjoy some exercise, meet other people, and become acquainted with a friendly, professional staff that will lead them to a fun, healthy lifestyle. These types of programming events will appeal to many of the niche market segments we identified earlier in this chapter. Seasonal programming is the first step in getting new members involved, inactive members reactivated, active members happy, and potential members eager to join. The secret is not that secret at all! It's about creating a programming calendar of events that remain consistent in date and content. Programming for profit and programming for retention are big business and must become your business culture. Holidays and special annual events will attract all four groups of people and encourage them to meet others like themselves with similar interests, skill levels, schedules, personalities, ages, and genders. These programs and others will give you constant opportunities to get new members, make people happy, sell more memberships, develop your business, and make a difference in peoples' lives.

For example, all holidays need to be programmed. Thanksgiving may seem like a day when everyone stays home to cook or eat, but a creative programmer will capitalize on the opportunity to market to those who would appreciate an organized activity for the day, or at least part of the day. Actually, many people would like to exercise to rationalize eating the Thanksgiving feast!

For example, years ago I organized a round-robin of eight male racquetball players to play on Thanksgiving Day. I promised they would be home in time for dinner. It was fun, it was competitive, it was special, and it was by invitation only. I charged an entry fee and gave three prizes to the winners—a turkey for first place, a chicken for second place, and a Cornish game hen for third place. I took pictures of everyone in the event and especially the three winners holding their "trophies." The next year on October 1, I put the pictures of the Thanksgiving event on the bulletin board and announced that we could accept 16 players for the Thanksgiving Day Turkey Shoot! The event was filled with 32 players. Each year for the next 20 years, the club had 100 percent occupancy of the racquetball courts every Thanksgiving Day for nearly six hours. Word of mouth helped fill the program, and the Thanksgiving Day event became a prototype for several other holiday tournaments throughout the year. Our club became known as the place to be for holiday events, and each holiday came to be thought of as an opportunity to do something special rather than downtime.

Everyone likes to dress up for Halloween and go to a Halloween party, but you can incorporate the Halloween fun into your programs too. Each year during the week of Halloween, have your group exercise instructors dress up for Halloween when teaching class. Encourage the members to dress up too, and have everyone bob for apples after the class. Choose special music for the class and call it "Ghost-aerobics!" Because this is a special class on a special holiday, encourage new members to bring guests or invite potential members to join the class that day for a fun experience at the club. You may find that you will have to add classes to the day's schedule to accommodate the numbers of participants. Holidays are special programming opportunities.

Programs and Programming Ideas

We learned three initial principles from part I as we explored what it takes to run a successful program:

- The goal of programming is retention.
- Every program should be adaptable.
- One program should always be used to promote another.

As we put together a series of actual programs, it will be interesting to note how you should apply each of these principles in every program.

One or more of the following groups of programs and program ideas in part II will touch every activity and niche—interest, skill level, schedule, personality, age, and gender—that would be a potential programming candidate in your club. Open your mind and be creative, innovative, and active as you implement these programs in your club. Picture your members and prospective members in the programs, and picture you and your staff creating the promotions for them. Most of all, think of adapting the programs to meet your needs. Professional programming should be adaptable for all types of recreational, health, fitness, and athletic facilities. Be aware of the variations presented in some of the program descriptions. They will often give you ideas and examples of totally separate programs, derived from the program featured.

Some of the programs presented in part II are very detailed, whereas others are presented as ideas for you to expand on. Some of the programs are presented with details that are important to their success. Others can be successful with several twists that you can provide. This book will help you be creative with such programs and make them your own.

The programs are presented with part or all of the following information:

- Title of the program.
- Description of the program: What it is, why it's important, or for whom the program is designed.
- Tips for success and points to consider: Things to add and things to avoid.
- Variations: Twists on the programming idea. One may work best for you.
- Supplemental materials: Forms, checklists, and logos on the CD-ROM that you can use to enhance your program.

As you know from part I, running a successful program is more than coming up with an idea and presenting it to your clientele. You must evaluate whether the program was effective. The final evaluation of any of the programs presented here will be your responsibility as you answer the five steps of programming success presented in chapter 1.

- The purpose: Was the program designed to meet the needs of a specific market or time frame? Was it intended to grow participation in a certain activity or department? Did you accomplish the purpose of the program or event? Why or why not?
- The goal: Did the program meet the goal number of participants needed to make this program a success? Did it reach the right type of member to make it a success? Why or why not?
- The plan: Were your promotions timely? Were they enough? Were they effective?
- The result: Are all the answers to the preceding questions positive? If yes, you are ready to make this program part of your programming agenda.
- The follow-up: What is next in the logical progression of programming? Do you intend to offer this program again? Why or why not? If yes, when?

You will be ready to grow your business with a new and productive programming calendar of events. Enjoy!

Court Sports

Many of the court sports programs are interchangeable between racquetball, tennis, volleyball, wallyball, and squash. Some of the programs presented here are written for racquetball but will work just as well with tennis, squash, or other court sports. The programs presented for court sports include introductory programs for beginning players (members) and follow-up programs to include intermediate and advanced players (members). The implementation of these programs will ensure retention of players (members) as well as growth of new participants and ultimately new members.

Although programs in court sports may seem specific to the recreational sports, many of the basic programming concepts should be adapted to programs in the fitness center or group exercise studio as well. The introductory programs, for example, will include many of the same features as the introductory programs for core cardio events in the fitness center, and the league programs will provide many of the same qualities found in circuit training or group exercise classes. You will also note that the court sports programs all fall into one of the stages of the wheel of logical progression.

Court sports programming opportunities are many and varied, going far beyond booking court time, organizing weekly leagues, and holding draw tournaments. Most clubs don't take advantage of additional programming ideas that help grow your business, enhance your court sports program, and increase retention, too. Your courts sports program is probably the largest and most successful program in your club and probably will have the most retained members of any programmed area, but you have to nurture it to keep it that way. The good news is that some of these special programs are also the most fun programs for you and your members.

The calendar can dictate when you should run a party or a mixer, a round-robin event, or a tournament in your court sports. Every holiday can be a celebration at your club, and your members will want to be part of every one of them. Don't miss the opportunities!

- New Year's Eve
- New Year's Day
- Super Bowl
- Valentine's Day
- President's Day
- Mardi Gras

- Cinco de Mayo
- St. Patrick's Day
- Easter
- School's Out!
- First Day of Summer
- Fourth of July
- Flag Day
- Mother's Day
- Father's Day
- Labor Day
- Columbus Day
- Halloween
- Thanksgiving Day
- Christmas

The court sports programs will guarantee exciting results and will include the following:

- Introductory programs
- Lessons
- League programs
- Rating systems
- Special events
- Tournaments

Racquetball

When our industry first started to grow, many clubs were built as racquetball facilities only. It was a new game that was marketed as easy to learn, fun to play, and appropriate for all ages, genders, and abilities. It proved to be a sport that captured the attention of everyone, so it was not long before beginning players became intermediate and advanced players and competition in leagues and tournaments dominated the game. Racquetball does not require a lot of athletic ability to get started, and there are a variety of programming opportunities for players. Here you will find a complete programming structure for a racquetball program in your club. You can run these programs with as few as two courts, so whether you are a small facility or a large sports club with eight or more courts, beginning to advanced players can enjoy racquetball in your club.

Racquetball Introductory Clinic

Description

The introductory racquetball clinic is for anyone who has never played racquetball before or who has never taken a good series of beginner lessons. The introductory clinic is designed to give every participant a positive, satisfying experience that will encourage further learning. It teaches basic racquetball skills and terminology. The format is fun and gives every participant a sense of personal achievement.

1. The introductory clinic is a group lesson. It is a one-time clinic for new members, players new to the game, or anyone who has played a few times but has not taken any lessons. Six to eight participants are ideal.
2. The clinic uses one court for one hour.
3. Each player must
   - hear her name often,
   - receive a compliment or words of praise, and
   - be encouraged to become involved in lessons, a round-robin event, or a league.
4. You must introduce yourself and shake hands with everyone.
5. Briefly explain equipment: racket, eye guards, ball.
6. Briefly explain basic rules: serve, volley, scoring.
7. Briefly lead the group in a few warm-up exercises, such as jumping jacks. (This releases tension and creates a congenial environment.)
8. Participants of the class take positions throughout the court with as much space between them as possible. You should be at the front of the class first

demonstrating the movements and then guiding the class through them. Show participants how to combine the forehand stroke and footwork, repeating with each action, "Racket back, step, swing." Repeat with the backhand stroke.

9. Begin drills. Participants line up against the wall and the instructor feeds the balls to each individual. Feed several balls for forehand hits only. After everyone has hit, repeat the drill using the backhand.

10. Repeat drills, giving each player five balls for forehand and five balls for backhand.

11. Demonstrate the serve and have each player serve a few balls.

12. Demonstrate the back wall shot and drill each player with back wall shots.

13. Teach vocabulary throughout the class: *kill shot, pass shot, pinch shot.*

14. For the final drill, each player hits one forehand shot and moves to the back of the line. As a class, see how many balls are hit in a row without a "skip." This is a great drill to establish a team spirit and camaraderie within the group. It's fun, too!

15. Use each person's name often and give compliments throughout the class: "good," "better," "great."

Tips for Success and Points to Consider

- You will have a variety of ages, abilities, schedules, and interests in the clinic. It is the responsibility of the instructor to categorize and document information about members (participants) for follow-up promotions and programs.

- Each person in your introductory clinic has a specific purpose for taking up the sport. Take note of these differences and prepare to deal with them in the clinic.

- You can give an introductory clinic as a private lesson, but the group concept is more fun, creates camaraderie, introduces new players to one another, and is a more productive use of time—serving six to eight times more members with one instructor for one hour on one court.

- It is best to establish a specific time each week for the introductory clinic. Calling new members and promoting the clinic to potential members should be an ongoing marketing effort that will increase racquetball activity and membership growth.

Racquetball Beginning Lesson Series

Description

The beginning lesson series is a follow-up program to the introductory clinic. It is a series of five group lessons, one hour each, for five weeks. During group lessons, people meet other players, socialize, practice the game, learn more, get better, get more confident, and, most important, prepare to get involved in a league, a round-robin, or a tournament. The racquetball beginning lesson series establishes regularity in playing and promotes retention. A group of four to eight players is ideal.

1. Lesson 1: forehand, backhand, and general game strategy. This lesson is basically the same format as the introductory clinic with a greater emphasis

on footwork, strokes, and court positioning. End the lesson with the final drill as in point 14 of the introductory clinic.

2. Lesson 2: back wall shot. Begin with a brief drill review of lesson 1 and discussion of practice. Combine the forehand and backhand shots off the back wall. End class with the final drill as in lesson one.

3. Lesson 3: ceiling ball. Begin with a brief drill review of lesson 2 and discussion of practice. Give drills on ceiling ball—forehand and backhand. Have players take turns playing a few points while the class views and the instructor critiques. End class with the final drill as in lesson 1.

4. Lesson 4: round-robin play. Briefly discuss practice sessions. Have players take turns playing each other.

5. Lesson 5: Refereeing instruction and singles play. Briefly discuss practice sessions. Players play against each other, and all players get a turn at refereeing with a real scorecard. Give a certificate of completion to each participant. Promote sign-ups for the beginners' tournament.

Tips for Success and Points to Consider

- Call each participant—confirmation call—for every lesson.
- Always stress safety and court etiquette during the lessons.
- The final drill in each session brings a sense of teamwork to the group. Always try to end the class with a better score than the previous week.

Variation

This beginning lesson format works well for squash, and with a few adjustments in technical aspects of the game, most court sports lesson plans can be adapted to this type of format.

 ### Supplemental Materials

Beginning Racquetball Series Scorecard

Racquetball Beginners' Tournament

Description

The beginners' tournament is a fun learning experience for the novice player who has never played in a tournament before. It should increase confidence, not be a humbling or discouraging experience. The beginners' tournament should entice players to join other tournaments or league competitions. The beginners' tournament should be the immediate follow-up program for those who participated in the beginning lesson series.

1. Instead of seeding players (the best against the worst for the first round), arrange matches between players that will result in a good experience of friendly competition.

2. Assess players' abilities and personalities and keep relatives or friends from eliminating each other immediately.

3. Use an authentic draw sheet and referee cards to give credibility to the tournament.

© Human Kinetics

4. Run a championship round, a consolation round, and a third-place playoff.

5. Require every participant to referee at least one match. Be sure all matches are refereed.

6. Provide small trophies—nothing else will do—for all the winners.

7. Don't assign starting times. Ask all players to meet for final instructions, questions, and a pep rally, then assign starting players and times. This format will encourage everyone to watch the players while waiting for their turn on the court. The entire tournament is a social experience.

8. Decide what constitutes a match: A match for the beginners' tournament can be one game to 15 points. With 16 players, the tournament can be completed in approximately two to three hours, depending on the number of courts you have.

9. Make the beginners' tournament a fun learning experience.

Tips for Success and Points to Consider

- There should be separate women's and men's divisions if possible, but if you don't have enough players it isn't necessary.

- This is an excellent program for junior players.

- Players who have played in leagues or have participated in other tournaments should not be allowed to play in the beginners' tournament.

- Take pictures of the players in the tournament and place on the bulletin board or on the draw sheet. Keep the photos displayed for a month.

- Guarantee two matches to every player and a fun, interesting, educational experience to boot.

- If promoted from the beginning, the beginners' tournament is a logical progression following the introductory clinic and the five-week lesson series.

Supplemental Materials

Racquetball Beginners' Tournament Draw Sheet

Racquetball League Program

Description

The purpose of the racquetball league program is to get every player in your club involved in a regularly scheduled activity. The league program is the pinnacle of your court sports program. The purpose of running league programs is to provide camaraderie, sociability, competition, recognition for achievement, and a fun way to exercise. It's a fact! Your league programs will have the highest retention rate of any group of members in your club. It should be your goal to get every player of any court sport in your club to join a league.

1. Leagues run for a series of weeks (6-10 weeks work best).
2. The success of the league depends entirely on the organization and follow-through of the program director.
   - Schedules must be accurate (e.g., names, phone numbers, and dates).
   - Rules must be clear, fair, complete, and written.
   - A staff person or program director must be responsible for following up with players to ensure that all games are played and that no-shows are eliminated.
   - Players must be placed in leagues that include players with similar abilities.
3. All scores must be posted weekly.
4. An end-of-league party or banquet is a must for providing sociability, giving out awards, and promoting more league activity, tournaments, and other programs.
5. See the CD-ROM for an example of a league program cover sheet to be given to all league players.

Tips for Success and Points to Consider

- Bonus points can be awarded to players who have played all their league games or made up missed games by a circled date on the league program scoring sheet. This is an incentive for the players to stay active and responsible to the league.
- The league program cover sheet and scoring sheet can be adapted to any court sport program (racquetball, tennis, squash, volleyball, wallyball).

Supplemental Materials

- League Program Cover Sheet
- League Program Scoring Sheet
- Racquetball Rating System

Racquetball Sponsored Leagues

Description

The sponsored leagues are team leagues rather than individual leagues. The purpose of a team is to create more relationships within the league system and, of course, to create a team spirit that adds to the commitment to the league. Each team has a sponsor that contributes money toward a special T-shirt for each of its players, usually advertising the sponsor's business. Many bonds and relationships make sponsored leagues special and unique.

1. Each team is made up of four players with graduating skill levels.
   - First position—A player
   - Second position—B player
   - Third position—C player
   - Fourth position—D player
2. Sponsors are recruited from members or from surrounding businesses.
3. Sponsors are given recognition in the club.
4. When one team competes with another team, the first-position players play, the second-position players compete, and the third-position players play one another, as do the fourth-position players.
5. The scores of the individual matches within the team are added, and the team's total score (all four matches) is posted and accumulated each week.
6. If the league has six teams, it will run for 10 weeks—each team playing each other twice. See the CD-ROM for an example of a sponsored league schedule.

Tips for Success and Points to Consider

- The racquetball program director should be present at the start of every league to distribute the T-shirts to the players.
- A "most valuable player" award can be given to the player on each team who accumulates the most points for the team at the end of the league. It's possible that the third- or fourth-position player can win that award. Also, it guarantees that someone on each team gets an award even if the team did not win the league.

Supplemental Materials

Sponsored League Schedule

Improvement Clinics

Description

Improvement clinics keep beginning players active, interested, and improving! Improvement clinics are part of the retention strategy of court sports programming. The clinics are a fun and very productive use of your time and space, because they are group clinics that easily serve four to six people for every court you have.

1. The group improvement clinics are two hours in length. The first hour is educational instruction, and the second hour is on-court practice.
2. The group improvement clinic goes for two weeks—clinic one is week one, and clinic two is week two.

3. The group gathers in one area as for a seminar, and using erase boards the instructors draw court positions and playing strategies depicting the lessons for the day, such as offensive shots, defensive shots, serves, and serve returns.

4. As each shot is described and drawn on the board, participants can ask questions and discuss the game with the instructor. This is an interesting and productive teaching format.

5. After the seminar, the group divides and moves on to the courts. Drills are set up on the courts to practice the material discussed in the seminars. Depending on the number of participants in the group, some players may watch, learn, and critique others while they wait their turn on the courts for the drills.

Tips for Success and Points to Consider

- If the group is a beginning to intermediate skill level, you can solicit some advanced players to demonstrate while you teach.

- You can charge a nominal fee for the improvement clinics but still make a good profit because of the number of participants.

- This is an excellent program to run in off periods—1 to 3 p.m. People will arrange their schedule to take part in these programs considering they are only offered one time per week for two weeks.

- If you have four to six courts available, you can easily handle 24 to 30 participants in the improvement clinics.

- The improvement clinics are excellent to offer a couple of weeks before a tournament. You most likely will increase the number of participants in the tournament.

- The improvement clinic format is a productive, enjoyable, profitable program that makes good use of your time and space while building your court sports program and increasing retention as well.

Round-Robin Events

Description

A round-robin is designed as a one-day event. It is a group event that encourages friendly competition and offers players the opportunity of meeting other players.

1. Everyone plays an equal number of games.
2. All players begin at approximately the same time.
3. All players end at approximately the same time.
4. All awards are presented in front of players' peers.
5. There is little waiting in between matches.
6. A round-robin provides great exposure for the club.
7. It's fun, fast paced, continuous, and interesting.
8. It encourages camaraderie.
9. It allows for several skill levels and ages, and for men and women, to play at the same time.

10. It is controllable by the program director or instructor.

11. It can be an event for all four groups of members: new members (players), existing members (players), dropouts (players who have been inactive), and potential members (nonmember players who are encouraged to join).

12. The round-robin event should promote participation in further instruction programs, league programs, and tournament play.

Tips for Success and Points to Consider

- Identifying skills and assigning skill levels to players can be interesting, challenging, and sometimes frustrating. Tennis uses a number system, and the levels are determined by a formula through the United States Tennis Association (USTA). Most everyone is familiar with the terms *novice (beginner), intermediate,* or *advanced.* Those three categories can be easily broken down into letters, which are also very familiar with most every player. See the CD-ROM for an example of how to help players identify their skill levels; using this system will also help you to promote further activity. Note: This rating system is appropriate to use for racquetball, squash, or tennis. It is very simple, but effective and sound.

- You can be very creative in using different scoring systems, especially in racquetball and squash. Changing scoring systems keeps the game fresh and interesting. Everyone won't like every system, but everyone will like some of them. You can change scoring procedures for different seasons of league play or types of leagues. You may prefer one scoring system over another in round-robin events to accommodate large or small numbers of players, a strict time schedule, or productive use of few available courts. See the CD-ROM for examples of a scoring system used in racquetball leagues, round-robins, and tournaments. The scoring systems are very adaptable to other court sports as well.

- This is a program that could be very effective if run four times per year, once during each quarter. The round-robin event can be run as a full club tournament accommodating up to 48 players by using six players at each of eight divisions (skill levels). The entire program can be run in a four-hour block of time.

Variation

Round-robins are excellent for doubles play as well as singles play.

Supplemental Materials

- Round-Robin Scorecard
- Racquetball Rating System
- Round-Robin Scoring System
- Round-Robin Racquetball Tournament

Racquetball Bingo

Description

Racquetball bingo is a fun one-day event that allows players to play racquetball with many different people and enjoy playing a game within a game.

1. Everyone has a bingo card, which is placed on a bulletin board. (See the CD-ROM for the Racquetball Bingo Card.)

2. Any number of players may play.

3. Players challenge each other at random to a match. The match should be as short as possible so that the players get to play many people and have many chances at winning bingo.

4. When the challenges are made, players choose a square on their cards that the match is being played for. The players put their opponent's initials in that square. The match is then played.

5. The winners put a foil star sticker on the designated square on their cards. The losers of the match leave the initials in the square but cannot play for that square again while trying to get a bingo.

6. A winning bingo card has a line of wins (stars) vertically, horizontally, or diagonally or stars in all four corners—just as in a real game of bingo.

7. Anyone getting a bingo gets a prize.

Tips for Success and Points to Consider

- Games to 11 points that include scoring on every volley go quickly and offer the opportunity for more challenges in the time allotted.
- Players may only challenge each player one time.
- Players can put their own names and a star in the "free space" (middle) and have one automatic win.

Variations

- Bingo can be played with racquetball, tennis, or squash.
- Bingo can be played as singles, doubles, or mixed doubles.
- With a little ingenuity, bingo can be played among volleyball teams or wallyball teams. Be creative! Have fun!

Supplemental Materials

Racquetball Bingo Card

Ridiculous Racquetball

Description

Ridiculous Racquetball is a great event for a one-day round-robin. It is a group event played in approximately one to one and a half hours. It promotes a fun, social experience, but it is also an excellent practice session and often results in lesson sign-ups.

1. Each round is played for a set period of time rather than to a certain point value. For example, each round can be 15 minutes.

2. The entire group of players is gathered together to begin the event.

3. The players challenge each other at random for each round of play.

4. Each round is designated for and focuses on one particular shot. In fact, a point can only be scored when using that particular shot. Following is an example:

- Round one—a point can only be scored with a backhand shot.
- Round two—a point can only be scored with a pinch shot.
- Round three—a point can only be scored with a ceiling ball.
- Round four—a point can only be scored with a kill shot.

5. Points scored are accumulated throughout the day (all four rounds) for each player.

6. After "time" is called, each player announces her score and the director records that number. A new challenge then takes place to begin the second round.

7. The third round is exhausting, but the players sure learn how to hit a ceiling ball!

8. For the fourth round, colored masking tape is placed on the front wall to designate the "kill shot" area. This should be your longest round.

Tips for Success and Points to Consider

- What happens if a player uses a forehand in round one (the backhand shot)? Nothing. Just keep playing. If a point was scored with a forehand, it doesn't count. Just start the next volley. Be flexible. This is a game for fun, exercise, and practice.

- Can players serve backhand? Of course.

- This event is best scored on every volley. This means playing as usual, but whenever the ball is down, someone gets a point whether she was serving or not. You would still change servers at the appropriate time. When scoring this way, more points are made, and it is possible for someone to accumulate 100 points by the end of the event. In fact, the first person to accumulate 100 points could be your winner!

- A one-minute mini–group lesson on executing each focus shot should be given to the group as a whole before the challenge. It helps the players practice correctly.

Supplemental Materials

Ridiculous Racquetball Flyer

Ladies' Challenge Luncheon

Description

Talk about niche programming! Here is a program that is designed for

- women only,
- daytime (not prime time) in the middle of the week,
- a one-day special event,
- an end-of-league party, or
- a seasonal event or holiday celebration.

The purpose of a ladies' challenge luncheon is to provide fun and camaraderie within a group of women (racquetball players) who have different skill levels, schedules, personalities, and ages.

1. The actual racquetball event begins at 9:30 a.m. All players arrive at the same time. The group is divided into two groups—the red group and the green group, for example.

2. Players from one group challenge any of the players from the opposing group to one game of racquetball to 11 points.

3. Everyone is to play as many different people as possible in one and a half hours.

4. A small prize may be given to the players on the team with the most wins.

5. At 11 or 11:30, the women meet in a lounge area of the club for a potluck luncheon. Prizes are awarded, pictures are taken for the bulletin board, and sign-ups begin for the next league, tournament, or lesson series.

Tips for Success and Points to Consider

- The luncheon part of this event is key. It should be programmed as much as the racquetball event itself. Rather than an ordinary potluck luncheon where the variety of dishes may be unconnected and uninteresting, issue a theme to guide the cooks in their choices. For example, consider the following:

  - Make the luncheon all appetizers.

  - Ask people to bring snacks of 100 calories or less.

  - Have a salad bar. Make a list of everything you would like to have on a salad bar and have the ladies sign up ahead of time under the ingredient they will bring. This will eliminate too much of one thing and not enough of another.

  - Have a taco luncheon. Make a list of taco toppings and other Mexican foods (rice, beans, and so on) and have sign-ups as for the salad bar.

  - Make your own sub sandwiches. Have a list available for the necessary ingredients and let the ladies choose what they will bring. Everyone can take part in putting the sandwiches together.

- For every luncheon give a certain number of ladies the opportunity to sign up to bring a bread or dessert. You may ask for just chocolate desserts, fruit desserts, or cookies.

- Signing up ahead of time for the luncheon participation will increase the commitment to the event.

- The luncheon provides a great atmosphere for giving out the prizes for the event and promoting other upcoming programs.

- Winners and losers alike will enjoy the camaraderie, sociability, and fun that the program was designed to give.

Variations

- The team colors should represent the day's theme.

  - End-of-league event: Two huge rackets made of poster board—one purple and one orange—are put on a wall. The players from each team write their names on their rackets. The player (purple or orange) who wins a challenge match to 11 points places a foil star sticker next to her name. The giant racket with the most stars at the end of the day wins the prize. The entire team is recognized collectively.

- Christmas: An untrimmed tree has two boxes of ornaments—one with red ornaments and one with green ornaments. After each challenge match, the winner puts her team color ornament on the tree.

- Easter or springtime: Players of the yellow or blue teams each sign construction paper eggs that are placed on a poster board basket. The player who wins a challenge match puts a foil star on her egg.

- This event can be played with doubles teams or even mixed-doubles teams on a weekend evening. Yes, even the men will be competitive enough to want the most stars for their team!

- This event can be adapted to tennis with no problem. Play three no-ad games for each challenge match.

Ladder Leagues

Description

Nearly every club that has a court sports program has a ladder league. It is a simple concept and presumably runs itself. Basically, players of any sport can sign up at any time. The players are placed on rungs of a "ladder" beginning with the most advanced (the players to beat) on the top and the players with lesser skill levels on the bottom. Additional players can sign up at any time but must begin at the bottom of the ladder.

Players challenge players above them and change places if they win. The object of the challenges is for a player to work his way up to the top of the ladder. The purpose of the ladder league is to allow players to play at their convenience, and it offers players the opportunity of having a game whenever they want one.

1. The ladder can be made up as a board with vertically placed hooks holding disks with players' names and phone numbers.

2. Players may challenge one, two, or three players above them to a match and arrange the court time with the club.

3. A challenge must be accepted within a designated time frame.

4. If the player on the lower rung wins, the players exchange places.

5. At designated times, a prize can be given to the player at the top of the ladder and to the player who has advanced the farthest.

Tips for Success and Points to Consider

- Players of reasonably equal skill levels must make up a ladder league.

- Several ladder leagues of various skill levels can be run at the same time.

- Although most clubs maintain a ladder league, very few of them are successful. By that, I mean that they often stall with no activity. People generally do not like to make the effort to call opponents and schedule their own games.

- Ladder leagues allow new members to immediately get involved in the court sports of your club even though a league season is already under way.

- Ladder leagues can be very successful if a program director or staff person is assigned to match the players, help them make the challenges, and schedule the games for them.

Variations

- Ladder leagues can be run as doubles as well as singles, but the need for a program director is even more important.
- Ladder leagues can be run within any court sport where a challenge match is appropriate.

Tennis

Tennis is truly the most elite court sport in the club business. The league system, tournament play, and round-robin events of court sports in general will apply to the entire tennis program. Innovation of programming will best be found in changing the scoring system to keep play interesting and fun for the recreational player and yet challenging for the more advanced and dedicated tennis enthusiast. The playing levels as set by the National Tennis Rating Program (NTRP) guidelines (see the sidebar on page 81) are paramount when you are placing players in tennis programs, but fun programs and party mixers help ease the tension of too serious competition and will help grow your club tennis program as well as offer opportunities to promote the quest for excellence.

Once playing level has been determined, round-robin play is a great way to set up games. For most round-robin play, the fun is in playing many different people, whether in a singles or a doubles format; therefore, you may want to deviate from the traditional scoring of love, 5, 15, 30, 40, deuce, and ad). To make things easier and quicker, numerical scoring—playing by the numbers, 1, 2, 3, 4—is acceptable, and allowing no ad games eliminates delays.

Instead of the traditional six-game set with a tie-breaker, popular Super Scoring programs are recommended to keep the tennis program in your club innovative and exciting for everyone. For example, best of two uses regular scoring, but should sets split, a super match tiebreaker (first to 10 points by a margin of 2) is in effect in lieu of playing a third set. The set tiebreaker—first to seven points, winning by a margin of two (i.e., 7–5)—is just as good. Compared with the standard best of three, best of two allows more play with more players.

Creative tennis programming is fun, challenging, and rewarding, but all too often programming is "same old, same old" and inhibits growth and excitement. Successful tennis programming ensures that all events are well attended, fun for the players, and enjoyed so much that the participants return again and again to play in similar activities. More people will want to take up the game of tennis simply because they will want to be part of the programming.

Although the events themselves are proven winners, their success (or failure) will be directly dependent on the upbeat personalities and organized professionalism of the individuals directing the events. Without enthusiastic promotion, attention to details, and constant on-site direction (who goes where, with whom, and when), the event will flop.

St. Patrick's Day Round-Robin

Description

The promotion for this event is almost as much fun as the execution. This should be a fun, mixed-doubles annual event that mixes the players, offers friendly competition, and provides memorable social time as well. As with many round-robins, the St. Patrick's Day Round-Robin allows participants to mix with one another, that is, change partners and opponents after each round is played. This allows players to meet new acquaintances, perhaps make new friends, and rotate partners and opponents so they do not get stuck playing with, or against, the same players during the entire event.

1. Require all participants to dress in green.
2. Reserve one court for every four players.

General Characteristics of NTRP Playing Levels

Following are the guidelines and general characteristics of various NTRP playing levels. Players in wheelchairs should use these same general characteristics to determine their NTRP skill level. The only difference observed is mobility and power on the serve.

1.0—This player is just starting to play tennis.

1.5—This player has limited experience and is still working primarily on getting the ball into play.

2.0—This player needs on-court experience. This player has obvious stroke weaknesses but is familiar with basic positions for singles and doubles play.

2.5—This player is learning to judge where the ball is going although court coverage is weak. This player can sustain a short rally of slow pace with other players of the same ability.

3.0—This player is fairly consistent when hitting medium-paced shots, but is not comfortable with all strokes and lacks execution when trying for directional control, depth, or power. Most common doubles formation is one up, one back.

3.5—This player has achieved improved stroke dependability with directional control on moderate shots, but still lacks depth and variety. This player exhibits more aggressive net play, has improved court coverage, and is developing teamwork in doubles.

4.0—This player has dependable strokes, including directional control and depth on both forehand and backhand sides on moderate shots, plus the ability to use lobs, overheads, approach shots, and volleys with some success. This player occasionally forces errors when serving. Rallies may be lost due to impatience. Teamwork in doubles is evident.

4.5—This player has begun to master the use of power and spins and is beginning to handle pace, has sound footwork, can control depth of shots, and is beginning to vary game plan according to opponents. This player can hit first serves with power and accuracy and place the second serve. This player tends to overhit on difficult shots. Aggressive net play is common in doubles.

5.0—This player has good shot anticipation and frequently has an outstanding shot or attribute around which a game may be structured. This player can regularly hit winners or force errors off of short balls, can put away volleys, can successfully execute lobs, drop shots, half volleys, and overhead smashes, and has good depth and spin on most second serves.

5.5—This player has developed power and consistency as a major weapon. This player can vary strategies and styles of play in a competitive situation and hits dependable shots in a stress situation.

6.0 to 7.0—The 6.0 player typically has had intensive training for national tournament competition at the junior and collegiate levels and has obtained a sectional and national ranking. The 6.5 and 7.0 player is a world-class player.

Courtesy of the United States Tennis Association (USTA).

3. Use an interchanging-partner mixed-doubles schedule that is easy to read and follow for all players.

4. Be flexible enough to handle the inevitable odd numbers of players—no-shows or surprise show-ups. Be prepared to handle byes.

5. Give every court a new can of balls.

6. Provide shamrocks and "Kiss me, I'm Irish" buttons for everyone—because everyone is Irish on St. Patrick's Day!

Tips for Success and Points to Consider

- Award prizes to the "best dressed" (in green) lad and lass.
- Provide snacks and drinks—corned beef and rye finger sandwiches, green beer (or the like).
- Use no-ad scoring for each game.
- For mixed-doubles play, number the women even and the men odd. Assign numbers to your players in chronological order as they show up.
- Determine your winners by how many total games they won. You won't know the winning couple till the very end!
- Make introductions part of the format and play: Mixers are great formats to break down tennis cliques that often form in clubs.
- Use mixers to allow players of varying ability levels to participate; as a result, the events themselves tend to be more socially fun than highly competitive.
- Be organized and make the schedule readable: Interchanging-partners mixed-doubles round-robins are fun to run as well as play. Enjoy!

Variation

Mixers are excellent round-robin format programs to run for your corporate events.

 **Supplemental Materials**

Interchanging-Partners Mixed-Doubles Round-Robin Scorecard

Tennis Parties and Mixers

Description

Your leagues have regularly brought many members together in your club for several weeks. It's time to celebrate! An end-of-league party or banquet is a perfect time to present league awards. Leaders should give players recognition in front of their peers, and this is a perfect setting! Play activity such as a round-robin event is a wonderful social environment for a party or celebration—for men's leagues, women's leagues, or junior leagues. A mixer is a play event (round-robin) with men and women—usually in the form of mixed doubles. It is the most fun, productive social program you can have, and it should be offered monthly, bimonthly, quarterly, or seasonally. Any excuse to run a mixer within any of the court sports is appropriate and will be beneficial—racquetball, tennis, squash, volleyball, or wallyball.

Any end-of-league party or mixer is a perfect opportunity to promote follow-up programs. Parties and mixers make new members feel welcome and at home. They are excellent opportunities for inviting inactive members back to the club, and, of course, they give recognition to your existing active members. But parties and mixers can also be available to guests, so these events can become programs for potential members too.

1. Always have an organized play activity to suit every skill level.
2. Always have a social hour (or two) to follow the event. Specific themes help make this part of the event even more successful.
   - A Mexican fiesta! Decorate the club with a Mexican flair. Serve tacos after the play.
   - Beach blanket bingo! After the round-robin event, serve hot dogs and hamburgers and have everyone sit on blankets on the floor.
   - Chili night! Serve hot steaming bowls of chili. If it's in the middle of winter, you could call this "Chilly Night!"
   - Pizza party! Need I say more?
   - Appetizer delights! Everyone brings an appetizer (pot luck).

Tips for Success and Points to Consider

- Always look for ways to make a good program better. Parties and mixers will create more interest and commitment if you solicit help from the members themselves; for example, for chili night you could ask four or five members to have a chili contest, cooking their own recipes for the group.
- Take pictures of the party and keep them on a bulletin board for at least one month or till the next party.
- Choose a day or night of the week that you consider your party time and stay consistent with that. For example, end-of-league parties would be on Wednesdays, mixers on Saturdays, and junior events on Sundays. You won't please everyone, but if you are consistent, members will adjust their schedules in advance to make room for these special events.

Variations

- Don't forget your early birds! An end-of-league breakfast is always a hit. (You will probably want to have them on Fridays.)
- A tennis program should always include an event called Breakfast at Wimbledon.
- Circuit training group programs and your core cardio programs can end with these same types of party events. It's almost like celebrating fitness leagues.

Wallyball and Volleyball

Two additional court sports we can't leave out are wallyball and volleyball.

Wallyball

Description

If you have never played wallyball, you have missed out on some fun. The name, *wallyball,* pretty much tells the story. It is played like volleyball (sort of) but using a racquetball court (sort of). Wallyball is a fun, social, team sport that can be competitive or strictly recreational. Wallyball is nationally recognized by the American Wallyball Association (AWA) and has been part of the industry since 1989. It was one of the first sports that offered a secondary use for the 800 square feet (244 square m) of a racquetball court, and it caught on big time.

Like all court sports in your club, wallyball can be very competitive or recreational. In most cases, clubs find recreational wallyball to be more popular, to be easier to promote, and to accommodate a wide variety of people. Wallyball is enjoyed by men and women, experienced and inexperienced players, athletic and nonathletic people, and adults and kids (as long as they are tall enough to get the ball over the net). Wallyball games or leagues offer terrific program opportunities for in-house special events or organized league play.

1. Wallyball uses an official AWA net that is easily installed across the width of a racquetball (or handball) court.

2. The ball is an official AWA ball approximately 27 inches (68 cm) in diameter weighing about 9 ounces (255 gm). There are many styles to choose from.

3. Each team consists of two, three, or four players.

4. Games are played to 15, 18, or 21 points, and a team must win by 2 points.

5. The ball is played much like a volleyball but is banked off the walls and the ceiling of the court.

Tips for Success and Points to Consider

* Wallyball, because of its versatility and relaxed rules, is a great activity to include at end-of-league parties, holiday parties, or open houses. It is lots of fun and very social.

* Clubs that invite corporations in to experience their facility will find that wallyball gets everyone active in something that is shared and enjoyed by a completely diverse group of people.

* Wallyball nights can be a drop-in program that gives every member an opportunity to use the club in a comfortable setting, and it's especially good for new members looking to get involved immediately.

* Wallyball leagues—lasting 6, 8, or 10 weeks—can be a great source of additional revenue from outside groups such as churches, community businesses, police officers, firefighters, and teachers. In addition to getting league fees from these groups, your club is being marketed to potential members as well.

Volleyball

Description

Volleyball is a sport that is enjoyed by all; is fun, social, and competitive; and offers an opportunity for recreational play to many diversified markets. Volleyball teams can be made up of two to eight players per team. Your volleyball program may be a drop-in program where several players sign up or drop in each week just for the fun of it, or it may be a six, or eight week program that runs like any other recreational league.

If it is a drop-in program, be sure to call new members each week and invite them to play. Volleyball is a sport that nearly everyone has experienced in their lives and is comfortable with. If it is an organized league program, volleyball is an excellent sport to provide the "club within a club" environment that will certainly lead to retention and growth for your business.

Tips for Success and Points to Consider

- Include a social event with food and drink after the games as often as possible.
- Think of reasons to give prizes:
    - Most improved player or team
    - The least wins as well as the most wins
    - The best sport
    - The most determined
    - The shortest and the tallest
    - The best server
    - MVP (Most Valuable Player)
    - Best attendance
- Be flexible. Read the type of members that are playing and perceive the correct action. If the group is strictly interested in serious volleyball, list the rules and follow them. Volleyball, however is a fun, social, recreational sport that can provide the experience that will bring people back again and again. If your group is open to enjoyment more than to a quest for championship, remember that rules are guidelines. Sometimes they are meant to bend without being broken.

Variation

The ultimate "fun in the sun" recreational sport is sand volleyball. Clubs can make arrangements with parks and recreation departments to offer sand volleyball off site: year-round, weather permitting, or in the summer months only. Sand volleyball is guaranteed to be a success for anyone, anytime. It is truly a sport—one of the only ones—that will accommodate every interest, skill level, schedule, personality, age, and gender. The key, of course, to making this court sport an over-the-top-success is the picnic, barbecue, hot dogs, and hamburgers that follow the fun! Guaranteed!

7

In and Around the Fitness Center

The fitness center is the focal point of every facility. Small facilities may be nothing *but* a fitness area with a line of equipment, and large multipurpose facilities will feature the fitness center as the center of all the club's activities. Almost all new members who join a club are encouraged to get started on a program in the fitness center. One type of program often presented begins with a meeting with a trainer to discuss the member's fitness status and short- and long-term goals. The member is then introduced to four to eight pieces of equipment, shown how to use them, and given a workout card that lists a series of repetitions and sets to do on the equipment three times a week for six weeks. The member is expected to execute the program and begin her commitment to a new lifestyle of fitness. Too many members never complete the initial six-week program, even though it may be well designed and potentially beneficial. The following programs, all designed to be used in and around the fitness center, will get more members involved in the fitness center, keep them coming in, and help them enjoy their fitness center workouts.

Core Cardio Programs

Description

These programs are designed to integrate the new member into the club immediately and comfortably and to be a stepping stone for further and ongoing participation. The cardiorespiratory area of the fitness center is the most popular area for most new members because it has the most popular and familiar equipment in it—the treadmill, the bike, and the stepper. When the three core cardio programs are presented, the member chooses one of the three pieces of equipment to use for eight weeks in one program, then chooses a second piece to use in the next eight-week program, and then uses the third piece in the next eight-week program. The three core cardio areas are Marathon Miles (or Kilometers), Tour de France, and Mountain Trek.

Courtesy of Center Court Fitness Club.

The three core cardio programs may be run simultaneously in an eight-week period or individually. You may run all three programs during the same eight-week period, but members may only sign up for one program per eight weeks.

1. Marathon Miles (Kilometers) is a treadmill program, Tour de France uses stationary bikes, and Mountain Trek uses stair climbers, elliptical machines, or cross-trainers.

2. Each program runs for eight weeks. The member must complete two 20-minute sessions per week. Everyone wins by completing the 16 sessions in eight weeks. It is not a race—everyone can win!

3. A member may only get credit for one 20-minute session per day but may record one session any or every day of the week if desired. A member may complete a 20-minute session at any time, at his convenience. The 20-minute session allows the member time to do other activities while visiting the club.

4. All participants must record their sessions on a tracking board with or without a trainer or on a tracking form. If a tracking form or activity card is used, I recommend that a trainer transfer the information to a tracking board that is prominently displayed in the fitness area. The tracking board is exciting for the members and is a fabulous marketing tool for the programs.

5. Each fitness trainer should be a captain for a team of players (to hold them accountable). Because all players can win, the captains must call their players to remind them to play.

6. All participants must be invited by their captains or trainers to attend the victory party for the core cardio programs.

7. All winners will receive a prize at the party—such as a T-shirt listing the three core cardio programs.

8. Sign-ups for the next core cardio program can be taken during the eight-week session and at the party.

9. Pictures of the participants during the event and at the party should be placed on the tracking board for promotional purposes.

Marathon Miles (Kilometers): (Core Cardio Program 1)

- Goal = 24 miles (38.6 km) total in eight weeks using a treadmill
- 20 minutes at any level or speed = 1.5 miles (2.4 km)
- 1.5 miles per session at two sessions per week = 3 miles (4.8 km) per week
- 3 miles per week for eight weeks = 24 miles

Tour de France: (Core Cardio Program 2)

- Goal = 2,400 miles (3,862 km) total in eight weeks using a stationary bike
- 20 minutes at any level or speed = 150 miles (241 km)
- 150 miles (241 km) per session at two sessions per week = 300 miles (483 km) per week
- 300 miles per week for 8 weeks = 2,400 miles

Mountain Trek: (Core Cardio Program 3)

- Goal = climbing up and down eight mountains in eight weeks
- 20 minutes at any level climbing up the mountain, and 20 minutes at any level climbing down the mountain
- Climb up one mountain once per week and down the mountain once per week

Tips for Success and Points to Consider

- It is recommended that a member participate in one program at a time because he likely will not complete the three programs simultaneously and therefore will consider himself a partial failure.
- A club should run only one of the core cardio programs for an eight-week period to get the experience of running the programs successfully.
- The goal of programming is retention! It is far better to keep a member active for 24 weeks than for eight.
- "New beginnings" for each program will encourage retention.
- Do not include *contest* or *challenge* in the title. The beauty of these programs is that everyone can win.
- The programs can be promoted with or without an entry fee; keeping the member on active status is the hidden profit behind the programs.
- The eight-week sessions should be run during a specific eight-week period with a beginning and an end—much like a sports league. Allowing random starts and stops is too difficult to track.
- It's possible that one third of all new members (members who have joined within the last 90 days) would be involved in a core cardio program. If you are selling 100 memberships per month, at least 90 (30 per month for the past three months) new members should get involved in one of the core cardio programs for an eight-week session and a victory party.

- The core cardio programs offer new members immediate, easy entry into a program at the club; therefore, they can be signed up at point of sale and begin using the club immediately.
- New members who participate in all three sessions will have regularly exercised for 24 weeks. This will happen if each program is promoted from within with as much enthusiasm as you used promoting the first program.
- Because the workouts are only 20 minutes in length, the new members will probably get involved in other activities during that time.
- With 20-minute sessions, members can join at almost any time during the eight weeks and make up the time lost.
- The programs are applicable to all new members who like to walk, run, bike, or climb . . . at their own comfort level and at their availability.
- The core cardio programs can be used to reactivate inactive members.
- The core cardio programs are also good to run as corporate programs where proof of use is required.

Variation

If you are a smaller club, you may consider one program titled Work Out and Win. In this scenario, a new member can choose the treadmill, bike, or climber for any workout. That workout will be recorded and at the end of 16 sessions—8 weeks—the participants enjoy a victory party.

Supplemental Materials

- Marathon Miles Flyer
- Marathon Miles Logo
- Tour de France Flyer
- Tour de France Logo
- Mountain Trek Flyer
- Mountain Trek Logo
- Core Cardio Tracking Sheet

New Member Equipment Orientations

Description

Group equipment orientations educate new members about all of the equipment, how to use it, and in general how to become familiar with the facility. Orientations also provide an enjoyable, educational, social, successful experience for the new member—so much so that the member will feel comfortable and eager to join an ongoing follow-up program.

1. The new member equipment orientations are presented in groups. The groups can be from 2 to 16 people or even more, depending on your size and the number of memberships sold each month. Also, depending on the size of your club, new member equipment orientations can be run daily, weekly, or monthly.

2. All orientations are done at specific scheduled times, not at random.

3. The new member group orientations should be no more than 45 minutes.

4. There must be enough choices of times so the new member has easy and immediate entry to an orientation. An example of times:

• Mondays	9:15 a.m.	7 p.m.
• Tuesdays	6 a.m.	5:30 p.m.
• Wednesdays	6 p.m.	
• Thursdays	9:30 a.m.	6 p.m.
• Fridays	12:30 p.m.	
• Saturdays	11 a.m.	
• Sundays	12:30 p.m.	

5. The orientations must be available for sign-up at the point of sale. Sales-people and trainers are held accountable for signing up new members.

6. The dates, times of orientations, and names of participants must be visibly displayed in the club to create excitement and commitment to attendance. A suggestion is to have a huge sign-up board on the wall in the fitness area.

© Bananastock

7. A staff person or trainer is assigned to a group of participants and is held accountable for getting the members to show up at the appointed time, by giving a reminder call or confirmation call.

8. The trainer or instructor gathers the group at the equipment and introduces herself to each person—including the handshake.

9. The trainer or instructor shows the group how to adjust the seats and has each person experience the piece of equipment.

10. Explain the intent:

• Make everyone comfortable with each piece of equipment.

• Give a fun experience and meet other people.

• Choose an ongoing fitness program to join. For example: "Welcome to (your club). I've reviewed your expressed interests and will suggest programs that will meet your needs. My goal is to make you comfortable with the facility and to help you understand what programs are available."

- Encourage participants to participate in an activity before leaving and identify their next contact with the club, such as tennis, racquetball, group exercise, fitness, or aquatics.

Tips for Success and Points to Consider

- You may provide two group orientations for members to experience. A member may do one or both. Here is an example of two orientations. You may mix and match the exercises depending on the equipment that is in your facility. Be your own programmer! Cardiorespiratory equipment can be included in the orientations.

Red Orientation

1. Leg press
2. Leg extension
3. Leg curl
4. Rowing

5. Ab machine
6. Rotary torso
7. Stationary bike
8. Treadmill

Blue Orientation

1. Chest press
2. Aided chin or dip
3. Stair climber
4. Calf raise

5. Shoulder press
6. Lat pull-down
7. Elliptical trainer
8. Adductor and abductor

- A member may sign up for only one orientation but will be encouraged to sign up for more than one. Any member may repeat any orientation as well.
- These are orientations only. At this point the total workout is not as important as becoming comfortable and familiar with a piece of equipment. The most important things to teach the participant are (1) getting on and off safely, (2) making seat adjustments, (3) starting and stopping a machine (if applicable), and (4) adjusting weights (if applicable).
- A general rule is that two thirds of all new members should go through at least one equipment orientation program.
- If confirmation calls are made, 80 percent of participants should show up.
- You should get approximately one half of all new members who participate in an orientation program to sign up for a follow-up program.
- Another title for the new member equipment orientations could be "Jump Start!"
- The new member equipment orientation can be adapted to other activity departments, for example, group exercise or court sports.
- These orientation programs are totally adaptable to any facility with any type of equipment.
- Depending on the number of people in the group, the number of staff trainers available, and the number of pieces of equipment, these programs can run from 30 minutes to one hour.
- Depending on the experience of the trainer in working with groups, more than one trainer may be necessary with large numbers of members.

- The new member equipment orientation could be extended to missed sales, guests, or trial members, otherwise known as potential members.

- Many existing, active members have not gone through an equipment orientation. Be sure to include them when promoting and marketing participation in these programs.

- Equipment orientation is an excellent program to invite inactive members to. Every quarter, send all inactive members an informational invitation to attend an equipment orientation, and follow up with a phone call and a more personal invitation to all members who have not used the club within a three-month period. Note: This step alone is likely to save many members from dropping out or quitting altogether. It is an easy reentry into fitness and your club. As explained in chapter 1, however, salespeople and fitness programmers must be held accountable for calling and confirming their goal share of inactive members.

Variations

- The new member equipment orientation can be an excellent program when you are introducing a new line of equipment at your club. The program will then simply be new equipment orientations (using the name of the new equipment). This becomes a program that gets many members using new equipment and using it properly. In addition, it uses staff time productively.

- This program is totally adaptable to a one-on-one orientation training program. However, logistics may make it very difficult to service all new members one on one. Using two or three trainers to serve 8 to 12 participants in one hour is far more beneficial than training one member with one instructor for one hour.

- If you prefer one-on-one orientation, limit the program to 30 minutes and promote it as a free personal training session. Encourage members to follow up with a group program or a personal training package with a personal trainer. (Always use one program to promote another.)

Fitathlon

Description

The Fitathlon is a cardio program in the fitness center that goes beyond the new member and offers the same fun group experience to the existing active member. It is the follow-up program to the core cardio programs encouraging adherence, commitment, and retention.

1. The Fitathlon is much like the core cardio programs but should be considered as a separate program unto itself. It is specifically designed for the more experienced, more active, or existing member rather than the inexperienced, inactive, or beginning member.

2. The Fitathlon is based in the cardio area of the fitness center and will use the treadmills, stationary bikes, and stair climbers or elliptical trainers.

3. The Fitathlon is a 30-minute workout to be done three times per week for eight weeks. A member must complete 10 minutes of walking or running on the treadmill, 10 minutes of biking on a stationary bike, and 10 minutes of stair climbing on a stair climber.

4. The goal of the Fitathlon is to complete 24 30-minute workouts using all three pieces of cardio equipment in eight weeks.

5. Participants may only get credit for one 30-minute workout per day but may record one session any or every day of the week if desired. A member may complete a 30-minute session at any time, at his convenience. The 30-minute session can easily be combined with other programs or activities at the club.

6. All participants must record their sessions on a tracking board with or without a trainer or on a tracking form. If a tracking form is used, I recommend that a trainer transfer the information to a tracking board. (Go to the CD-ROM for an example of a tracking form.)

7. Each fitness trainer should be a captain (accountable) for a team of players. Because all players can win, the captains must call their players to remind them to play.

8. All participants must be invited by their captain (by phone if necessary) to attend a victory party at the end of the eight weeks.

   - All winners will receive a prize at the party.
   - Sign-ups for follow-up programs can be taken during the eight-week session and at the party. (Always use one program to promote another.)
   - Place pictures of the participants during the event and at the party on the tracking board for promotional purposes.

Tips for Success and Points to Consider

- One third of all members who complete any of the core cardio programs should sign up and complete the Fitathlon.
- One third of the total number of players per eight-week session should be active existing members.
- One third of the total number of players per eight-week session should be inactive members invited to come back to the club by participating in the Fitathlon.
- You can require just two 30-minute sessions per week—16 workouts to complete the Fitathlon.
- You can require that a member complete one of the core cardio programs before joining the Fitathlon. It can be called "The Graduation Program."
- Present the program so that everyone can win. Here is a good rule to include: "If you miss a few days, we might be able to help you catch up. Here's how: Minutes accumulated during week eight will be doubled!" Set your member up for success. This same rule can be applied to the core cardio programs.
- If a member has already won a T-shirt, offer an alternative prize.

Variations

- You can adjust the goals and make them more specific—for example, an eight-week program could consist of 20 miles (32 km) of running, 100 miles (161 km) of biking, and climbing up and down four mountains. A member would receive 2.5 miles (4 km) for every 30 minutes of using the treadmill, would receive 12.5 miles (20 km) for every 30 minutes on any exercise bike, and would be considered to have gone up or down a mountain for every 30 minutes of climbing.

- The Fitathlon is a good program to use for a one-day event or for an activity at a party. The times can be adjusted from 5 to 15 minutes per activity and can accommodate many people in a reasonable time slot.

Supplemental Materials

Fitathlon Tracking Form

Fit in Thirty

Description

Fit in Thirty is an easy tracking program designed to get a member to exercise regularly and be recognized for doing so. This program also keeps your staff accountable to the members' participation.

1. Fit in Thirty is one of the most fun workouts for your members and can be fun for you too.
2. It is a 30-minute cardio workout in a group setting.
3. This program is best run one or two times a week only. The programs should run for 30 days only. It adds diversification to a regular workout routine or offers a beginning or new beginning to a fitness lifestyle.
4. The number of participants will depend on the number of treadmills, bikes, and climbers you have. This program is run at specific times, so you do not want to tie up every piece of equipment, if possible.
5. Example: If you have four treadmills, four bikes, and four climbers available, the group is 12 people. The 12 participants sign up for a specific time. The participants begin together and exercise on their piece of equipment for 10 minutes. Each group moves to the next piece of equipment (treadmills to bikes, bikes to climbers, and climbers to treadmills) and exercises for 10 minutes. This process is repeated for the third 10-minute segment.

Tips for Success and Points to Consider

- This is an excellent program to offer at the early bird time (6-9 a.m.).
- It is an ideal program for new members.
- It is an ideal program for bringing back inactive members.
- It can be regulated to challenge active, fit members. Instead of allowing members to work at their own pace, you can require them to reach a challenging level on each piece of equipment.
- The group or niche that participates must be called and specifically invited to join the program.
- A small fee can be charged for a reserved spot for the 30 days.
- Each 30-minute program must be run by a trainer, instructor, or fitness staff member. The program's success is determined by the amount of energy, enthusiasm, and excitement put into running it. This will only be generated by a leader.
- This program is done in 30 days only. Run the program only from day 1 to day 30 (or 31) of a specific month. Do not start it mid-month. This makes it clearer and simpler to understand and promote.

Variations

- A group can sign up for four weeks (30 days) and each participant will have a reserved spot.
- You may allow sign-ups from week to week.

Three for Three

Description

The Three for Three program is a way to get members to work out at your club three times a week for three weeks. It is a retention program designed to get the member to exercise consistently, form a habit, and create a schedule that includes regular exercise. Anyone who signs up for Three for Three should complete the program. A staff member or trainer must be in charge of the program and follow up with participants if they miss a workout. The staff person must reschedule so the participant makes up the missed day.

1. Three for Three is ideal for any type of member: the new member, the inactive member, or the active, existing member.
2. It is a short program (three weeks) so the success rate is high.
3. Each workout must be tracked on a member's activity card. (Go to the CD-ROM for this activity card.)
4. The Three for Three program can include any type of workout in the fitness center done three times per week for three weeks.

Tips for Success and Points to Consider

- Some clubs have tried to run this program as three times per week for three months. That is too long! Too many members fail to finish. It is better to set your member up for success and then use this program to promote participation in another follow-up program.
- Offer some kind of prize, award, or incentive at the completion of the program. It can be a T-shirt, a water bottle, or a gift certificate to a pro shop.
- Charge a small fee if a larger prize is to be given. If you offer the program free of charge, perhaps hold a drawing for a prize at the end of a three-week period.
- This is a quick program that can be offered between seasons or between larger programs.

Variations

- Three for Three can be a project program at any time for any staff member or trainer. He or she would set a goal of 20 participants and call them to promote the program. It is much like running a fitness league. If all 20 participants complete the program, the staff member would be eligible for a bonus, a prize, or an award as well.
- Three for Three can be a full program run within the fitness center during a specific three-week period. With this scenario, 5 or 10 fitness trainers would each take on 20 members each as their goal. If five trainers participated, 100 members—new or inactive—would be working out at your club regularly for 3 weeks. Rewarding the successful trainers for their programming efforts as well as the members will be well worth it.

- One step further—you can establish a Three for Three club. Any member who completes the program would be a member of the Three for Three club. The club could run from January through December of every year so, for example, a member can become a member of "T4T Club, 2007."

Supplemental Material

- Three for Three Flyer
- Three for Three Activity Card

Circuit Training Classes

Description

The purpose of circuit training classes is to provide a fun, exhilarating, group workout for up to 20 members at a time in the fitness center using a variety of equipment. The program is to encourage weekly exercise.

1. Circuit training classes (groups) combine muscular strength exercises and endurance (cardio or aerobic) training exercises in the fitness center using a variety of equipment.

2. The pieces of equipment are reserved for the registered participants during the class time, and a trainer is provided to instruct and motivate the group.

3. The classes are best run in 30-minute blocks on the equipment. A 45-minute period is scheduled to accommodate a group warm-up and a group cool-down. One hour is suggested if the trainer or instructor also takes time to meet, greet, answer questions, give recognition for personal achievements, and promote ongoing participation.

4. Circuit training classes are fast, fun, and effective.

5. At the beginning of the class, all participants are stationed at a piece of equipment. Everyone begins at the same time and does as many reps as comfortable within a given time period. The time periods may vary—from one minute to three minutes.

6. Everyone in the group follows one another around the circuit until completed.

7. Cardio equipment (bikes, climbers, treadmills) is not used in circuit training classes. (See core cardio programs on page 88 for programming ideas that use cardio equipment.)

8. If a cardio (aerobic) exercise is included in the circuit, the class becomes an interval program. This is recommended because it is more fun, more interesting, and more challenging. It also allows twice as many participants in the class. The cardio exercises are done between each piece of strength training equipment. Examples include the following:

   - Step
   - Bosu
   - Jump rope
   - Trampoline
   - Sit-ups
   - Jog in place
   - Push-ups
   - Climbing up and down a staircase

Tips for Success and Points to Consider

- Circuit training classes are most effective when they are instructor driven—rather than using red and green lights or music cues—and when they involve a specific group.
- Depending on the number of pieces of equipment you will use, the participants can go through the circuit once, twice, or three times to complete the 30 minutes.
- Circuit training classes can run continuously as group exercise classes and be available on a first-come, first-served basis.
- Circuit training classes can run for six or eight weeks and include a specific group of members who signed up to participate. If this format is used, making this a fee-based program is appropriate because of the reserved time, equipment, and instructor. If a fee is required, the commitment to the program increases.
- Success and retention will be increased if a trainer or instructor is held accountable for attendance.
- Classes can run for six weeks with a two-week break to accommodate drop-in users and trial participants. These trial classes are great to allow guests or trial memberships to experience your club and programs.

Variation

Circuit training classes are great opportunities to market to specific niches—beginning, intermediate, or advanced classes; 50+ classes; women only or men only; or specific times such as early morning, noon hour, or late evening.

WOW! Women on Weights
Introductory Class

Description

The purpose of the WOW! Women on Weights class is to encourage women who are not familiar with weight training to use that area of your facility.

1. This program is designed to target a niche market—women.
2. The WOW! introductory class is free.
3. The WOW! program should be promoted by encouraging women to sign up in pairs (with a friend or relative), but you must guarantee that you will provide a partner if needed. The women will be able to meet partners at the introductory class.
4. The WOW! introductory class can be promoted throughout the club and with the help of the staff, as discussed in chapter 4. The slogan "Ask about WOW! Join us now!" can be used for promotions such as posters or promotional buttons. (See the CD-ROM for the WOW! logo.)
5. The purpose of the WOW! introductory class is to get sign-ups for the six-week follow-up program. (Always use one program to promote another.)
6. The WOW! introductory class
   - explains the benefits of weight training,
   - introduces a free weight class as a social program emphasizing the partner concept, and
   - introduces vocabulary, terminology, and general weight room etiquette.

7. Keep the class in the free weight area specifically.

8. Demonstrate the use of some equipment.

9. Have all participants experience at least one exercise using at least one piece of equipment, such as barbells or weight bar, and have them experience spotting.

Tips for Success and Points to Consider

- Give a coupon for a pair of free weightlifting gloves to everyone who signs up for the six-week WOW! program.

- Show participants or have the staff wear the T-shirts that will be given to everyone who completes the six-week WOW! program. The T-shirts can say, "WOW! I Did It!"

- Get everyone to sign in at the WOW! introductory class so you can follow up with phone calls inviting them to join the six-week WOW! program.

Supplemental Materials

- WOW! Introductory Class Flyer
- WOW! Coupon for Free Gloves

WOW! Women on Weights
Six-Week Program

Description

The WOW! Women on Weights six-week program helps women to become comfortable and familiar with the free weight area and experience the benefits of strength training. The most important goal for each participant is to have perfect attendance for all 12 sessions. The progress that is seen on participants' log sheets will guarantee commitment to exercise, strength training, and your club.

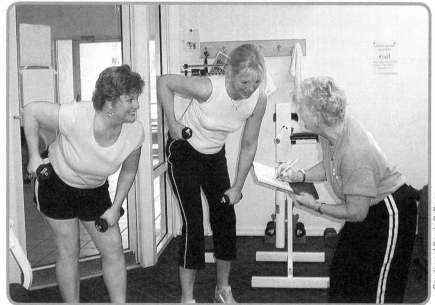

Courtesy of Sandy Coffman

1. The classes are conducted much like a group personal training program.
2. The classes are in groups to promote camaraderie, sociability, and fun.
3. Organizing the class in partners keeps each other committed, promotes friendship and sociability, and provides spotters.
4. WOW! Women on Weights is a six-week program.
5. Women are to sign up with a partner (relative or friend), but one will be assigned if needed.
6. The class will meet two times per week for six weeks.
7. The cost of the class is $45 per person per session.
8. A free pair of weightlifting gloves is included in the fee.
9. A T-shirt (WOW! I Did It!) at the end of the session is awarded to each participant and is included in the fee.
10. Each participant will keep a log of her weekly progress. (See the CD-ROM for a WOW! tracking log.)
11. Snapshots of the teams will be placed on the WOW! Women on Weights bulletin board.

Tips for Success and Points to Consider

- Except for a few machines that may be necessary, the class should be kept inside the free weight area. It will give more credibility, exclusivity, and uniqueness to the program.
- Each participant should be given a log to complete after each class. The log will list and track these items:
  - The exercise
  - Piece of equipment
  - Amount of weight
  - Number of reps
  - Number of sets
- Four teams are manageable for an experienced instructor. More than four teams may require a second instructor.
- This is a very worthwhile program in that it gets inexperienced and beginner-level women involved in weight training and also uses instructors' time well.
- Because the program is valuable to the member and to the business, extra care must be given to ensure success. Instructors or trainers should call each participant (confirmation call) before each class for the first three weeks. This call will encourage commitment, retention, and success.
- The key to the six-week WOW! Women on Weights program is a well-run WOW! Women on Weights introductory program.

Variations

- This is an excellent program to run with a coed group such as couples (husband and wife, significant others, or friends). It has the feeling of a mixed-doubles program. The program would then be called WOW! Work Out on Weights.
- This is an excellent program to run as a senior program, titled WOW! Work Out on Weights.

◉ *Supplemental Materials*

- WOW! Six-Week Program Flyer
- Ask About WOW! Join Us Now Logo
- WOW—I Did It! Logo
- WOW! Six-Week Program Tracking Log

Weight Training 101

Description

Weight Training 101 is the everyday program in the fitness center of every club. It's a program that is absolutely necessary, yet often ineffective. The program is offered to new members who are just getting started on an exercise program or who are new to weight training equipment. It is the program that usually follows a fitness assessment or evaluation and an equipment orientation. The member tracks his or her visits on a workout card that is kept at the club. The purpose of Weight Training 101 is to get your members into a healthy habit of weight training on a regular schedule and to work at increasing weights, reps, and sets periodically (usually every six to eight weeks) after being reassessed by a trainer.

1. The member is shown several pieces of equipment that exercise large muscles, small muscles, upper body, and lower body. The trainer assigns an appropriate weight, number of repetitions, and number of sets for the member to do three times per week.

2. Members are given a card that is kept on file in the fitness center. Members pull their card at every visit—ideally at the beginning of their weight training workout. They log the date and the weights and reps done during that specific workout on their card.

3. The members are encouraged to take their card around the entire workout as a continuous reference to their performance and goals.

4. If the card is used regularly and the member continues to perform the exercises as prescribed, the member is to call the club (or trainer) and get an increased performance level of weights and repetitions for the next period of weeks. This program would obviously encourage a good fitness routine for the member.

Tips for Success and Points to Consider

- The cards are filed alphabetically, but many clubs divide them into two boxes or files—one for men and one for women—to make it easier for the member to find his or her card. Option: Have color-coded cards for various types of members, such as pink cards for women, blue cards for men, green cards for 55+, and yellow cards for new members (first three months).

- Members tend to lose interest or get bored with basic weight training because it often lacks ongoing encouragement from the trainers, the members don't get recognition for their achievements, and the responsibility of the reassessment is left up to the member. Weight Training 101 has a beginning and an end. It also has a tracking system for recognition and a trainer accountable for the members' participation, which contributes to its success.

Successful Programs for Fitness and Health Clubs

- This program works best when trainers are assigned specific numbers of members to track. Trainers must track and contact the members they are accountable for to ensure that they stay on track with their weight training program. Trainers then are held accountable for reassessing their programs and promoting other programs as well.
- Weight Training 101 is a perfect program to use in promoting follow-up programs such as WOW! Women on Weights. You will move (or add on) the free weight program to the basic weight training on selectorized equipment.

Variations

- Trainers can form groups of four members and encourage them to work out together at set times during the week. The group will form a club within the club and feel as committed to each other and the specific time slot as they are to the weight training workout.
- Trainers can use the members logging on to Weight Training 101 as potential clients for their personal training programs.
- Trainers can form groups of four members and offer to take them through their workouts in a group personal training format, thereby keeping the members on track and selling a personal training package as well.

Supplemental Materials

- Training Log 1
- Training Log 2
- Training Log 3

Balance Your Fall

Description

Balance Your Fall is designed to bring members back to the club after the summer months. It is designed to encourage working out with a buddy or friend, and it helps members meet other members.

1. Balance Your Fall is presented here as a seven-week program but can be adapted to any number of weeks that will take the members from September to Thanksgiving.
2. Balance Your Fall is a retention program because it keeps your members coming into the club regularly for several weeks.
3. Balance Your Fall is a great program to reactivate members who did not use the club in the summer months.
4. Balance Your Fall promotes sociability and camaraderie, because it encourages exercising with others (family, friends, new friends).
5. The program uses a team concept that can be adapted to many combinations—it's a takeoff on the word *balance.* Each member of the team must balance the other member. Team options include
   - a new member and an existing member,
   - a couple—husband and wife (mixed doubles), or
   - any two people to make up a team.

102

6. The program is based on two workout visits to the club each week.
    • One visit must include a cardio workout—with cardio equipment.
    • One visit must include a strength workout—with machines or free weights.
7. A workout consists of a 30-minute session.
8. The team must work out together.
9. If one member of the team can't make the workout, a makeup time will be allowed within a one-week period. No more than three makeups are allowed per person.
10. Each team has a tracking card.
11. Photos of the teams are placed on a promotional bulletin board.

Tips for Success and Points to Consider

• This is a relatively simple program in concept yet very beneficial to the club. It capitalizes on the time of year by incorporating *fall* into the program title.

• Get new members involved—an attainable goal would be to get one fourth of all the new members who joined the club in June, July, and August to get into the Balance Your Fall program.

• Reactivate dropouts—pair dropouts from June, July, and August with a friend, relative, or new member.

• Promotional idea: Use a picture of a turkey holding a balance scale.

• Have a drawing for all participants for a free turkey at the end of the session.

• Telephone campaigns and proactive pairings from the programming staff will be necessary to make this program successful, but it will be well worth the effort for your business. It is unlikely that people would sign up for this program without the marketing effort.

Supplemental Materials

• Balance Your Fall Flyer
• Balance Your Fall Tracking Card

Race Across America

Description

Race Across America is a great program for retention. It offers a reason for members to keep coming to the club regularly. It offers them a goal and an incentive. Everyone can win, and prizes along the way or at the end of the journey are incentives for people to work out regularly. Watching themselves progress across the nation with every visit to the club makes the workout fun. There is also a sense of belonging—participants feel that they are part of a club within the club. Making the staff responsible for ensuring that the members complete one visit for every state keeps them actively communicating with members and creates accountability. Anyone can participate in the Race Across America. If presented correctly, it will encourage participation from members who aren't involved in other programs. Finally, this is a program that is easy to organize and will keep members active and exercising.

1. The program as presented here uses the 50 states of the United States to represent 50 visits to the club.

2. A 30-minute workout completes one visit to the club—and to a state. A member may work out by himself or participate in a program such as a circuit training class to get credit on the program.

3. Everyone can win—just by completing the 50 visits.

4. This can be a very simple program that requires only one visit per week.

5. A party is held at the end of the program for all the participants.

Tips for Success and Points to Consider

- You should have a big map of the United States on a wall in the fitness center to promote the program and constantly encourage the participants.

- A question pertaining to geography at various parts of the program will add to the challenge. Prizes for the correct answers make it more fun. Another way of using the geographical questions is to use them to qualify for the program.

- Teams can include 5, 10, 15, or 20 members. A staff person (trainer) is captain of a team and is held accountable for each team member to complete the race. List the teams on the wall next to the map.

- This can be an actual race. One way of presenting this program is to see which team (or individual) completes 50 visits first. With this format, the winner is usually an existing, active member, and it can be quite discouraging for the new, less active members who joined the program. One way around this dilemma is to limit the program to new members and inactive members who are recommitting to the club after not using it for, say, one month or more.

- If you run the program so that everyone can win by completing 50 visits, you will get more participants and probably more of the participants who need an incentive to exercise. With this format, the program is open to new members, existing members, and inactive members coming back to the club. When forming teams, include some of each group of members on every team.

- It is wise to note in the rules of the game that only one state per day can be visited or counted.

- A grand prize can be given at the party. One suggestion is a trip to somewhere in the United States. The prize could be donated by a travel agency in exchange for displaying their company logo next to the map.

- If a grand prize is given, the winner is determined by a drawing. The name of every participant who completed the program is put in the drawing.

- For every geographical question answered correctly, the participant's name is placed in the drawing again.

- You may want to charge an entry fee for this program and give everyone a T-shirt with the map of the United States on the back. It's not only an incentive but a great marketing tool as well.

- This is quite a long program if one visit equals one state—50 visits. If you consider two visits a week average, the program will take 25 weeks—nearly six months. This is very difficult to monitor, and without incentives along the way, and without the staff (captains) staying in touch with the members, participants are likely to lose interest.

- If the program is offered to new members only, clubs often leave this program (or others like it) up to the individual. For example, whenever a member joins the club, he or she is encouraged to participate in the Race Across America but there is no follow-up. This will usually end in failure because it is too difficult to track and individuals lose interest.

- A good time to offer this program is at the beginning of the year (January) until the end of the year (December). If a member registers one visit a week, it will take 50 weeks to complete. Although this is a fun way to get and keep members using the club, it will not discourage them from joining other programs along the way.

Variations

- You can create similar programs that focus on different continents, such as Race Across Europe or Race Across South America.

- You can run this program in your aquatics program, measuring attendance in your aquatics classes.

- You can also run this program for your lap swimmers.

- This program is excellent to run in your group exercise program.

- This program is an effective addition to your walking or running club within your club.

Supplemental Materials

Race Across America Tracking Form

Congratulations!

Description

A Congratulations! program is an example of a program in the achievement phase on the wheel of logical progression. Quite simply, it is a terrific retention program because it recognizes people for their attendance or performance. It's important enough to list here as a program unto itself.

1. Specific programs with the purpose of saying congratulations are necessary to encourage retention of any member.

2. Congratulations! is especially beneficial to the new member who has completed (been active during) the first month of membership.

3. Congratulations! is very encouraging for any active member who has completed a fitness program.

4. Congratulations! is also helpful to retain those who are new but inactive, for example, "Congratulations for joining the ABC Club. You've made an excellent decision!"

5. Whether members are active or inactive, Congratulations! cards should be sent to members in the mail. It is a marketing tool (direct mail) that is specific and personal. It is relatively inexpensive because the recipients are not in the thousands and they are already members who have indicated that they want to be at your club.

6. Congratulations! cards should include a list of current programs available at the club.

7. Congratulations! cards should include a voucher for a free drink, an energy bar, a massage, or a program fee.

8. Congratulations! cards could include a "fit fact," a statement or question for the member to answer. If the member brings the card into the club with the correct answer, she gets a prize—a free drink, an energy bar, a massage, or a program fee.

9. In addition, if the member brings the card into the club with the correct answer, she puts the card in a drawing box. One or more cards will be drawn at a specific time and the winners will receive a prize.

10. Despite your best efforts, it is inevitable that some people will be hesitant to become involved in the club in the first place or will become inactive after a short period of time. These cards can be important tools in the process of winning them back.

Tips for Success and Points to Consider

- The cards should be signed by the salesperson, the program director, and the manager.
- The cards can be sent by e-mail.
- Congratulations! cards must be followed up with a phone call!
- About 80 percent of active new member cards will probably be returned.
- About 60 percent of inactive new member cards will probably be returned.
- The staff is held accountable for sending the cards to all new members in a timely manner, with the appropriate information, and to follow up with one or more phone calls inviting them back to the club.

DJ Nights

Description

The purpose of this program is strictly to generate excitement and activity in the fitness center with a unique use of music.

1. Instead of piping in the normal music, bring a live DJ to the fitness center.
2. You can even include request sheets so that everyone can choose the music they like.
3. If you hold this program one time per month or even one time per quarter, you will bring a crowd of members into the fitness center and provide positive word of mouth regarding the excitement at your club.

Tips for Success and Points to Consider

- DJ Nights work especially well on the nights that activity is usually low, such as Friday, Saturday, or Sunday nights.
- DJ Nights work especially well during off-peak times of the year—summer months, or December, for example.
- This could be a program that you offer at the beginning of every quarter or at the beginning of a season or to kick off an important retention program.

- If the DJ Nights get too popular, you may have to ask members to reserve a workout time.
- You may be able to find your DJ within your membership.
- Guests coming to the club on a DJ Night will probably be interested in joining your club.
- DJ Nights are not likely something that your competition offers . . . at least not at first!

Variations

- Design DJ Nights specifically for your youth members (have the DJ play current songs and artists) or specifically for older adults (have the DJ play big band music or oldies).
- Have a theme, such as love songs during February or holiday music during December.
- Offer food and drink to create a party atmosphere.

Walking or Running Clubs

Description

The purpose of any walking or running program is to get people moving and help them to create an active lifestyle both in and out of the club.

1. Encourage and promote the walking or running programs as clubs, more specifically, clubs within your club.
2. Form walking and running clubs with niches in mind:
   - Time periods: early morning, noon hour, or early evening—title the groups "Early Birds," "The Nooners," or "Happy Hours."
   - Skill levels: beginners, intermediates, or advanced walkers and runners
   - Age groups: 30-somethings, over 40, baby boomers, over 60.
3. Give the walkers guidelines that teach the correct walking stature and stride for optimum results. (See the CD-ROM for Walkers' Workout Teaching Guidelines.) The instructor or trainer will walk with the group and throughout the group to remind the participants of the guidelines.

Tips for Success and Points to Consider

- Walking and running programs are often offered as individual activities, but group participation will encourage retention and create commitment to your club.
- Fun titles or names for the groups encourage participation. One of my favorite names is "Walkie Talkies."
- During inclement weather, the group could meet on the club track or make up the time on a treadmill.
- Promotion for the walking clubs can include a map of a specific route that will change monthly. The map of the month would be displayed on the walking and running club bulletin board.
- Formal start dates and ending dates give you the opportunity to provide recognition or prizes as incentives.

- A formal start date and ending date give your members who dropped out a new beginning.
- A formal start date and ending date give your members an opportunity to move from one program level (beginning) to another (intermediate).
- Athletic shoe retail stores in your area may sponsor a running and walking club for your club or give healthy discounts to your participants.
- Program cards for each participant to keep track of date, time, distance, and speed will encourage retention and provide pride and satisfaction with the program.
- Prizes (incentives) for participants can include discounts on apparel from your club's pro shop.

Variations

- A walking group would meet at a specific time two to three times per week and walk as a group for 45 minutes. The program will be more successful if an instructor or trainer leads the group. The program should run six to eight weeks maximum. A prize can be given to those who attend 80 percent of the classes.
- Walking or running programs can be ongoing programs that are available for members to join at any time. However, this format makes it very difficult for the club to track participation. Participation is mainly left to the individual, which will result in greater attrition rates than a program with an official starting date and an ending date.
- A fee for the program could be justified if each participant receives a pedometer. A fee may also be justified if the members receive a T-shirt at the conclusion of the program and if an instructor or trainer leads the group and gives educational materials and tips for success along the way.
- A running club from your club could train together for a marathon in your area, or the group could run a 10K race wearing your club's T-shirt and representing (and thus promoting) your club.

Supplemental Materials

Walkers' Workout Teaching Guidelines

Sport-Specific Programs

Description

Sport-specific programming offers excellent opportunities to encourage young athletes to enjoy competition and develop pride and self-esteem as they work toward their goals. Sport-specific programming also combines good fitness practices for anyone interested in developing better form, agility, and, of course, better performance in the recreational sport of their choice. The example presented here is for golf, but any sport can fit this program.

1. The promotion could say, "Join us for a golf conditioning program that will develop flexibility, power, and coordination for greater distance! You will improve your performance, your swing, and your score."
2. This group personal training fee-based program will be approximately eight weeks in length.

3. The fee will include a book such as *Complete Conditioning for Golf* by Pete Draovitch and Wayne Westcott.

4. The fitness program will partner with a golf club and golf professional.

5. The course will include exercises for strength and power but will increase flexibility and postural stability as well.

Tips for Success and Points to Consider

- Discounted lessons and possibly membership dues are exchanged between a local country club and your fitness club for participants in the program.
- Sport-specific programs can be one-on-one programs—designed to increase the performance and fitness of an individual.
- Sport-specific programs are excellent for team sports. In football or basketball, for example, the trainer can work specifically on offense or defense skills. With any team sport, working together to achieve success will enhance team spirit.

Variation

Other personal training sport-specific opportunities include these:

- Skiing
- Hockey
- Tennis
- Football
- Basketball

Corporate Membership Programs

Description

Get corporations to commit to exercise and become members of your club or facility with group orientations or one-on-one orientations as their entry program.

1. Give a trial membership—1 week to 30 days—to your chosen corporations.

2. Send an invitation and follow up with phone calls inviting all employees to sign up for either a group equipment orientation or a one-on-one orientation program. You may want to have a special sign-up board with specific times that suit the hours of the corporation, such as early morning, noon hours, after 5 p.m., or late night. Corporations may want to have the exclusive training.

3. Try to convert 30-day potential members to new members.

Tips for Success and Points to Consider

- If a 30-day pass is issued, add a separate group cardio orientation.
- Assign each corporate employee to a club fitness staff programmer who will follow up with the employee activity.
- Include an open house or happy hour event for the corporation to get complete tours and explanations of programs within the entire club.

- If the corporation joins your club with more than 50 percent of their employees, offer to announce to the media (newspaper) that the corporation you are working with has committed to a healthy lifestyle by joining your club and your programs.
- Be aware of the calendar! Prepare for your corporate program to run around National Employee Health and Fitness Day, Administrative Professionals' Day, and Boss' Day.
- Set goals before you begin and then measure how well you met the goals. Evaluate how well you met your goals by analyzing how well you followed the systems to guarantee success, such as the 10 keys to retention: (1) communication, (2) responsibility, (3) recognition, (4) sociability, (5) commitment, (6) diversification, (7) progression, (8) promotion, (9) reliability, and (10) accountability.

Variations

- Include either a fitness assessment or a needs analysis at the beginning of the 30 days.
- Include a 30-minute personal training session for each employee.
- Include a special gift to every employee who joins at the end of the 30-day trial, such as a gift certificate to a local restaurant. The restaurant will probably give you the gift certificates with no charge to promote their business, and you, in turn, can offer them the same corporate membership package. (Always use one program to promote another.)

Abs and Stretch

Description

The purpose of an Abs and Stretch class is to encourage more people to add valuable stretching to their exercise routines on a regular basis and to promote involvement in other like programs, for example, the Breathe and Stretch program or yoga.

1. Too often members do not take the time to stretch properly, before or after a workout. Most members do not know how to breathe and stretch correctly.
2. Visual aids at a specific stretching area will encourage your members to make stretching part of their regular routine, but instructor-driven classes will better educate your members, make stretching more enjoyable, and contribute to retention as well.
3. Abs and Stretch classes are very effective when offered for short periods—10 or 15 minutes at the stretching area of your club. Post a schedule for three or four times a day during which an instructor will be available to take a group of members through a stretch routine: for example, 7 a.m., 12 p.m., 5 p.m., and 8 p.m.

Tips for Success and Points to Consider

- At scheduled times during the day, make announcements throughout the club, over a PA system if possible, inviting members to the stretching area for an Abs and Stretch workout. "Don't have time for a stretching class? Stop by our stretching area at the times posted for a fun, fast, free Abs and Stretch class."

- Walk through the club at the scheduled times of the day inviting members to the stretching area for a stretching workout.
- Designate a separate stretching area near or adjacent to the fitness center of your club to remind members that stretching (warming up and cooling down) should be a part of their fitness routine.

Supplemental Materials

Abs and Stretch Guide

Breathe and Stretch

Description

The purpose behind the Breathe and Stretch class is twofold. First, it can be a lighter alternative to a yoga class, will attract many members, and may lead many of those members into yoga—the next phase. Second, Breathe and Stretch is a natural follow-up for those who have experienced the Abs and Stretch program. (Always use one program to promote another.)

1. The 30- to 40-minute classes will include a long, intense abdominal workout and concentrated breathing techniques along with stretching routines. It is a great addition to the group exercise program.
2. The class includes a three- to five-minute warm-up followed by the presentation of a variety of relaxing stretches and poses (postures) to refresh and energize.

Tips for Success and Points to Consider

A Breathe and Stretch class can be included in your group exercise program.

Group Exercise

Our objective as programmers in the fitness industry is to provide a facility with fitness programs and to provide members with leadership that will encourage exercise adherence. Years of experience in the industry has repeatedly shown that adherence to exercise is enhanced when camaraderie and sociability are added to exercise routines, and research has also shown that most people join clubs because they would prefer to work out in a group environment. It isn't surprising, then, that when group exercise (formerly known as aerobics) came into the industry, it was a booming success. Yet, within the 10-year period of the 1990s, group exercise participation dropped dramatically; many clubs report that participation dropped by fifty percent or more. This is puzzling, because group exercise programs got better, offering a greater variety of classes, more professional music, better trained instructors, specially built studios, and even better attire for the participants to wear. Ten to fifty participants or more come together in a social atmosphere to move, dance, and exercise with high energy to exhilarating music, following a leader who motivates them throughout the routine. What's not to like?

The good news is that we now have many new types of programs available—mostly in the mind–body–spirit arena—that are attracting many new participants and many different types of participants (niches). We also have professional, licensed group exercise programs available to clubs that need outside help to grow their business. Body Training Systems and Les Mills, both of which are described in this chapter, are good examples. Considerable commitment and additional expense are involved with these programs. I am including a few that I think you should know about and that I endorse highly, but they are not for every club or facility. It will depend on your size, your location, your demographics, and your business plan. They are presented here to be part of your programming reference book.

As this book suggests, programming is more than an idea! It's all about how the program is presented, promoted, marketed, and implemented. It's all about the relationship built between the instructor and the class and the sense of belonging, success, and acceptance within the group. The following group exercise programs are examples of many types of classes in our clubs today. Some are more popular than others, but every one of them has the potential to offer a fun, energizing, intense, workout that will give results. The group exercise program can be a tremendous retention program if the principles of programming are followed with as much dedication as execution of the specific exercises themselves.

Following are some general guidelines to follow when leading a group exercise class:

• The key to a successful group exercise program is often found in the personality of the instructor. The instructor should greet the class properly, using the professional greeting, addressing new members and guests specifically and enthusiastically, and introducing himself. This will build an immediate rapport with the members.

• Explaining the class agenda and reiterating its goal throughout the class educates the members and keeps them interested and the instructor interesting.

• A rapport occurs when there is response from the members. A group experience needs questions, answers, comments, and laughter. Yes, you can have fun and exercise too. That's exactly what the group exercise program makes possible.

• The instructor must be aware of and take advantage of opportunities to give recognition to those who are performing well or even just trying hard. Recognition given by the leader in front of peers is always a winning strategy.

• Educating the members on the benefits of a particular program encourages people to work harder, gives purpose to the exercise, and builds a trust between the instructor and the group. Education can be ongoing throughout the class.

• Choosing music that the members in a specific class enjoy is more productive than choosing music that the instructor enjoys.

• The instructor should say a formal good-bye and always use the opportunity to end the class with a promotion, congratulations, and an invitation to return.

• Variety is the spice of . . . the group exercise program! With the many types of group exercise classes available, there is no reason that this program should not be filled with every type of member at your club—new members (looking for a fun way of getting started), existing active members (wanting an interesting exercise program), inactive members (returning to the club with ease and enjoyment), and potential members (seeking fun, music, sociability, exercise). Who wouldn't want to be part of it?

• The class should be promoted and marketed to all your members—not just the existing active ones. Active members make up approximately 20 percent of your total members and are already exercise adherent, are familiar with the routines, and are probably using several different activity departments. Check out your group exercise schedules and class descriptions. Are the majority of classes geared for the top 20 percent of your membership—advanced, experienced, active, retained? Do you have an equal number of beginning and intermediate-level programs offered in prime time as you do advanced and high-intensity programs?

• The 30-minute workout is most workable for most people. Why? The number one reason people quit our clubs is that they don't have time. It's a real issue in today's world. For the majority of members, 80 percent, exercise classes are too long and often too exhausting. You may find it very beneficial to change your group exercise program to include several choices of 30-minute classes.

Introductory Classes

Description

The introductory program may be the catalyst that turns the new member into a retained member. Most of the attrition in our industry occurs because new members never get started. Most clubs have some group exercise classes available, but too often they are intimidating to new or inexperienced members, who are hesitant to get involved for fear of failure or simply a fear of not knowing what to do or what to expect. The introductory program is to get your new members involved in the club immediately and comfortably. These classes apply to any type of activity that is in your group exercise department. The introductory class gives you the perfect opportunity to promote other programs and activity departments in your club.

1. Personally invite every new member to experience a sense of belonging by taking part in an introductory program of group exercise classes. The class should be no longer than one hour and must include time for socialization and time for sign-ups too!

2. Have as many instructors as possible participate in the introductory class and socialize with the members.

3. During the introductory class, explain your class schedule and further describe the type of classes offered and the skill level needed to perform them. Most important, tell people what to expect . . . later, deliver on your promise!

4. Give everyone a chance to try the movements, exercises, and equipment. This class is not intended to deliver a full workout but instead to increase awareness and interest in the group exercise programs.

Tips for Success and Points to Consider

- Explain the difference between all the types of classes offered in your group exercise curriculum.
- Teach participants how to take a resting heart rate and how to calculate a target heart rate.
- Explain warm-ups and cool-downs.
- Include classes such as these in one session:
  - High- and low-impact aerobics
  - Stepping
  - Yoga
  - Other equipment—balls, weights, bands, body bars
  - Pilates
  - Kickboxing
  - Stretching

Group Cycling

Description

Group cycling came to group exercise in the 1990s and had the same sort of impact that the step program did much earlier. An indoor cycling class! This group exercise program combines music, camaraderie, and visualization along with a high-calorie-burning workout. With visualization tools, participants can ride on journeys through mountains, seasides, and other countries. It's a phenomenal concept and one of the best programming ideas that ever entered our industry. I must add, however, that it can be good, great, or best depending on how the program is presented, how it is run, and, most important, how it is perceived—by the programmers as well as the members. There have been some real flaws in some programs, and I'll present the group cycling program with a few additions and variations that you can adapt to make your group cycling program the best it can be.

Most brands of group cycling bikes will be fine for your program. Again, it is how you run the program, how you market it, and whom you run it for that count. It is very easy to promote and market group cycling. It is basically a stationary bike program

© Human Kinetics

that is designed for all members—any ability, amount of experience, schedule, age, or interest. Participants choose a schedule within the class menu, join the group, and follow the instructor's lesson plan, but they perform the class at the speed, intensity, and duration that suit them individually. "Everyone, ride at your own comfort level," is the message heard. This is the simple concept of group cycling and it certainly makes sense initially and sounds attractive to almost everyone. Here are some of the situations that evolved from this concept, and if you want to make your group cycling program go from good to great, consider making adaptations to the program as you think about these issues.

- In the beginning, everyone was new to the program so no matter what skill level you were at, the safety issues and technicalities of the bikes were of interest to everyone. The program grew so rapidly that the classes filled up with members wanting to come back and get the "cycling high" as they pushed harder and longer through the workout journeys.

- The popularity of cycling became rampant with the high-intensity crowds. Every class became another challenge. For the fit, the experienced, and the cycling enthusiasts, the group cycling program became and still is exciting, fun, a great workout, and a social experience. It's good.

- Safety issues and bike adjustments are still part of every class designed to accommodate the beginner, but the reality is that true beginners are the minority in most classes and they feel very intimidated among the regulars. When the majority of the class is standing and hammering "up the hill," a beginner is not comfortable sitting down and coasting back to a normal breathing pattern. Most beginners who have looked forward to getting involved with a group stationary program don't come back for a second or third class full of experienced cyclers.

Such a situation can easily happen because the avid group cyclists remain excited and continue to fill the classes. Group cycling programmers should present a program for every type of member (beginning, intermediate, and advanced), offer classes that are adapted for various niches (seniors, women), and work on growing the program by offering separate introductory clinics that prepare a group of people to comfortably get involved with a cycling group. People feel most comfortable with other people like themselves.

1. The beginner group cycling program should run for no more than 30 minutes. It will include five minutes of warm-up and discussion of safety and technical issues, 15 minutes of cycling, and 10 minutes of cooling down and stretching.

   This class is designed for the individual just starting out in cycling and will possibly consist mainly of new members.

   The cycling portion of the class will be done in a seated position only. The intensity of the class will be light to moderate.

   The class will prioritize basic grips, body positions, and drills, with no more than 10 seconds of hammering.

   The beginner group cycling program can be drop-in, sign-up, by invitation, or a combination of all (recommended).

2. The intermediate group cycling program should run for 30 minutes and include a 5-minute warm-up, 20 minutes of cycling, and 5 minutes of cooling down and stretching.

   A moderate intensity will attract individuals who want to add variety to their workouts.

   Some standing, more aggressive positions, and hammering for 20 to 30 seconds are appropriate.

3. The advanced group cycling program should run for 30 to 45 minutes with at least a 5-minute warm-up and 5-minute cool-down.

   Group cycling classes are best when designed to add variety to the exercise program of even the most experienced exerciser.

   The advanced class will be of moderate to high intensity with up to a minute of hammering and will use a variety of grips, body positions, and stand-up drills.

Tips for Success and Points to Consider

- All instructors should go through an orientation program that covers the content of the various classes to keep the different classes consistent and credible. Set guidelines for all levels of classes.

- Various classes should be given equal time slots of daytime and prime-time hours, and the level of participant skill should be appropriate for the level of class offered. It will be easy to slip into having every class dominated by the advanced members.

- The growth of the group cycling program will continue if the program is presented specifically to the needs of the niches.

- Thirty-minute classes are best for encouraging retention and growth of the group cycling program.

- The Four Star Program, which is presented in detail in the specialty programs section, is ideal for measuring and rewarding the participation and retention of participants in your group cycling program.
- Because of the equipment, the instructor, the music, and the visualization tools, the group cycling program can be a fee-based program.

Variations

- The introductory group cycling class is an excellent class to offer at your parties. It can be an extremely good marketing tool within your party program. The introductory class can be about 15 minutes long and would look like this:

  - The instructor smiles and introduces himself to each participant, shakes the participants' hands, and uses their names.

  - The instructor tells them about the program, demonstrates the actions, and involves them in participation: "In this class you will learn how to adjust the bike for your size; you'll learn two or three grips, two or three body positions, and two or three cycling drills that we use in our programs. My goal is to make you feel comfortable with the equipment. I will explain and demonstrate it for you, and you will get on the bike and try it yourself."

  - The instructor encourages people to get involved with the group cycling class of their choice.

  - The instructor thanks the participants and congratulates them.

- Group cycling classes are wonderful additions to your Baby Boomers and Beyond market and the after-school kids' program.

- Special one-hour or longer classes should be offered periodically to the very intense, advanced cyclists. Offer these programs on a Friday night, Saturday, Sunday, or holiday. Offer them monthly, bimonthly, or quarterly. Keep them special and unique.

- A more sophisticated form of the core cardio programs in your fitness center, the group cycling program can be a lead-in for a trekking program or a rowing program. The trekking program is a group program on your treadmills with an instructor and music. This is an advanced program because it will have the participants running, jogging, doing a sidestep, lunging, and climbing hills—all on the treadmill. It can be very exciting for those who can do it and also for those who watch it!

Step

Description

The step program certainly revolutionized the group exercise department of our entire industry, and although it has taken a back seat to many other programs available nowadays, the step is still a popular cardio class on any group exercise schedule. In addition to providing several options to members, however, the step program also became too complicated and advanced. After many years of "stepping," instructors got bored with the same movements, as did many of the members who took the classes regularly. As the routines got more and more familiar, even the next level of choreography seemed too easy. Turns, hops, kicks, and 32-count "build-on" routines got to be the norm, and soon new members who would ordinarily want to take a step class were intimidated and confused by the complexity of it all. The step program is valuable, however, because it offers a fun cardiorespiratory workout in the group exercise studio. Depending on the design of the specific class, a step workout can be beneficial for and executed by almost anyone.

1. The step can be adjusted in height from approximately 4 to 12 inches (10 to 30 cm). Increasing the height increases the intensity of the workout.
2. The addition of handheld weights will further increase the intensity of the workout.
3. Step routines are set to music with eight-count beats, which adds to the enjoyment of the workout.

Tips for Success and Points to Consider

- Step fundamentals classes should be scheduled at popular times. Because retention must begin with new members, the step program should be available for a new member, beginner, or first-time stepper.
- A 30-minute beginning step class can be beneficial and satisfying. It should include a 5-minute warm-up, 20 minutes of stepping, and a 5-minute cool-down.
- Proper form and safety factors must be taught as well as the coordination of arm work and footwork.
- The building blocks of stepping are eight-count routines. In beginning classes, changing in fewer than eight counts often becomes confusing, and safety in execution may be compromised. Eight-count routines do not have to be boring.
- Adding three to four eight-count routines can be challenging and fun and will usually bring new members back regularly.
- Most new members will want to use too many risers too soon, making participants vulnerable to sore knees and backs. This often happens in large classes with advanced students who use two and three risers.
- Experienced steppers will love to use step for their regular cardiorespiratory workout and will appreciate a high-energy step class with creative, innovative patterns of advanced movements. Steps and routines are layered using a variety of changes including rhythm, direction, and intensity. The challenging movements change rapidly and build up to 64 counts in length.

Variations

- The step is a wonderful piece of cardio equipment to add to any group exercise class for variety.
- The step is a great tool to use in an interval circuit training program.

Old-Time Rock 'n' Roll Aerobics (Aerobic Dance)

Description

Sometimes it's best to go back to basics. What was it that made group exercise part of our industry? Aerobic dance, of course. Why wouldn't anyone want to get fit and healthy by being in a group environment, moving to upbeat and exciting music, while following an energetic, empathetic instructor who leads you through the exercises as though you were a pro. Laughing, singing, dancing, jumping, hopping, kicking, sliding, marching, punching, swinging, bending, twisting, turning, stretching, reaching, walking, and jogging . . . what's not to like? This is not funk fusion! Aerobic dance is simply exercising to the familiar music that filled dance floors and aerobic dance studios for years. The music is put into routines that require ordinary movements instead of coordination challenges.

1. The word *aerobic* tells you that this class is a fun, exciting, and high-energy class.
2. The instructor must face the class and bring out the personality of the class as much as lead the participants in exercises.
3. Familiar rock 'n' roll music such as "Old-Time Rock 'n' Roll," upbeat country classics, and Top 40 songs of the 1980s and '90s are best when shuffled through the class. Variety is key here.
4. Dance exercises that are used to create the right environment will include the grapevine, step kicks, jogging in place, jumping jacks, sliding to the right and sliding to the left, crossover reaches to the opposite foot, punching right and left, and clapping hands while jogging forward and back.
5. The class begins with a warm-up, ends with a cool-down, and has 20 to 30 minutes of a combination of high- and low-impact moves.

Tips for Success and Points to Consider

- Dance aerobics is a very fun class to wake up the morning people. Early risers will look forward to the energy and uplifting spirit that greet them at the club each morning.
- Many of the easy-to-perform moves can be done over and over without being boring if you change the types of songs throughout the class.
- In this class, unlike any cardio class that uses equipment, the room can be used creatively. Formations such as circles and lines keep the class interesting, and using partner moves—and changing partners—is fun too.
- An easy, fun-filled energetic class like dance aerobics or Old-Time Rock 'n' Roll Aerobics is a great stress releaser; offer it as a quick noon hour exercise class for the 9 to 5 working crowd.

Variations

- This class, if run for an eight-week session, is great because the participants feel a real sense of belonging, familiarity with the music and moves, and camaraderie with all the participants because of the format.
- To make this class a coveted part of your group exercise program, you can make Fridays special. On Friday morning, for example, provide bagels, juice, and coffee to help the participants get on with their day. Friday at noon hour offer a yogurt, piece of fruit, and an energy bar for lunch. Charge a nominal fee to cover the cost of the breakfast or lunch at the beginning of the session, and you will be sure to have a waiting list for the next eight-week Old-Time Rock 'n' Roll Aerobics program.
- The fun that participants have in a class like Old-Time Rock 'n' Roll Aerobics is contagious and will automatically turn the shy, apprehensive, inhibited member into a full-fledged enthusiast. This class is primed to enjoy group experiences

like "crazy hat days" or "vacation T-shirt days" (everyone wears a T-shirt that they brought back from a holiday vacation). It certainly becomes a club within a club.

Let's Have a Ball

Description

Fitness professionals can use a variety of props and equipment in the group exercise studio to teach a productive class that will include cardiorespiratory activity, strength training techniques, flexibility exercises, and balance and core-stabilizing techniques. The purpose of a program like Let's Have a Ball is just that. It offers variety in one class, and every class can be different and exciting.

1. This class is different from the normal fusion class that would combine two or more specific programs. It is strictly prop focused, which will be the main attraction to your members.
2. Stability balls are now a staple in most clubs and are some of the most versatile pieces of exercise equipment on the market. These balls are used in exercises for balance, core, strength, and flexibility routines.
3. Dumbbells, medicine balls, and resistance tubes can be added for variety.
4. The Bosu offers strength and balance exercises that accommodate all levels of fitness. Members find great satisfaction in increasing their ability on the Bosu quickly.
5. Portable fitness bars offer exercises designed to increase mobility in muscles and joints and develop strength as well.

Tips for Success and Points to Consider

- This program can be run as a circuit class using each piece of equipment as a station.
- Because of the use of the equipment and the concentrated effort of the instructor, this program is excellent when offered as a group personal training program.

Variation

Create an eight-week session using only one specific piece of equipment (your choice) in each class for 30 minutes. At the end of the eight-week session—the ninth week—have a special one-hour class in a circuit format combining all the props and various pieces of equipment used during the eight-week session.

HAT and Upper Armor

Description

The HAT class involves specific exercises done for hips, abdomen, and thighs. The Upper Armor class consists of specific exercises for the arms, shoulders, and upper back. A 30-minute session for each of these classes can be very popular.

1. The HAT class is a 30-minute class using weights, cables, rings, fit balls, and body bars to tone and strengthen the muscles of the hip, abdomen, and thigh.

2. The HAT class includes a 3- to 5-minute warm-up, 20 minutes of muscle toning and strengthening exercises, and a 3- to 5-minute cool-down. This class is very popular, especially with women, and often will be a great cross-training program for a cardiorespiratory (aerobic) class.

3. Upper Armor is a 30-minute class geared toward toning and strengthening the muscles of the upper body. These muscle groups will be trained using weights, cables, rings, fit balls, and body bars. It will also have a 3- to 5-minute warm-up and cool-down.

Tips for Success and Points to Consider

• You will get more participation and cross-training from your members if you keep these two programs separate and limit each to 30 minutes.

• You can also call these two programs Above the Belt and Below the Belt. The fun titles tell it all!

Variation

These two programs are great to offer in a personal training program. In group personal training (four or more participants), the two programs combined would make an excellent 60-minute program. An individual personal training program could separate or combine the two programs, but separately the programs should be kept at 30 minutes.

Jam, Jab, 'n' Kick

Description

Jam, Jab, 'n' Kick is definitely offered as a cardio and strength training class. A challenging and yet doable introduction to kickboxing, this class is good for men and women and will specifically attract the younger adult crowd looking for a serious cardio workout.

© Human Kinetics

1. Jam, Jab, 'n' Kick is kickboxing at a slower pace and can be taught without the boxing props or apparatus.
2. The class emphasizes the form and technique associated with the basic movements of boxing and martial arts.
3. The class uses jump ropes as the only additional equipment but will certainly emphasize the cardiorespiratory training involved in boxing.
4. The punches require lots of upper-body technique, and the lower-body kicks require strength, endurance, stamina, and flexibility. Participants are usually very competitive in nature, and keeping skill levels fairly equal in this class works best.

Tips for Success and Points to Consider

- A beginning or introductory class to Jab, Jam, 'n' Kick is a good idea. It may evolve into a program of its own or can simply prepare members to feel more comfortable in the regular program.

Variation

An actual kickboxing class would be the follow-up program to Jam, Jab, 'n' Kick, but gloves would be a must because equipment such as boxing bags would be used.

Dancing Like the Stars

Description

The purpose behind group exercise dance classes is definitely to provide a cardiorespiratory exercise program in a group setting, but many more attributes of this program make it a worthwhile part of your group exercise menu. Dance classes automatically create a congenial, sociable atmosphere whether members are partnering or not. Dance classes taught in a group exercise format appeal to men as well as women, and it's important to find programs in group exercise that get men involved. Dance classes will definitely require the best music available, because music moves the soul and so does a group dance class. Dance exercise classes appeal to all ages and abilities—only energy and a desire for having fun are required, and the result is a great cardiorespiratory workout. Here are some dance classes to consider.

1. Moving to a Latin beat will offer many types of dances that will take lots of practice and exercise to master. A salsa, samba, rumba, cha-cha, or tango rhythm will demand lots of arm work and extra hip movements and is guaranteed to break a sweat.
2. Intervals of cardio movements and core conditioning are put to music in a fusion-style class that alternates low-impact ballet movements and dynamic balance sequences with challenging muscular endurance, flexibility, and core-strengthening exercises. This class combines dance, Pilates, and fitness, focusing on body awareness and controlled movement.
3. Another high-energy dance cardio workout that combines hip-hop and jazz steps will be especially attractive to those who already know most of the moves.

4. A remix of aerobic dance choreography can be one of the most challenging workouts ever. Jazz, hip-hop, and a little bit of Latin are taught, slowly at first, to the beat of hot, up-to-the-minute nightclub music or good old disco beats. Once the sequences are learned, the tempo is raised and . . . wow! It's fast paced, fun, and definitely aerobic!

5. The real dance challenge for the toughest of dance enthusiasts is street dancing. Funky moves, thrilling spins, balancing tricks, coordination challenges, and syncopated rhythms demand the most advanced and daring dance maneuvers ever. Conditioning is a given.

6. Eight and eight are 16—beats that is! The best way to introduce the dance exercise craze to new members, beginners, and others new to dance is to teach short routines with 16 beats each. Each routine would have two portions of eight counts each put together with music that matches. This class is fun, easy to learn, and good exercise to boot. Absolutely any type of dance can be taught with this terrific concept.

Tips for Success and Points to Consider

- This group exercise phenomenon can be placed right in your group exercise menu of classes or can be offered separately in six- to eight-week sessions. The sessions should be run by sign-ups or reservations only and can be fee-based for added profit.

- You can bring local professional dancers into your club to teach the various dance sessions. You would probably be able to get some free publicity with this type of format.

- A special ballroom dance event could be a kick-off for promotion of the sessions and should certainly be offered as a grand finale to an eight-week program. Open it up to nonmembers and boost your new member campaigns as well.

- In May or June, your club prom is a natural for a fun annual event to promote your group exercise dance program.

Variations

- Add some spice, some twists, some bumps, and some grinds to a ho-hum step class. You'll have to change the music and be aware that it will be a bit more challenging, but you may increase the participation of the step program by stepping to a Latin beat.

- Dancing is fun for kids and important for them to learn. Go back to the basics of an eight-count routine; with the right music, kids will learn coordination, rhythm, and creative movement while exercising.

- A dance class in the water does not mean water ballet. Dancing in the water can be a dynamic cardio class that improves body awareness, coordination, and endurance. This may be a good start to dancing on land.

Aerobic Championships

Description

With all the different types of group exercise programs available in our clubs today, this program can take on many forms, but it is patterned here after the original aerobic championships that popularized aerobic classes in our industry and motivated and inspired the newest as well as the most experienced aerobic exercise participant. As a special event, the Aerobic Championships will become a fantastic promotional and marketing tool for your entire group exercise program. It is offered as both a spectator event and a participatory event. The Aerobic Championships give the top 20 percent of the group exercise participants a chance to show off and be recognized for their commitment to the program, diligence, perseverance, and expertise. The Aerobic Championships give you an opportunity to invite the media in and therefore get recognized in the community through newspapers, radio, or TV.

1. The Aerobic Championships should be an annual event, best offered in April or May. Your heaviest participation will be in the first quarter of the year, so the promotion of this event would encourage retention during that period, but the extravagance of the event will probably promote participation for the following spring and summer months.

2. The event should include at least three divisions:
   - Singles competition (male or female)
   - Mixed-pair competition (one male, one female)
   - Team event (groups of three to five participants, male or female)

3. The competition guidelines include the following:
   - Each event should be no less than two minutes and no more than three minutes long.
   - Each demonstration is to include at least one floor exercise.
   - There is no mandatory warm-up or cool-down period. The demonstration is strictly for performance.
   - Each entry chooses his or her own music.
   - All movements must be safe and properly executed.
   - Judging will be based on creativity, form, energy, and overall performance.
   - Awards will be presented to the top two finishers in each event for two to four entries and the top three finishers in each event for five or more entries.
   - Participants may enter up to two events.

4. The presentations should be judged on the following criteria—using a scale of 1 to 10 (10 being the best):
   - Overall presentation—general appearance, smile, eye contact, attitude
   - Energy—enthusiasm
   - Form—legs and arms, movements defined and crisp
   - Conditioning—flexibility, strength, agility, coordination
   - Choreography—floor usage, flow of movements, creativity

5. This event should require an entry fee, which would cover the awards, food, and beverages at the ending reception (party), door prizes, and a participant gift such as a T-shirt and possibly a goody bag containing small promotional items.

Tips for Success and Points to Consider

- The Aerobic Championships can be a small, in-house event, drawing all participants, spectators, and judges from the membership and staff.

- The Aerobic Championships can be marketed to the outside by inviting members from other clubs to participate in the competition.
- If the event is large enough, members of the community media may be invited to be the judges. This would obviously evolve into a great PR opportunity for the club.
- Sponsors can be solicited for door prizes, food, and awards.

Variations

- Presentations other than aerobics can be included in this special event program or become separate championships:
  - The use of a step
  - The use of weight equipment, such as barbells
  - The use of bands and balance apparatus
  - The use of all kinds of balls
- Various age groups can make up separate divisions:
  - 6- to 12-year-olds
  - Ages 55+
  - Ages 17 to 24
  - Families—all ages
  - 30-somethings

Martial Arts and Other Mind-Body-Spirit Programs

Most clubs will incorporate a martial arts program into the group fitness repertoire. They are specialized programs that are adaptable for men, women, children, and seniors. Martial arts include a huge variety of programs and a variety of ancient Asian influences. Specialized training is required to become a martial arts instructor, and most clubs find that hiring an outside contractor works well. Martial arts programs are very popular, and the expectation is that the popularity and variety of programs will increase. Martial arts programs are indeed beyond the traditional group exercise classes but are an excellent complement to aerobic dance classes or step classes.

Martial arts programs are seldom put on an ongoing schedule. They will run for a series of weeks, usually 6-, 8-, or 12-week sessions with participation at least twice per week, and they will be fee-based. The fee will usually be paid up front and for the entire session rather than per class. Because a martial arts instructor is often brought in as an independent contractor, the martial arts sessions are often open to nonmembers (potential members), who may be required to pay more for the sessions than a member.

One of the reasons martial arts programs are growing in popularity is that they all require a concentrated effort of mind, body, and spirit, the essence of true fitness. The term often used nowadays is *fusion*—the combination of two or more mind, body, spirit, or ancient Asian influences that make up a class or program.

Some of the martial arts and other mind–body–spirit programming ideas are presented here for you to consider.

Yoga

Yoga is an ancient art based on developing the mind–body–spirit connection. Classes consist of various postures known as asanas. Yoga is definitely one of the most popular group exercise classes of our time. At the beginning, intermediate, or advanced level, yoga improves respiratory, circulatory, digestive, and hormonal systems of the body; strengthens, tones, and restores muscle; and greatly increases flexibility and balance. Yoga participants will probably be required to purchase their own yoga mat, belt, and block. The cost can be incorporated into the fee of the program.

A variety of yoga programs are available, each with its own emphasis and description. Again, specially trained instructors will be necessary to teach all the types of yoga classes. Some types of yoga classes to consider are these:

- Kripalu yoga—People take their postures off the mat and incorporate movements into their daily lives. Kripalu yoga uses several breathing techniques that the member is encouraged to practice in daily life.
- Power yoga—This is the more advanced form of yoga, as the name indicates. Much more physical than regular yoga, it works to sculpt and tone every muscle of the body.
- Vinyasa yoga—This is another challenging form of yoga where strong poses flow from one to another to dynamic, upbeat music.
- Yoga fusion—The combinations of various forms of yoga can accomplish many goals.
- Yoga for relaxation—This is used to calm the mind and restore a feeling of well-being. It focuses on back and neck problems and is excellent for the beginner or intermediate yoga participant.
- Yoga for rejuvenation—A mixture of asanas (postures), breathing techniques, and mediation exercises works on relieving muscular pain and stress.

Taekwondo

Tae means *foot,* kwon means *hand,* and do means *techniques* of the martial art. Taekwondo is a Korean art of self-defense that is taught to children as a discipline and to adults as a practical way of building confidence, strength, and dexterity. Taekwondo is a vigorous activity that enhances concentration and combines flexibility and strength. Taekwondo offers a systematic approach to advancing and achieving goals and is a very popular sport for teenagers as well. As children and adults progress, they wear colored belts in accordance with their knowledge and skill. Advancing in taekwondo is exciting, and retention is built into recognition.

As participants are tested, different colored belts are awarded. In addition to passing the physical test, students must attend a minimum number of classes, learn factual taekwondo knowledge, and demonstrate appropriate self-defense moves and form. The belts are a visible and recognizable part of the mandatory uniform, which is worn for every class and is considered required equipment.

- White belt—This belt notes the beginner, whether adult or child. Children as young as 5 years old can begin to learn the techniques of taekwondo.
- White and yellow belts—This class covers a more advanced level of the introduction to taekwondo, and students are expected to perform with a high level of self-control. There is no sparring in these classes, but an emphasis is placed on physical fitness, form, and self-defense tactics.

- Green and above belts—These classes build on the skills learned in the white and yellow belt class. In this class, sparring with protective gear is introduced for the first time. Students will begin sparring with punch and kick combinations using heavy bags and sparring gloves.
- Blue belts and above—These classes will include board breaking in the training and will introduce other taekwondo weapons as well.

Taekwondo testing occurs about every three months if classes are held twice a week. Testing and award ceremonies naturally encourage advancement and retention of the students. Participants tend to stay together in their groups as they advance through the ranks and achieve the colored belts. The bonding, sociability, camaraderie, and respect for the sport and for each other are excellent examples of the benefits of the best of group fitness programs. Discipline, fitness, and rewards for achievement are the goals of taekwondo. The classes will require a session charge, a mandatory uniform charge, and testing charges for the opportunity of achieving higher level (colored) belts. Taekwondo will be a fee-based program and can be offered to non-members (potential members) for an additional cost per session.

Tai Chi

Tai chi is a Chinese martial art form that consists of a series of slow, gentle flowing movements designed to increase strength and flexibility, align the body, and improve balance. It can be used as a preventive measure to maintain good health. Tai chi is the ultimate low-impact exercise and may have a significant effect on your posture, strength, and balance. It is the perfect exercise for those with arthritis, circulation problems, high blood pressure, and stress. Tai chi is a wonderful group exercise for anyone but is especially beneficial to the older adult.

Karate

Karate uses Okinawan techniques, which emphasizes simple, aggressive attacks using hands, elbows, and feet. Conditioning exercises will have to be included in this very aggressive program.

Pilates

Description

Pilates is a very sophisticated mind–body program that can be taught with or without the reformer, one of several specialized pieces of equipment used to enhance the Pilates movements. Pilates must be taught by a certified instructor and can be part of the menu of group exercise classes if taught as a mat class (without the reformer) or used with the reformer as a fee-based program. Portions of Pilates exercises are ideal to include in your personal training program.

Work on the Pilates mat is the fundamental building block of Pilates. It is an innovative system of mind–body exercises evolved from the principles of Joseph Pilates and done on the floor. Pilates dramatically transforms the way your body looks, feels, and performs. It builds strength without excess bulk, creating a sleek, toned body with leaner legs and a flat abdomen. It teaches body awareness, good posture, and easy, graceful movement. Pilates improves flexibility, agility, and economy of motion. It can even help alleviate back pain.

Pilates exercises can even be brought into the water for aqua Pilates. It will combine core strength training with balance and conditioning in the water. The Pilates program on land or in the water produces long, lithe bodies and solid abs.

1. The mat-based Pilates class helps to restore muscular balance and improve strength. Pilates teaches how to stabilize the pelvis by using the back and abdominal muscles, which allow you to control and move your body freely. Proper breathing is emphasized.
2. Pilates mat work uses small equipment or apparatus, including stability balls, medicine balls, foam rollers, straps, and bands.
3. Pilates with the reformer includes fundamentals of exercises in kneeling, sitting, and standing positions.
4. Increased levels of Pilates will enhance precision of movements and provide core strength, balance, coordination and flexibility.

Tips for Success and Points to Consider

- Formal introductory educational classes for Pilates should be offered to members.
- The Pilates program can definitely be a revenue-producing program for your club.

Variations

- Pilates is paired with many other types of group exercise programs, allowing the programs to fuse together (fusion classes) for more diversified programs, variety, and challenges.
- Aqua Pilates combines core strength training with balance and conditioning in the water.
- Pilates exercises on land can include a fusion of tai chi, yoga, and Pilates—a true mind–body–spirit program.

Branded Group Exercise

Professionalism, the key to success, is the bell ringing message that this book conveys. The marketing, training, and knowledge behind your programs, especially your group exercise program, can not be taken for granted. I believe the future of successful and profitable group exercise programs will include the use of licensed, trademarked, and proven companies. You have choices and more will become available. The best of the best—Body Training Systems and Les Mills—are offered here and I strongly endorse them.

Body Training Systems

Body Training Systems is a registered trademarked group exercise program that is sold to clubs throughout the United States and Canada. Body Training Systems (BTS) is a division of The Step Company, the inventors of the step, one of the most popular group exercise phenomena of our time. Almost every person who takes a group exercise class of any kind becomes involved with or at least tries a step class. It is fun and easy to do at first, but over the years the regular step classes lost participants along with group exercise in general. Beginning classes went by the wayside and bored instructors began making the choreography so complicated that the majority of the new members and beginning exercisers couldn't keep up the pace. The programming went beyond the average member's capability and enjoyment, promotions totally lost their impact, new and innovative moves were abandoned, and the classes and leaders became boring. The decline in the participation of the very popular step program is a prime example of the decline of participation in group exercise in general. It became increasingly difficult to bring back the group exercise excitement of old. In fact, American Sports Data, Inc., reports that after its peak in the 1980s, group fitness participation dropped by 50 percent by the year 2000.

What really went wrong? In a nutshell, group fitness is only as successful as the professional programming efforts behind it. Successful group exercise classes need professionally chosen music; exciting, energetic, and empathetic instructors; and fun, diversity, and new beginnings. Let's face it: Group exercise is all about a group experience. That experience is automatically expected to be sociable, uplifting, and fun as well as effective. In general, group exercise today lacks freshness in programming, professional personalities of instructors, and professional teaching techniques to get new members into classes and keep existing members coming back for more. This is, of course, true in every activity department of a club, and this book gives the recipes for success in any program you choose to run. As I've stated before, there is no reason why any program should fail if you follow some or all of the systems offered in this text, including the group exercise program.

Body Training Systems has brought the issues of group exercise to the forefront and has developed a turnkey group exercise system that incorporates all of the professionalism needed to run a profitable successful program. It has revitalized declining group exercise programs in clubs that were unable to or chose not to work the systems themselves. BTS is a proven example of programming success, and for that reason I believe it is a vital part of this book. Many group exercise classes offered in clubs are similar in nature to the BTS programs, but the actual, genuine BTS programs, with all of their marketing and promotional campaigns, music selections, choreography, and teaching techniques, are licensed to clubs and instructors and are specialized for those who become licensees. Visit www.bodytraining systems.com for more information.

All the programs in this section, whether BTS or similar in nature, should be part of any group exercise menu. The reason BTS is featured in this book is that the company guarantees the quality, productivity, and effectiveness of programming in your group exercise department.

- BTS trains your trainers to become professional personalities and helps you evaluate their effectiveness. BTS trains all instructors to teach classes by facing their classes. This in itself will enhance your programs. BTS training will eliminate the fight between you and your instructors regarding this and similar teaching issues.
- BTS has quarterly meetings and training sessions to maintain growth and consistency in your programs.
- BTS has a wide variety of campaigns and resources appealing to three major demographics: 30 and under, 30 to 50, and 5 +.
- BTS has branding resources and marketing material for your continuing promotions. As a member of BTS you will receive banners, posters, and free experience cards, with specific program tag lines.
- BTS provides program marketing campaigns to increase guest traffic and memberships to your club such as direct mailers, door hangers, and e-mails. These are specifically designed to appeal to nearly 87 percent of the nonclub population.
- BTS provides professionally selected music that is guaranteed to motivate and inspire your participants in each of their programs.
- BTS provides professionally designed choreography and exercises to deliver fun and success to all participants.
- BTS delivers new music and new choreography every few months. Each new program is called a launch and will include all the marketing and promotional tools necessary to fill your classes.
- BTS provides a professional management system that is focused on increasing the number of people participating in group fitness.
- BTS has a quality assessment system that keeps your group fitness instructors, classes, and programs at a professional level and keeps you in touch with how the members are feeling and reacting. This system is evaluated regularly and appropriate changes are made to ensure success.

As this book continually stresses, professionalism must be evident in everything you do, from the programs themselves, to the marketing efforts, and especially the training of the trainers. All aspects of your programs must inspire trust and must convey reliance, consistency, and sincerity as well as knowledge. If you can't do this, Body Training Systems can help you, which is why the company is featured here. Note that in every program, the instructor must face the class directly and must arrive early and stay late for every class in every program. Without proper communication, the programs will be ineffective, they will absolutely lack growth, and the success of your club will be compromised. Some of the communication between the instructor and the participants must include the following questions. Keep in mind that the answers are just as important as the questions and must be followed up with the proper actions.

- Have you ever exercised?
- Have you ever participated in group fitness?
- Do you have any injuries or problems that might affect your ability to participate?
- Have you ever weight trained?
- Have you ever done any step-based workouts?
- Have you ever experienced a mind–body workout?
- Have you ever participated in group cycling?

Group fitness and group exercise work only as well as the programming behind them: the moves,

the music, the instruction, the fun, and the diversity. Control all that and you have a group fitness phenomenon that truly delivers. For the individual, this means fitness results that are actually fun. For the club, it means member participation and member retention at all-time record highs. Variations of these and other programs are included elsewhere in this book. All programs presented can be effective using professionally based systems of preparation, checks, and balances as presented in part I of *Successful Programs for Fitness and Health Clubs*.

BTS offers the following programs in its trademarked licensed program agreement. For more information on these programs or BTS in general, please contact

Body Training Systems
2130 Newmarket Parkway
Marietta, GA 30067
Info@bodytrainingsystems.com
www.bodytrainingsystems.com

Group Step

Description

This is an energetic and exciting 60-minute cardio program. It is designed to give many options to new exercisers as well as experienced ones. Adjusting the height (risers) and including some movement variations make the class appeal to everyone. The purpose of Group Step is to offer cross-training opportunities for those who would like to add variety to their routines or to offer a start-up cardiorespiratory training class that can be done once a week or every day. It is designed to teach participants how to self-regulate their progression. Group Step should offer immediate success and fun to the new participant.

1. The class starts with a fun warm-up, continues with 10 songs with specific training objectives, and ends with a well-earned stretch.
2. Group Step teaches the movements and the basic terminology. Foot placement is one of the key things to learn so that stepping is done safely and easily . . . without the complexity that confused and turned away too many people in the past.
3. Group Step is effective with no risers or one, two, or three, depending on the individual. One height does not fit all! Movement variations and intensity are also individually controlled, but only if the instructor educates the class and is aware of each participant.
4. The experienced, advanced stepper can perform all the same movements, without changing choreography, but with up to three risers and an increased workout intensity.
5. Group Step is created for a fun group experience and a good cardio workout.

Tips for Success and Points to Consider

- Advise participants to concentrate on footwork and leave out any arm movements until comfortable with the foot movements.
- Advise beginning steppers to stand in the middle of the class and to avoid the mirrors, because they can be distracting.
- Arrive early to meet all new participants. Address these members after each class too.
- Face the class directly.

Courtesy of Body Training Systems, a division of The Step Company, LLC.

Group Power

Description

Group Power is a 60-minute barbell program that strengthens all major muscles in a motivating group environment inspired by preselected music. The class is designed for all ages and fitness levels because it uses simple, athletic movements such as squats, lunges, presses, and curls. The purpose of Group Power is to use traditional strength training routines to create programmed fun movements to music—in groups rather than as individual workouts. Group Power aims to remove the barriers to strength training such as age, gender, and fitness background, and it enthuses even the inactive person looking to start a fitness program.

1. The class starts with a comprehensive warm-up, followed by eight songs that focus on specific muscle groups, and finishes with a well-earned stretch.
2. The class includes weight-bearing exercises that have been proven to reduce the incidence of osteoporosis. These exercises are part of the education that is included in the class.
3. The class is a good cross-training program for members who want to add strength training to their fitness routines.
4. The class is designed to give results when done only twice a week.
5. Everybody is responsible for setting up his or her own equipment for the class. The equipment needed is
   - a step and four risers,
   - a bar,
   - two collars, and
   - weights—small, medium, and large plates.
6. Group Power emphasizes working within the class structure, becoming familiar with the equipment, and understanding the basic techniques rather than focusing on lifting as much weight as possible.

Tips for Success and Points to Consider

- Explain to the group that this class is not meant to suggest that the more you do the better. Two to three times a week is sufficient, and a rest between class experiences is ideal.
- Tell the class that weight training gloves may be helpful, but they are not essential. A personal note: Weight training gloves give women and first-time exercisers a real boost of confidence. It's fun to feel confident and "in," to have a sense of belonging.

- Educate the class on the degree of muscle soreness to expect. This class is likely to place new demands on the muscles.
- Explain that this class is designed to be conservative, and recommend lighter weights in the beginning and increasing them slowly. Enjoying a strength training workout is the object of this class.
- Arrive early and stay a few minutes after class to converse with new members and answer any questions.
- Face the class directly.

Courtesy of Body Training Systems, a division of The Step Company, LLC.

Group Centergy

Description

Centergy is an example of the fusion of two classes—yoga and Pilates. It is a 60-minute class focusing on the mind–body–spirit form of exercising. It concentrates on the core and helping the participant to grow longer and stronger. The purpose of Centergy is to center energy and reduce stress and, yes, to actually smile while doing it. Centergy should offer individual improvements in the general health and well-being of the participants. The class is meant to leave everyone rejuvenated and centered. It is truly meant for everyone—new exercisers, occasional exercisers, and fitness enthusiasts. Centergy offers men the opportunity to enjoy the physical and mental benefits of a mind–body discipline as well.

1. Classes start with a general warm-up, followed by tracks with specific training objectives.
2. Even in a group setting, Centergy includes modifications for new exercisers to work at their own pace. Instructors for Centergy (the fusion of yoga and Pilates) are trained to look after each participant personally.
3. Centergy works on flexibility and relaxation techniques.
4. Group Centergy helps fight injury and allows for quick recovery if necessary, again allowing for individual needs.
5. Wearing comfortable and appropriate exercise attire is always important, but for Group Centergy it is especially comfortable because you do not need shoes.
6. Bringing a yoga mat is very worthwhile. Most clubs will provide yoga mats for participants who do not have their own.

Tips for Success and Points to Consider

- Group Centergy, although a popular concept, is a very new form of exercise for most people and will tend to make people feel apprehensive or nervous. Instructors must be sensitive of this and be prepared to deal with it individually, empathetically, and professionally.
- Mirrors can be very distracting because they tend to show movements or postures that look awkward. The Centergy instructor must keep the class focused on him and on themselves.
- Instructors should arrive early and stay late, especially to learn of any injuries or problems that might affect the performance.

- Terminology and movements of Centergy are usually new and unfamiliar. Instructors should take the time to teach terminology so that the participants can talk about their experiences with one another . . . and others.

Courtesy of Body Training Systems, a division of The Step Company, LLC.

Group Kick

Description

Group Kick is for anyone wanting a challenging, athletic, and motivating workout. It is a very energetic cardiorespiratory training class that is offered as a total alternative to the traditional aerobics class. Group Kick is a program that will appeal to the male members of your club, and women who are a bit more experienced with intense exercise routines will appreciate the punching and kicking movements. Group Kick works the upper body, giving shoulder and arm definition, and focuses on movements that require timing techniques and precision. The purpose of the class is to fuse martial arts and boxing movements in a 60-minute workout format. It's definitely a class that enhances self-confidence and control and provides a challenging workout.

1. Group Kick borrows movements from boxing, kickboxing, and various martial art disciplines and then programs the movements to music.
2. The class starts out with a comprehensive warm-up and then moves to specific songs that offer effective sequencing for quick learning and a suitable work-to-rest ratio. The class ends with a stretch and cool-down that offer not only physical but mental and relaxation benefits.
3. It's imperative to teach the terminology along with the movements for the participants to feel comfortable talking about the class and asking appropriate questions.
4. Cross-training shoes are recommended because they provide the necessary support during a lot of lateral movement in Group Kick.
5. There is no contact involved in Group Kick.
6. Wearing lightweight boxing gloves gives people a feeling of authenticity when holding the wrist and fist in the correct position.
7. The first few classes should concentrate on the names and objectives of the moves. Foot placement is one of the important things to learn so that the participants kick safely.
8. As the classes progress, participants concentrate on target zones and focus on aiming their punches and kicks at a specific point.

Tips for Success and Points to Consider

- Beginning exercisers should not do too much too soon. Once a week for those who are new to the program will be sufficient, and workout frequency will increase as will the participant's level of fitness.
- The majority of participants will be sore after their first class. This is normal as their bodies adjust to new exercises that work new muscles.
- If new to the class, exercisers must be shown, with care and concern, how to adjust the level of the class to their individual needs and capacities.
- Group Kick is fast paced and uses new terminology. The movements are somewhat unfamiliar to most participants, and the instructors must consider that in their teaching.

- Correct attire is important. Typically with martial arts–based workouts, loose pants are recommended to accommodate kicking.
- Boxing gloves are by no means essential but are recommended.
- Group Kick has a slightly steeper learning curve compared with other programs, such as Group Power.
- The instructor should keep track of new participants and encourage them to take three to four classes; instructors then discuss the experience with them and help them decide if this class is right for them.
- Instructors must arrive early and stay a bit after class to talk with participants.

Courtesy of Body Training Systems, a division of The Step Company, LLC.

Group Ride

Description

Group Ride is a cycling (stationary bike) program geared for anyone who can ride a bike. It is a cardiorespiratory program that attracts many different users because of the ability to ride their own bikes and control the gears. The purpose of Group Ride is to burn calories, burn fat, shape and strengthen the lower body . . . and provide fun and excitement while doing all these things. The program is appropriate for all types of members. New exercisers are successful because of the simplicity, controlled speeds, and ability to work at one's own level, so it is a great program for your new members. Group Ride is great for men and women, conditioned and deconditioned, experienced or inexperienced. Even avid cyclists are attracted to Group Ride because it is a 60-minute program that allows the participants to work as hard as they want.

1. Group Ride uses cycling principles and matches speeds, positions, and resistance levels to music, creating a simple, fun, and effective way to cardio train in groups.
2. The class is broken up into nine songs for different terrains, speeds, and intensity. One minute you will be climbing the Alps, the next minute just cruising.
3. Group Ride has very controlled speeds to ensure that everyone can keep up. Participants need to gain confidence, and as they do so, each rider increases resistance to make the ride more challenging.
4. As in every program, but particularly in this class, the right exhilarating music and an inspiring instructor are key.
5. Periodically it may be necessary to stay seated on the bike and pedal slowly to help in recovery. The instructor should recommend it!
6. Wearing appropriate cycling attire is a must. Cycling shorts are padded and give a little extra comfort where needed. They should be recommended.

Tips for Success and Points to Consider

- The objective in the first few classes is to focus on learning the terminology and how to actually ride the bike. Learning how to adjust the resistance is more important than keeping up.
- Group Ride can be quite challenging because the pedaling never stops! Participants should feel comfortable stopping if they have had enough.

- Hydration is extremely important in Group Ride. Everyone should have a water bottle.
- It is extremely important for the instructor to arrive early to make sure all participants set their bikes up correctly.
- It is very common for the participants to be sore, especially in the rear end; it gets better!
- People perspire a lot in group ride, so they should prepare for this with shirts that breathe and are conducive to sweating.
- Regular shoes are fine to wear for the average cyclist. Actual cycling shoes should be a matter of preference.

Courtesy of Body Training Systems, a division of The Step Company, LLC.

Group Active

Description

Group Active is a 60-minute program that incorporates cardio, strength, balance, and flexibility training. Group Active primarily targets the deconditioned market and can be a launching pad into other BTS programs for new or infrequent members in their 30s, 40s, 50s, and 60s. It can also become a home or permanent program for those who feel one hour of a single format, such as Group Power, might be too much.

Group Active's first 20 minutes focus on a warm-up and cardio fitness using floor and step training movements. After recovering and restoring the body, the next 20 minutes are spent building strength in the back, chest, arms, and core using adjustable dumbbells. The remainder of the class is allocated to improving balance, symmetry, and flexibility. The Group Active format includes the following:

1. Warm-up
2. Cardio 1
3. Cardio 2
4. Cardio 3
5. Recover and restore
6. Back
7. Chest
8. Arms
9. Core
10. Balance
11. Flexibility

Tips for Success and Points to Consider

- Music selection must suit a wide variety of musical tastes with special consideration given to baby boomers.
- Incorporate cardio fitness, strength training, balance, and flexibility elements to the program so that new or infrequent exercisers are not overwhelmed.
- Include the balance segment of the class near the end because members will tend to be fatigued or tired at this stage of the workout. When muscles fatigue, other bodily structures are forced into action.
- Group Active instructors need to be very caring individuals who are focused on participant success. They should possess strong coaching skills and a real love for exercise and people.

Courtesy of Body Training Systems, a division of The Step Company, LLC.

Les Mills International

Les Mills is the world's largest distributor of branded group exercise-to-music programs. Choreographed programs are produced at Les Mills' global headquarters in Auckland, New Zealand, and distributed through agents to nearly 11,000 licensed health and fitness clubs in more than 70 countries (as of May 2007). More than four million people participate in the programs every week. For more information on these programs or about Les Mills in general, please contact the company by mail, e-mail, or internet at the following addresses:

Les Mills International
Level 2, Ranger House
150 Victoria Street West
Auckland, New Zealand
info@lesmills.com
www.lesmills.com

Bodyattack

Bodyattack is the sports-inspired cardio workout for building strength and stamina. This high-energy interval training class combines athletic aerobic movements with strength and stabilization exercises. Dynamic instructors and powerful music motivate everyone toward their fitness goals—from the weekend athlete to the hard-core competitor!

Courtesy of Les Mills International.

Bodybalance

Bodybalance is the yoga, tai chi, and Pilates workout that builds flexibility and strength and leaves you feeling centered and calm. Controlled breathing, concentration, and a carefully structured series of stretches, moves, and poses to music create a holistic workout that brings the body into a state of harmony and balance. (For copyright reasons, Bodybalance is known as Bodyflow in the United States.)

Courtesy of Les Mills International.

Bodypump

Bodypump is the original barbell class that strengthens your entire body. This 60-minute workout challenges all your major muscle groups by using the best weightroom exercises like squats, presses, lifts, and curls. Great music, awesome instructors, and your choice of weight inspire you to get the results you came for—and fast!

Courtesy of Les Mills International.

Bodystep

Bodystep is the energizing step workout that makes you feel liberated and alive. Using a height-adjustable step and simple movements on, over, and around the step, you get huge motivation from sing-a-long music and approachable instructors. Cardio blocks push fat burning systems into high gear followed by muscle conditioning tracks that shape and tone your body.

Courtesy of Les Mills International.

RPM

RPM is the indoor cycling workout where you ride to the rhythm of powerful music. Take on the terrain with your inspiring team coach who leads the pack through hills, flats, mountain peaks, time trials, and interval training. Discover your athlete within. Sweat and burn to reach your endorphin high.

Courtesy of Les Mills International.

Bodyjam

Bodyjam is the cardio workout where you are free to enjoy the sensation of dance. An addictive fusion of the latest dance styles and hottest new sounds puts the emphasis as much on having fun as breaking a sweat. Funky instructors teach you to move with attitude through this 55-minute class. So grab a friend, get front and center, and get high on the feeling of dance.

Courtesy of Les Mills International.

Bodycombat

Bodycombat is the empowering cardio workout where you are totally unleashed. This fiercely energetic program is inspired by martial arts and draws from a wide array of disciplines such as karate, boxing, taekwondo, tai chi, and muay thai. Supported by driving music and powerful role model instructors, strike, punch, kick, and kata your way through calories to superior cardio fitness.

Courtesy of Les Mills International.

Bodyvive

Bodyvive is the low-impact group fitness workout that lets you choose just how hard you work. Using the VIVE balls, tubes, and optional hand weights you're talked step-by-step through the entire class by a skilled instructor, all while listening to uplifting and inspiring music. Best of all, you finish feeling thoroughly rejuvenated and fizzing with energy.

Courtesy of Les Mills International.

Aquatics

The pool—it isn't just for lap swimmers anymore! Lap swimming is just one of the many aquatic activities that can be done in your pool. You don't want to tie up your swimming pool just with people swimming back and forth. Scheduling a wide variety of programs can involve more people and generate revenue for your facility. Children's learn-to-swim classes and water exercise classes are usually the biggest producers of revenue for swimming pools. Why not build up your aquatic program to include a wide variety of aquatic activities that attract a wide variety of age groups and interests? Pool aerobics and aquatic exercises offer many great benefits and just as many programs. In fact, water workouts are considered by many people, especially in the medical field, to be the best exercise routines for just about anyone wanting to get fit and stay healthy.

When water exercise classes first came on the scene, they were considered to be programs only for the elderly and those with arthritis. Well, that was partly right! Water exercise programs provide amazing results for that market and will continue to do so, but many other people of various ages and skill levels can benefit as well.

Exercising in water is effective for several reasons, the first being that it's easy on the body. There is no impact on the joints and it is very difficult to get injured. Second, you have to breathe deeply, which is great for your body. Third, for many people, water exercise is more tolerable than other types of exercise. A person can get a full workout in water and not feel discomfort because the water provides constant resistance to the muscles. Jogging in the water, for example, gives a lot of resistance to arms and legs and yet people perceive a much lower level of exertion because the water is cooling and takes away sweat. The motion of water also assists in getting blood back to the heart. Aquatic programming improves and maintains muscular strength, flexibility, and cardiorespiratory endurance and is often the exercise of choice after surgery, illness, or accidents.

Water exercise, because it is generally done in groups, has a social component that motivates participants to stay with it. It's fun! For example, participants tread water with plastic noodles, which are long tubular flotation devices, and when this exercise is done in deep water, it works the core muscles just as with land exercises, only more comfortably. Special flotation belts also help people to jog in deep water. A multitude of flotation and weight devices are available for use in your aquatic program. The key is to have enough programs that accommodate all levels, ages, interests, and needs.

A menu of classes could be available for all ages, preschool children to elderly and arthritic people. For example, aquatic programs for children can begin at age 6 months with parents and progress through the ages with a multitude of classes based on stroke mastery, competition, and lifeguard preparation.

Aquatic programs can also fuse with other programs such as Pilates to form classes like "Aquates," "Pilaqua," or "Aqua Sculpt." Members often will take a stretching class or beginners' Pilates before aquatics, thereby getting cross-training in their exercise program. The fusion of activities with aquatics can include tai chi, yoga, walking, running, stretching, and even biking. The programs are born when participants, instructors, and trainers ask, "Why can't we do this in the water?"

Detailed information about aquatic programs is available from the United States Water Fitness Association, P.O. Box 243279, Boynton Beach, FL 33424; e-mail, info@uswfa.org; or on the Web, www.uswfa.com. You may also order the Aquatic Directors Manual from USWFA, which contains 50 chapters and includes more than 350 pages of aquatic programming information.

There are too many aquatic supplies for the various aquatic programs to list here, and most programs will have many types of equipment from which to choose. Several product catalogs are available on request to guide you in your needs. One example is Aquatics by Sprint, a product catalog for aquatic supplies. Check the Web site at www.sprintaquatics.com. Another source for products in your aquatic programs is SPRI products; for more information visit www.spriproducts.com.

Supplies that you should consider having for your general aquatic programs include goggles, caps, kickboards, balance boards, water polo gear, bags, swim fins, masks and snorkels, aqua weights, gloves, aqua shoes, aqua toys, aqua balls, aqua games, and flotation devices. Safety gear such as CPR rescue tubes, whistles, and lanyards are also available as are videos, DVDs, and educational literature.

The following are some aquatic programming ideas for your facility. Each has a general description of the program and the market that the program will attract. Most important, you will see that a veritable paradise of programs are available for your pool area. You may even want to consider renaming your swimming pool area as the aquatic fitness center, the aquatic water fun center, or the aquatic program area.

Aquacize

An Aquacize class is a water aerobics exercise program for people not comfortable in deep water and those who want a light, relatively easy workout. This level is popular with those with arthritis. Exercises include jogging, cross-country ski motions, and variations on jumping jacks. A general Aquacize program is often called Aqua Aerobics. It is considered a mild to moderately strenuous program and is good for all-around conditioning.

Deep Water Aerobics

Deep water aerobics classes take Aquacize to the next level and are usually done using a belt and other equipment. The deep water aerobics program is for persons who want to jog or run in deep water. The exercises focus on overall body conditioning, especially arms and legs. The program uses a variety of cardio skills to promote endurance training and power development. Deep water aerobics can be extremely strenuous.

Aqua Circuit Training

Circuit training in the pool! This program is run just like a circuit training class in the fitness center except pool props are used instead of huge pieces of equipment or exercise machines. Balls, steps, bands, paddles, and weights provide an all-around workout. No equipment, seat, or weight adjustments are necessary, and no swimming skills are required. Participants move from station to station, doing a specific exercise or using a ball or band at each stop. All participants work at their own level at each station, so the class is designed for beginners as well as intermediate-level students.

Aqua Cardio Sculpt

This fusion aquatic program is based on the principles of Pilates and core strengthening and conditioning. Exercises are done with flotation devices in deep water. The object is to either get a cardiorespiratory workout or use abdominal muscles to lift and strengthen various parts of the body. This program is moderate to quite strenuous and requires comfort in deep water.

Aqua Kick

If martial arts seem a bit too strenuous, you can experience the fusion of martial arts training and water exercise with a variety of kicks, jabs, and punches that are challenging, safe, and effective without the high impact of the floor routine. Kickboxing routines in the water are probably best for advanced exercisers.

Water Walking and Water Jogging

This is a terrific program designed to teach safe and healthy movements in the water that will increase flexibility, balance, and coordination. Participants walk forward, backward, and sideways. They lunge, jump, and jog. This program is excellent for anyone and requires no swimming skills.

Lap Swimming and More

This is a lap swimming group program that starts with a warm-up, ends with a cooldown, and has a challenging, organized, interval lap swimming routine that combines different strokes throughout the class. Participants will work on stroke improvement and develop endurance, which will make ordinary lap swimming more interesting, fun, and beneficial.

Master Swim Program

The Master swim program includes structured workouts to improve stroke technique, teach flip turns, and help participants gain strength, stamina, and flexibility. This class is for the serious swimmer.

Arthritis Foundation Aquatic Program

The Arthritis Foundation Aquatic Program consists of water activities designed to maintain or increase range of motion and to promote muscle strengthening for anyone suffering from arthritis. The AFAP has developed 68 separate exercises to enable participants to improve and then maintain joint flexibility, thereby enhancing their abilities to perform daily tasks, increasing their independence, and improving their overall sense of well-being. Consult your local Arthritis Foundation to learn how you can offer this program at your club.

Children's and Junior Swim Programs

Junior swim programs have fun titles that explain the progression of ages and classes. This is a good retention tool because kids love to move from being a "guppy" to achieving "tadpole" status. It's much more fun than moving from junior beginning level I to junior beginning level II. Some other ideas include sea horses, sea turtles, starfish, flounders, swordfish, dolphins, barracudas, sharks, whales, Orca, or jaws. Can you think of some awards that children would appreciate after graduating from these classes? Can you think of some promotional pieces that would attract children to these aquatic programs?

Swimfants

The Swimfants program is for children ages six months to two and a half years. Parents have as much fun as the children blowing bubbles, kicking, and splashing. Children learn to have fun in the water as well as to respect the water while achieving a great bonding experience with their mom, dad, grandma, grandpa, or caregiver.

© Human Kinetics

You and Me, Baby

You and Me Baby is a great follow-up program for children ages three to five years. Children can learn breath taking, submerging, and movement skills.

Toddler Splash

Children ages four to six years can learn floating, kicking, and stroking skills such as crawl strokes and backstrokes. The goal of this class may be to swim 25 yards unassisted.

Bronze-Level Youth Swimming

Students who can swim the front crawl and the back crawl unassisted will now learn side breathing, breaststroke, flip turns, and water safety skills. Learning to be "torpedoes" in the water and retrieve objects beneath the water is challenging and fun.

Silver-Level Youth Swimming

At this level, students can add the sidestroke and the butterfly stroke and learn to increase their distance. The goal of the swimming lessons now becomes fitness. Instructors can teach competitive strokes and work with students to increase speed and endurance. Classes will combine aerobic conditioning with stroke development. Some of the skills taught will include these:

- Rhythmic breathing
- Retrieving objects in deep water
- Being long-range torpedoes (swimming half the length of the pool)
- Using kickboards and other flotation devices
- Practicing friendly competitive heats and relays

Gold-Level Youth Swimming

At this level, the active aquatic youth may be preparing to become lifeguards. Class includes endurance swimming, lifeguard strokes, and safety skills. Contact the American Red Cross for help and direction in teaching a basic water rescue course and preparing participants to become lifeguards. A gold-level youth swimming program may also be advantageous for participants who are preparing for local swim team competitions or for their school swim team.

10

Baby Boomers and Beyond

The senior population, the baby boomers—people in their 40s, 50s, 60s, 70s, 80s—are categories or niches of the aging market. Each age group is a niche within a niche, and members are diverse, ranging from the physically weak to the physically strong. So be aware that marketing and programming for seniors nowadays go far beyond water exercises for people with arthritis. Some programs are more strenuous than others, depending on the age, experience, or condition of the group, but despite those differences we can identify similarities in the wants and needs of the aging population.

The largest and most influential niche of this population is the baby boomers, born between 1946 and 1964. As of 2007, however, the oldest of this group are turning 61; U.S. Census statistics state that those 65 and older will be 63 million strong by 2025, and they will be more affluent and healthier than any elderly generation before them. On the other hand, many—even most—of these people have never been involved in a regular fitness program, and they are not familiar with or comfortable with our clubs.

Research has also taught us that it is never too late to get fit. Seventy- and eighty-year-olds are coming to our clubs, community centers, and fitness facilities at an enormous rate. They know that instead of avoiding exercise because of diabetes or arthritis, they need to get *more* exercise into their daily and weekly routines.

Senior programming deserves its own identity and its own chapter in this book just as it deserves its own programming menu or department in your club. Some requirements of the baby boomers and beyond market are met by all the programs presented here. You need to be apprised of these qualities to develop your programs for the aging population in your club, whether beginning or advanced. The wants and needs of the baby boomers and beyond are these:

- **Socialization and fun.** Active aging includes eliminating loneliness, depression, apprehension, and possible pain. The joy of friendship, playfulness, laughter, spontaneity, games, and recreational activities are key. Programs that include socialization and fun will result in happiness, a quality that will make the difference to them for the rest of their lives. When creating and marketing our programs to seniors, we must establish an atmosphere of excitement and energy that includes socialization, conversation, and relationship building.

• **A sense of belonging.** Activities should be offered in groups to give participants the feeling of being in a club within your club. Group experiences lead participants to want to become active members. They will want to join in. A sense of belonging gives confidence, provides energy, and enhances performance in any activity.

• **Leadership.** To create a fun environment, we must be fun leaders with engaging personalities who convince seniors that we want them in our facilities and are willing to give of ourselves to make them feel comfortable. Our energy level must be tenfold to theirs to draw them in. Making fitness fun is the key to success with everyone in our business, but with the aging population it is even more important. Let's face it, having a good quality of life is the definition of successful aging, yet it becomes increasingly difficult to achieve. We make the difference—as leaders, in our clubs, within our programs. Empathy and sincerity must dominate the leadership that we bring to the programs and must be delivered in a professional, mature manner.

• **Mind stimulation.** When giving directions, remember to take enough time to explain why we do things as well as how to do them. Teaching techniques that are the most beneficial to seniors include singing, chanting, and dancing; yes, an excited, energizing experience. Having said that, I must add that this population needs and wants to learn about exercise physiology, vocabulary and terminology, and the latest in fitness technology. Including education within the activity will be necessary for a successful program.

• **Time, comfort, and convenience.** Seniors will have many concerns. Are specific areas set aside in the club for me to socialize with friends and other program participants? Are locker rooms designed for privacy? Is the equipment designed for easy access and weight adjustments? Is the music played at a comfortable volume? Are specific times and programs set aside for my needs and abilities? Will dedicated leaders be available who support me and whom I can trust? Are there programs designed for me to get started? Will there be other people there like me? Will I have fun?

For more information on the aging market, please visit The International Council on Active Aging at www.icaa.cc.

Fun and Fitness for the Aging Population

This program is guaranteed to put a smile on your face and new energy into the aging population of your club and community. Fun and Fitness for the Aging Population is an exercise program that begins with chair exercises for the older, inexperienced, deconditioned, or beginning exerciser and proceeds through a progression of programming ideas including strength training, aerobic exercises, floor routines (land aerobics), and even a little line dancing.

Fun and Fitness for the Aging Population is designed to develop initial interest in your facility and your programs and to entice this population to come into your clubs in the first place. This program offers a vast variety of exercises that are doable and fun, using group concepts, special props, and music appropriate to the age and activity. The program is best offered as a special event that delivers new and innovative ideas for follow-up programs. Fun and Fitness for the Aging Population is adaptable to every type of facility including large coed fitness clubs, women-only clubs, community recreation centers, retirement centers, senior living facilities, and assisted living facilities. It is an excellent program for ages 45 to 90, for the obese, for those going through rehabilitation, for the first-time exerciser, and for the friends who brought them. Fun and Fitness for the Aging Population promises to

- increase participants' ability to add physical activity to their daily living,
- improve joint range of motion,
- improve self-esteem and self-image,
- increase positive social interaction, and
- allow participants to enjoy themselves!

1. Exercises in chairs offer participants security and allow for good posture and balance. The participants can concentrate on maintaining a positive attitude, working on range of motion, and learning, feeling, and enjoying the movements.

2. Here are some examples of choreography:

Warm-Up: Head

* Move head side to side and up and down (nodding yes and no).
* Drop ear to shoulder.
* Move chin forward and back.
* Smile broadly and "kiss the air."

Shoulders

* Raise up and down—both together, one at a time, and alternating.
* Squeeze front and back and then circle forward and back.

Arms

* Stretch arms forward. Making a fist with fingers facing up to work biceps, bend both arms and release for several repetitions—then alternate right and left. Repeat with arms stretched out to side.
* With arms stretched out to side, open hands and point thumbs up and down (rotating arms from the shoulder).
* Do joggers' arms, perhaps while marching in place.

Hands and Wrists

* With arms stretched out in front of body, palms facing front, fingers up, make a fist and open hand, repeating, "Open, shut, open, shut."
* With hands open, spread fingers apart and then together, repeating, "Open, close, open, close."
* Circle fingers one at a time . . . thumb, index, middle, ring, pinky.
* Circle wrists in each direction.
* "Wave" with hands from the wrists—saying hi and 'bye.
* Touch a finger on one hand to the thumb, each finger, one at a time. Repeat with the other hand and then do both hands together.

Dancing While in the Chair

* Reach both arms to the right side while touching the right foot to the floor on the right side eight times, then repeat to the left. Repeat sequence in fours, twos, and singles.
* Slap thighs eight times and then clap eight times. Repeat sequence in fours, twos, and singles.
* March in place with joggers' arms for a count of eight.
* Roll hands over each other, circling forward for a count of eight and ten circling backward for a count of eight.
* Combine all of the preceding in a sequence of movements.

Feet and Ankles

- Point and touch toes to the floor—alternating right and left.
- Reach and touch heels to the floor—alternating right and left.
- Pronate and supinate the feet, touching the floor with each movement.
- Circle the right ankle in the air and then the left.
- Step to the floor with the right foot and kick the left foot out straight. Repeat on other side.
- Add these to the dancing routine already described.
- Roll hands over each other, circling forward as previously but this time leaning forward toward the floor. Then circle hands backward and come back to a sitting position. Circle hands forward again, raising them high over the head and backward down to center.

Exercises and Sports Movements

- Do jumping jack movements with the feet while sitting in the chair. Add arm movements.
- Do swim strokes with the arms while sitting in a chair—dog paddle, front crawl, sidestroke, breaststroke, backstroke, butterfly stroke.
- Hold onto chair with hands and kick feet as though splashing in a pool.
- Hold onto chair with hands and kick feet as though riding a bicycle.
- Using the arms with a make-believe jump rope, raise both feet off the floor and return as though jumping, but stay seated in the chair.
- Do the same movement but circle the rope backward.
- Do the same jump rope movements but alternate right and left feet as though jumping on one foot.
- Pretend to dribble a basketball and perform two free throws—remain seated.

Add Strength Training Exercises Using Bands and Light Weights

- Arrange participants in a circle and play kickball—kicking a ball across the circle to one another.
- Play basketball—throwing a basketball (or a lighter ball) into a big hoop in the middle of the circle.
- Add floor routines—marching forward and back, sliding side to side, walking in a circle, kicking side to side, toe tapping, and heel tapping.

Variations

- A line dance can occur before you know it!
- Those with physical limitations can continue the exercises in their chairs.

Tips for Success and Points to Consider

- Use as many props as possible—balls, balloons, weights, bands, discs.
- Use music such as big band, rock 'n' roll, folk music, country, show tunes, marches, and the like.
- Give ribbons or buttons for excellence, perseverance, or determination.
- Give a ribbon or button for birthdays.

- Include a sing-along . . . even singing rounds of "Row, Row, Row Your Boat."
- Invite potential members—relatives, neighbors, friends.
- Have a social hour after the class and serve lunch or snacks.
- Take pictures.

Senior Day With a New Beginning

Senior Day With a New Beginning is a one-day special event designed for clubs that want to increase their membership, grow their senior programs, and provide visibility to the community as well. The program will reenergize the existing senior program in your club, reenergize its existing participants, encourage existing members to bring a guest for the day, reactivate dropouts, get inactive members involved, get new members involved in scheduled programming, and encourage potential members to become new members. The day's event will include many activities and experiences, but the core event of the program will be the fun and fitness chair exercise class.

The day's agenda: 9 a.m. to 3 p.m.

1. The day begins at 9 a.m., when the entire staff comes together for a short pep rally to instill team spirit and emphasize similarities of purpose rather than individual agendas. The greeting at the front desk is echoed by the trainers in the fitness area, the sales team, and the maintenance crew.
2. The participants enjoy coffee and cookies at the reception gathering.
3. Various booths and health screenings are set up throughout the club for the participants.
4. Small groups of participants attend 15-minute seminars to learn how to use specific equipment for the knees, back, and shoulders. The groups listen to the trainer's educational material, watch the trainer's demonstration, and try each piece of equipment.
5. A light lunch is provided for all.
6. Door prizes are given out.
7. Pictures are taken.
8. Demonstrations of programs (many already scheduled) go on throughout the day, such as aquatics, group exercise, and tai chi.
9. An added feature can include a nonfitness event such as flower arranging or a sketching or painting class.
10. Fitness assessments should be offered throughout the day—either free or for a fee.
11. The event of the day is the chair exercise class, scheduled from 10:30 to 11:30.
12. Most important, a membership table and a program table are visible, accessible, and staffed for the entire day!

Tips for Success and Points to Consider

- To set your goals for the program, consider what you need to achieve from the event. Evaluate the results as you compare them with your goals as in the following examples:

- The number of existing 50+ members attending

- The number of guests of existing members attending

- The number of inactive members attending

- The number of new members (first three months) attending

- The total number of guests attending

- The total number of nonmembers (potential members) attending as a result of the promotions themselves (not guests)

- This program is an excellent way to get your staff involved. Encourage all the staff members to personally invite someone they know to attend this event.

- Have a minimum goal of enrolling 10 percent of the total guests as members of the club. The total number of guests will depend on your location, community, and demographics, but 100 is an attainable number to shoot for.

- Promotions appealing to your existing senior members to come to the event with guests must begin three weeks before the event.

- Include a line dancing class.

- Include a sing-along segment.

- Include a 20-minute demonstration of a class performed with your club's existing active senior members.

- Invite the media—radio personalities, TV reporters, and newspaper reporters—to the event. Offer to give pictures and on-site interviews. Radio stations will be happy to come on site to talk about the activity—live.

- Ask the police and fire departments to provide booths where attendees can receive safety tips. This will entice the media to attend as well.

- If you have multiple clubs (sites), have one event at each site throughout the year.

- Follow up! Follow up! Follow up!

Variations

- This special event—Senior Day With a New Beginning—is often run as a health fair. Obviously, a health fair would include more booths providing health screenings—eyes, ears, blood pressure, diabetes, and cholesterol. I strongly encourage the inclusion of these screenings, but health fairs are common, and the addition of the fun and fitness class as well as the other events makes this program unique. The purpose of this event is to grow your membership and to grow your programs in addition to attracting the inactive potential senior market to fitness.

- Several marketing strategies can be used to entice people to health screenings. Often the title of programs can help attract participants: "Oh, Say, Can You See?" (vision screening) or "Say What?" (hearing screening).

- The program can be broken down into several smaller units and run specifically for recreational sports, nutrition, health screenings, group exercise, aquatics, or strength training.

- A full day with a variety of events pertaining to a specific market, the preparation of the staff, and the promotions and marketing techniques can work for other populations as well:

- Women only: emphasizing women's issues

- Toddlers: emphasizing parent–child classes

- 5- to 10-year-olds: emphasizing martial arts classes, aquatics programming, or recreational sports such as racquetball and tennis

- 11- to- 15-year-olds: emphasizing sport-specific training

- Overweight or obese children: emphasizing fun ways to get fit

I Love a Parade

A good, old-fashioned parade is an excellent way to promote a variety of fitness activities. It can appeal to persons of every interest, skill level, personality, age, and gender. The marketing advantages are endless. It certainly will attract the potential member and the inactive member while focusing on the existing member and getting the new member comfortably integrated. A parade takes the stress and seriousness out of fitness.

The purpose of a parade is to portray different programs and groups of people who share the fun experience of exercising at your club. It will inspire activity and probably increase your revenues by adding more members and retaining existing members. A parade makes fitness fun—especially for the aging population.

1. The leader must be energetic, organized, and willing to participate in the parade. Every program department must be involved in the parade.

2. Choosing a theme, such as the Fourth of July, St. Patrick's Day, or Easter (the Easter Parade), will encourage creativity and excitement.

3. Costumes can be used that reflect the theme (red, white, and blue for the Fourth of July or green for St. Patrick's Day). When dressing alike, participants get a sense of belonging.

4. Each group can choose its own music for the march down the street, and everyone will be in a festive mood.

5. There is seldom a parade that wouldn't include a picnic. The events following the parade can bring the various groups together, such as a Frisbee toss or a beanbag toss. This is also an opportunity to recognize individual performances and give recognition to people. T-shirts, ribbons, water bottles, and towels are all inexpensive prizes that are appreciated at an event such as a parade or a picnic.

Courtesy of Sandy Coffman

6. Pictures say a thousand words. Any follow-up program will be easily promoted with pictures of your participants. Not only will all the members who participated in the first parade want to participate in the follow-up activity, but any spectator or anyone seeing the fun had by everyone in the pictures will want to get involved the next time. Pictures will tell your story. Pictures will market your programs.

Tips for Success and Points to Consider

- Have staff involved in the parade—each group should be represented by staff.
- Tell the media about the parade. You are sure to get coverage from the newspaper, radio, and probably TV.
- Have all the participants invite relatives, neighbors, and friends to the parade and to the picnic to make this event intergenerational.
- Include sing-alongs.
- At the picnic, include a bake sale and a craft sale, but more important have program tables available with staff to take program registrations and a club table available with staff to take appointments for tours. Tip: Have the bake sale run by the spectators only. It will give them a sense of belonging as well, and they will feel as much a part of the program as the parade participants.
- Follow up, follow up, follow up!
- Make this an annual event.

Variations

- Include kids' programs in the parade.
- Have a separate parade for kids' programming.

May Day! May Day!

May is Senior Health and Fitness Month. Designate every Wednesday in May as May Day—a free program for seniors. The program would consist of an educational seminar, an activity, and a social time. Each Wednesday the seminars are on different topics and the activity changes. Each program would be approximately two hours in length, offering beverages and light snacks before or after the seminar. The seminars and activities could be open to members, guests, or nonmembers in the community. Examples of seminars and activities could include these:

- First Wednesday of May—"Ask the Pharmacist." Invite a local pharmacist to be a guest speaker to discuss the many over-the-counter pills and supplements available today. This is always a very popular seminar and will guarantee many questions from the audience. The activity could be line dancing.
- Second Wednesday of May—"A Balancing Act." Ask a physical therapist to hold a seminar to educate members about how to keep their bodies aligned and balanced in daily life. The activity would be exercises for balance and posture from a fitness trainer.
- Third Wednesday of May—"Diabetes? Arthritis? How Exercise Can Help." This would be a seminar to explain the what, whys, and hows of exercises for people with diabetes or arthritis. The activity would be a walk (outside if weather permits).

- Fourth Wednesday of May—"Heart-Healthy Exercises." This seminar, given by a local physician, would cover ways that exercise can help prevent heart disease as well as how to exercise safely if you have heart disease. The activity could be a demonstration of light exercises in the pool.
- Fifth Wednesday of May—"What's for Lunch?" A seminar by a dietitian would enlighten the participants on good nutrition. The activity could be a chair exercise class or a sampling of tai chi or yoga.

Tips for Success and Points to Consider

- This program is for all four groups of members—new, existing, inactive, and potential. Every Wednesday will be a great opportunity for the sales department to introduce themselves to the guests and follow up with membership information.
- May Day! May Day! becomes a great community outreach program because it offers the local population a chance to learn about the benefits of exercising and about the wellness programs offered at your club.
- By incorporating samplings of your current programs into the activity hours of the program, you will be promoting cross-training opportunities to your senior population and, of course, using one program to promote another.

Variations

- May Day! May Day! can be the annual event for Senior Health and Fitness Month, but to promote the program all year long you may want to devote the first Wednesday in August, November, and February to seniors, leading up to the events in May.
- May Day! May Day! also could be offered every Wednesday for members only until May of the following year.
- An additional suggestion for the social part of the program is to ask everyone to bring a bag lunch or charge a nominal fee and provide a lunch for everyone. This idea will make reservations a must.

Supplemental Material

May Day Flyer

Welcome Back to Tennis

The 50+ population is the largest segment of our market today! They are here—ready, willing, eager, and able to get onto the tennis court for the first time or definitely excited about getting back onto the court after 5, 10, 15, or 20 years. The USTA reports that the tennis industry during the last five years of the 1990s lost more than 5,000,000 players, many of whom were aging persons who became injured or worried about injuring or adding stress to their bodies. In an effort to recapture these players and offer them a new beginning to tennis, the USTA, AARP, and the International Council on Active Aging (ICAA) initiated the Welcome Back to Tennis program (trademarked by the USTA). This program provides instructors who demonstrate and teach participants how to ease back into tennis safely, comfortably, and enjoyably. The program is a three-hour party in a safe and fun environment. It includes socializing, music, food, drinks, advice on new racket technology, safety considerations, warm-up and cool-down activities, a refresher course on basic tips, on-court tennis activities, prizes, and sign-up opportunities for continuing tennis programs. The Welcome Back to Tennis program format is successful for as few as 10 or as many as 100 participants.

Presented here are the basic concept and key characteristics of Welcome Back to Tennis. A shorter, general format of the program is being offered here, and it is suggested that you include this program in your programming agenda. The general format is considered an excellent example of a 50+ program and can be adapted as you see fit. It is a successful program format to follow for tennis and possibly other activities and opportunities for the 50+ market. The general program could be called "Tennis Again."

The Welcome Back to Tennis program is a trademarked program designed by and administered through the USTA. For information and specific training on the Welcome Back to Tennis program, you may contact your local USTA branch or log onto www.usta.com for detailed information.

Welcome Back to Tennis promotes a healthy lifestyle for seniors by providing them with an exciting social tennis event

© Human Kinetics

and offering them opportunities to join a specifically designed continuing tennis program. The target audience is people older than 50 years who used to play tennis but stopped playing or who would like to get started. This event is not intended for individuals who are currently involved in a local tennis program or league. Another objective of Welcome Back to Tennis is to grow the tennis participation in your facility by involving new players (specifically 50+ players) in a new programming format. And finally, a prime objective of this program is to get participants to commit to a follow-up program of instruction and play. How do you get started?

1. Call or send a personal invitation to all 50+ people in your club or your community. The promotion must inform recipients that this event will get participants involved in group round-robins rather than the traditional private lesson format that encourages ranking, competition, and tournament play. Socialization, fun, and the opportunity to meet new friends are the key ingredients.

2. The example used here is an event held on Saturday morning from 9 a.m. to noon. Participants arrive at 9 a.m., check in, and enjoy social interaction. Plenty of staff and volunteers must be on hand to introduce people and engage in conversation. Light refreshments are served to encourage a more active social time.

3. 9:30 a.m.: Welcome. The group is welcomed and given an outline of the day's events and goals for the party. The welcome includes information on new equipment, attire, technology, and lesson and play plans specifically designed for the 50+ market. Some humor here goes well too. This group will almost always be apprehensive, intimidated, and unsure of their ability to participate or keep up. Providing a lighthearted atmosphere is essential. Explain how the game has changed to accommodate how the people have changed; this can be an easy and fun way to put everyone at ease and supply needed education as well.

4. 9:50 a.m.: Warm-up. The group gathers en masse on a court with upbeat, age-related music to do dynamic stretching with footwork and leg, hand, and arm movements.

5. 10:05 a.m.: On-court tennis activity. In one large group, or several smaller groups, instructors take the participants from working the balls and rackets individually to small friendly rallies. Key instructional tips are given periodically and reviewed at the end of the on-court session. Most important, the participants change partners frequently. The objective is to ensure that everyone, from beginner to a more skilled player, experiences success, has fun, practices rallying, and meets a number of new people. The activities on the court must keep everyone moving and taking turns just hitting the ball over the net. During the one-hour or less period, participants should be given the opportunity to stop and introduce themselves to new people at least every 10 minutes. People will laugh and become more active as energy levels rise.

6. 10:50 a.m.: Cool-down. All participants perform static stretching to prevent stiffness and soreness.

7. 11:00 a.m.: Social time and program sign-ups. Program tables are set up for participants to sign up for follow-up programs specifically designed for this audience. This is the all-important follow-up to this event. Two options may be available—doubles play, either mixed or not—for more socialization. These programs last four to six weeks, beginning the road to retention. Examples: (1) Learn to Play Doubles—entry-level play focusing on skill development and basic doubles positioning; (2) Doubles Strategy and Play—intermediate program that places more emphasis on strategy and playing the game.

8. 11:00 a.m. to noon—Lunch! Door prizes! Sign-ups! This is the hour of opportunity. Participants should have met new people with whom they would enjoy playing. They also should have experienced success on the court with easy, fun play and no competition or demanding skills. They should definitely feel that they are ready to come back to tennis, or, more important, that tennis has been reintroduced to them at their level and with their needs and wants in mind. At this point, signing up for a six-week program of doubles instruction and play should be a given.

9. Follow up with participants and begin doubles programs the next week.

10. The Welcome Back to Tennis program as a whole is obviously a hit on its own, but running a Welcome Back to Tennis Program quarterly or even every two months will be beneficial to the senior market, your business, and the promotion of health and fitness.

Here are suggested guidelines for setting up the two follow-up instructional programs for the participants in the Welcome Back to Tennis program.

Learn to Play Doubles

Learn to Play Doubles is designed for those who have never played tennis or have not played for a number of years. It emphasizes the skills of rallying, serving, and playing at the net. Participants play actual games, sometimes modified, by the second session. New friends and playing partners are introduced and relationships formed.

Doubles Strategy and Play

Doubles Strategy and Play is for people who played fairly regularly in the past. It emphasizes learning the strategy and tactics of play and applying them to game situations. Activities include practice on executing repetitive game situations. Supervised play follows. All programs for 50+ will center on doubles play for several key reasons:

- Most adult players naturally gravitate to doubles play.
- Doubles encourage social interaction and meeting new partners and opponents.
- Doubles requires less physical exertion, because players need to cover only half the court.
- Court space is maximized, and the costs of court time or the program itself are reduced per player, because more players are accommodated on one tennis court.
- Doubles strategy and tactics are more stimulating and achievable, even at more modest skill levels.
- Doubles open up many more opportunities for mixing partners and opponents between males and females, spouses, and groups of friends, thereby enlarging the pool of potential playing partners.
- Because less physical movement is required than in singles, the risk of injury is lower.

Tips for Success and Points to Consider

- You should look for at least 60 to 70 percent of the participants to sign up for the follow-up doubles programs.
- Keep the doubles programs to four to six weeks and have the next set of programs ready to promote during that time—2.5 leagues, round-robin play, or additional lessons.
- You must have a training session before the event for all the staff involved in the program. Everyone on board must understand the nuances of the 50+ market and know how to greet the participants with the professional greeting. Staff must learn to keep the event social by introducing people to one another during the tennis activities as well as the social activities.
- Hold a training session before the event for all the instructors who will implement the on-court portion of the program. Many tennis pros may not automatically be as enthusiastic about this event or the market as they should be. The on-court training should not be administered as lessons or the kind of drills used in the past. The tennis pros must be fully apprised of the market and goals of the program, and they must demonstrate buy-in. Sometimes it is very difficult to keep things simple, make them fun, and provide a successful experience as well.

- Be sure everyone has name tags.
- Take pictures of the participants and put them on a bulletin board with the flyer and the invitation to the next event.
- Have one person be the host or hostess (emcee) of the event to keep everyone moving and to make sure no one is left sitting or standing alone.
- Have participants bring their old rackets to the event and give a prize to each player who tells the story behind the racket.
- Have rackets available for everyone to use. You may want to go to your local manufacturer's rep and ask to use their demo rackets. Don't expect participants to bring their own racket.
- Definitely alert all media to this program. It may very well be considered a good PR piece for the radio, TV, or newspapers.
- Contact wbtt@usta.com for the complete event planning guide.

Variation

This program is incredibly successful as a senior tennis program. It is an excellent format to follow and adapt for other markets and other programs as well, such as the corporate market, aquatics programming, and family programs.

Supplemental Material

- Learn to Play Doubles Flyer and Registration Form
- Doubles Strategy and Play Flyer and Registration Form

Courtesy of the United States Tennis Association (USTA).

SilverSneakers Fitness Program

The SilverSneakers Fitness Program is a registered trademarked program available to fitness centers nationwide through Axia Health Management. The SilverSneakers Fitness Program offers a group exercise program designed exclusively for older adults. Founded in 1992, Axia Health Management promotes health through unique physical activity programs in partnership with health insurance companies and other large consumer groups to offer programs to their members. At the writing of this book, SilverSneakers is available to more than 2.5 million members in 44 U.S. states.

The SilverSneakers Fitness Program is a socially oriented program offered to Medicare-eligible members of Axia's partnering health plans. Eligible health plan members receive a basic membership at no charge at a participating fitness center that is part of a nationwide network. Members can participate in the customized SilverSneakers classes and use all other amenities associated with a basic membership, including exercise equipment, weight training equipment, and pools. Fitness centers participating in the SilverSneakers program are subject to the following benefits and obligations:

1. All tools and equipment for classes are provided free of charge.
2. Free accredited instructor training, choreography exchanges, and seminars are offered, and qualifying instructors receive continuing education credits.
3. Targeted mailing and promotions to members within the service area of a fitness center are available on a Web listing and include full-color brochures, postcards, posters, and flyers.

4. There is zero cost to the fitness center to acquire new members.

5. Participation initiatives, fun activities, and awards are offered at a fitness center to promote members' adherence to exercise through healthy competition and goal setting.

6. A fitness center must track and verify eligibility to the program each month.

SilverSneakers Muscular Strength & Range of Movement is the program's core class and is a multilevel, equipment-based format designed to increase muscular strength and range of movement in older adults. This total body conditioning class uses handheld weights, elastic tubing with handles, a SilverSneakers ball, and a chair for seated or standing support. Exercises include work for all major muscle groups addressing strength, flexibility, muscular endurance, balance, coordination, agility, speed, and power.

The class format includes a warm-up, rhythmic range of movement stretches, muscular conditioning exercises with resistance tools, a cool-down, and a final stretch and relaxation segment. All class formats and choreography options meet industry standards for older adult fitness as outlined by all accrediting professional organizations and curriculum guidelines from the International Society for Aging and Physical Activity (ISAPA).

Tips for Success and Points to Consider

- Axia account managers are based in your community, and the program has a toll-free support line. Online options will educate your participants about senior health topics, exercise and healthy lifestyle, and chronic condition management and provide you with access to wellness professionals to speak at your location.

- You may take advantage of special events planned, staffed, and advertised at no cost to your fitness center to drive new members into the program. Additionally, members can visit any network fitness center across the nation at no additional cost.

- SilverSneakers classes are traditionally offered between 10 a.m. and 2 p.m., usually a good time for fitness centers. Classes provide an opportunity for older adult participants to meet one another and form enjoyable friendships. A good incentive for active ongoing participation is to offer a prize such as a signature T-shirt or water bottle after a student has attended 8, 10, or 12 classes within a four-, five-, or six-week period.

Variations

- The SilverSneakers Cardio Circuit is an advanced group exercise class designed for participants who have expressed a desire for more cardiorespiratory work in addition to exercises for agility, balance, and coordination. This nonimpact cardiorespiratory conditioning class is presented in a circuit format with alternating resistance work and aerobic conditioning choreography.

- SilverSneakers YogaStretch is a blend of three yoga styles creating harmony of movement for the whole body. YogaStretch is performed from seated and standing positions to enhance flow and energy in combination with restorative breathing exercises. The class offers a variety of safe and effective options designed to increase flexibility and balance to improve each individual's sense of well-being.

- SilverSplash is Axia Health Management's new older adult group water fitness program designed to enhance each individual's quality of life and daily function. SilverSplash uses the physical properties of the water and a SilverSneakers kickboard to enhance strength, agility, range of motion, and cardiorespiratory conditioning.

For more information, please visit www.silversneakers.com or www.axiahealth.com. You may also use the following contact information:

Axia Health Management
Network Development Department
800-295-4993
networkdev@axiahealth.com

Courtesy of Healthways, Inc.

Youth and Teens

Our industry has an opportunity and a responsibility to create and implement programs for children of all ages—9 months to 90 years! Like any other population, children fall into niches (in this case based on age) that determine the best programs for happy, healthy lives. If children are active in their early years, they lay a solid foundation for a healthier adult life; therefore, a book on fitness programming would be remiss if it did not feature some specific programming ideas for children in their formative years, say 1 to 16. Just like adults, children respond and react best when they experience an activity with other kids like them, who have similar interests, skill levels, schedules, personalities, ages, and genders. Age group is the most important factor to consider when placing children in programs that will generate results and ongoing enthusiasm. It's another case of programming (age-related activities) to niches (certain age groups) within the niche (all children ages 1 to 16). As with most successful programs, the sociability factor is huge with children, as are variety and fun. As children grow older, their body awareness, personal goals, and competitive spirit become more important. Children who are brought up in a physically active world that combines creativity, imagination, and fitness challenges are more likely to participate and enjoy sports activities of all kinds as they grow older and to maintain a healthy lifestyle all their lives.

How important are fitness activities to children? Society is dictating that it will be up to the individual to seek out fitness opportunities and to take the initiative to exercise regularly, so parents will take on the responsibility of developing exercise as a way of life for their children from day one. It's clear that kids' programming must be an integral part of your programming calendar, and it may begin with fitness programs that require parent and child involvement. In fact, in the beginning years, parent–child classes tend to nurture healthy bonds between child and parent as well as develop healthy bodies and minds.

Perhaps as you focus for a moment on kids' programs, you will discover the child in yourself, while remaining the expert, the guide, and the protector, and will become even more productive and creative in the development of your adult programs. Here are a few programming ideas to get your creative juices flowing.

Each programming idea includes a general description of the program as well as an indication of the age market that the program will attract. Some include tips for success and points to consider, and some offer variations of the program. Most important, you will see that there are a multitude of kids' programming opportunities for you to include if you have the type of facility and demographics for this market. Your kids' programming classes are prime-time opportunities for growing the programs and your membership too. Nearly every kids' program should end with "Bring a friend." The words *children* and *friends* simply go together! Regardless of whether your program is for one day or a full week, it's sure to be a success for the kids and the club.

Yoga Bears

Description

The Yoga Bears class is created for two- to four-year-olds and their parents. The purpose is to provide a fun, unique experience for children and their parents or caregivers, combining creativity and imagination with fitness. Movement, balance, and body awareness are inspired by simple yoga postures and poses and performed with parents and children working together, holding hands or supporting one another.

1. Identify body parts and experience their movements.
2. Experience the difference between moving in a personal space rather than a general space.
3. Recognize and move in various directions—right, left, forward, backward.
4. Execute simple but specific locomotor movements such as walking, running, and jumping. Learn body control by starting, stopping, and holding still.
5. Execute simple nonlocomotor patterns such as bending, reaching, pushing, pulling, stretching, turning, lifting, and twisting.
6. Move to music—starting and stopping with music cues, for example, and reaching high or bending low with music cues.
7. Use props such as soft balls to develop eye–hand coordination, hoops to learn space control, and balls or objects to kick. Learn how to catch, roll, bounce, bat, or toss a soft ball.
8. Learn how to participate cooperatively in movement group activities by moving together—holding hands, sitting down and standing up, or moving a big circle in and then out. The group activity will teach emotional control, sharing, and patience.

Tips for Success and Points to Consider

- The music and fun sounds will be key to getting the children to move enthusiastically, but they will also help to teach consistent reaction. For example, play the same music that creates or demands the same movement every time.
- Specific music selections are a must: Try movie or television themes such as Pink Panther or the Charlie Brown theme. All the Disney songs are terrific.
- A multitude of good, safe equipment is designed specifically for children's activities. Many items are inflatable and can be used for many activities and age groups. If your facility is small, and so is your budget, implement your kids' programs with simple equipment that is readily available, such as colorful hoops, balls, parachutes, and tambourines. Simple activities can be fun, educational,

and challenging, such as balancing a bean bag on your head or on your knee or foot, throwing it in the air and catching it, or throwing it to another person to play catch.

- Having a mat, such as a yoga mat, for each child teaches the use of space and movement. Each child could have his own step to work on as well.

- Constant and positive reinforcement by the leaders—parents and teachers—is important, but group cheers go a long way too.

- Recognition and awards using ribbons or buttons will always encourage a child to try harder. Find a reason to reward every child for something at one time or another. Many awards can be given for reasons other than performance, such as perfect attendance, good sporting behavior, friendliness, helpfulness, courtesy, perseverance, being the most improved, and . . . birthdays! Building self-esteem is a sure way to build a life of fitness that incorporates the mind, body, and spirit.

- At young ages, two to six years, the ratio of students to teachers is best at about six to eight students per teacher; therefore, the parent–child setup enables the class to be bigger. A larger class size encourages more sociability and will encourage children to make friends in the fitness world.

- Yoga Bears is a friendly title for a class and suggests that the content will include child-friendly yoga poses. A key to kids' programming, however, is to offer variety within the class and to introduce other forms of exercise that will encourage retention, commitment to the exercise, and, most important, an interest in sports, recreational activities, or more advanced programs such as gymnastics. Be aware of children who show strong aptitude and commitment to specialized sports, and your kids' programming menu will grow as will your business.

- Having a club mascot, such as a big Yogi Bear, will give you lots of marketing opportunities and will surely be a fun and unique addition to your kids' programs.

Courtesy of Sandy Coffman

Gymnastics

As the children leave toddlerhood behind, the groups will range from three- to five-year-olds, four- to six-year-olds, and five- to seven-year-olds, and the parents will not be part of the program. More difficult locomotor patterns can be introduced in a gymnastics program, and more challenging routines make up the class content. You can have lots of sophisticated apparatus for a gymnastics class or you can improvise easily with the equipment you have. A gymnastics program will introduce increased range of motion exercises and develop balance, coordination, and the ability to perform tumbling skills. Children will learn to work individually as well as begin to experience competition. Challenging activities, learning to follow instructions, and social interaction are all part of becoming involved in a gymnastics program.

- Agility courses—weaving in and out of cones on the floor, walking on a balance beam or over stepping-stones
- Obstacle courses—crawling through a tunnel, jumping through a hoop, stepping over a step, jumping over ropes, throwing a ball into a basket

Games, Music, and Crafts

Kids' programming, gymnastics, or other activities must include variety.

- Cooking healthy snacks can be educational and fun as well. It's also a great treat for the kids to bring home.
- One specific day each week or one specific week each session can emphasize music and movement, as the children learn routines with rhythm and coordination.
- One specific day or week can emphasize making a craft item, learning creativity, dexterity, color, and patience. It's a great opportunity to make something tangible to show at home or at school.
- One specific day or week can emphasize game playing, such as Monopoly or Shoots and Ladders. Making big boards of these games really creates a

Courtesy of Health Quest

fun atmosphere. As each child rolls (or throws) the dice (often made of large Nerf-type material), they move to a square or place on the game board that dictates an exercise, movement, or use of apparatus or equipment.

Incorporating a variety of gym games encourages regular gym usage, alleviates boredom, and stimulates social interaction. Most important, the kids learn about the importance of exercise and discover how easy and fun it is to bring movement into their lives.

It's a Family Affair

Kids' programming will undoubtedly evolve into family activities. Families that play together stay together. Families that exercise together stay fit together! Picnics and fun 5K walks are great for promoting your club, your programs, and a healthy lifestyle as well. A picnic or a fun walk will not only generate member interest but community interest too, and often your local media will publicize your events. Organize a 5K walk for your families. They can even include babies in strollers and tykes on bikes. A good old-fashioned barbecue or picnic to end the walk will complete the perfect family program.

- This can be a charity event such as "Walking for Breast Cancer," with proceeds from an entry fee to be donated to the charity.
- Local sponsors will be happy to get involved by paying for T-shirts, water bottles, or food and beverages.

Courtesy of Health Quest

Parents' Night Out

Description

Kids age 12 months to 12 years can enjoy an evening of fun and games every Friday or Saturday night from 6 to 11 p.m. while their parents enjoy a night out on the town. The night for the kids would include the following:

- Snacks and possibly pizza
- Interactive games for the younger kids
- Line dancing, hip-hop, or other dance activities
- Some craft projects
- Movies for the older kids
- Swimming for kids six years and older
- Sports for the older kids such as basketball, soccer, and badminton

Tips for Success and Points to Consider

- Potential members could take advantage of this night for an additional fee. It might be a good way to introduce your club to potential members.
- Choosing one specific Friday night and one Saturday night every month—such as the last weekend of every month—will help regular users to promote the program and therefore the club by word of mouth.

Junior Weight Training

Children age 11 to 15, for example, are brought to the fitness center and taught weight room safety and etiquette. A basic cardio and weight training after-school program twice a week not only will get the youth at your club working out regularly but will encourage and inspire their parents to use your club as well. This is an especially good program to run in the mid-afternoon, right after school and before your prime time.

Introduction to Sports

Each week a different sport is presented in a fun, exciting group event:

- Week 1—Tennis
- Week 2—Racquetball
- Week 3—Track and field
- Week 4—Volleyball
- Week 5—Wallyball
- Week 6—Basketball

This could be a once a week program for six weeks. It also works well as a summer camp program offered twice a week for three weeks or three times a week for two weeks.

Outdoor Activities

Weather permitting, your club can be the place where children will want to be, especially if programs have been offered to them throughout their formative years. Your clubs offer a healthy lifestyle for a healthy lifetime activity, and active children will want to participate in programs that include:

- Outdoor swim programs
- Basketball
- Outdoor tennis programs
- Soccer
- Biking programs

- Volleyball
- Hiking programs
- Football
- Track
- Baseball

Girls' Club

A very successful program in your club will be a girls' club for ages 10 to 15. The program could be an eight-week session or a special birthday party (or other special day). The program would include fitness center activities, swimming, gymnastics, cheerleading, and dancing as well as activities designed exclusively for girls:

- Special fashion tips—clothes and hair
- A modeling class
- An arts and crafts day (flower arranging? jewelry making?)
- Manicures
- Pedicures

Variations

- Do you think a girls' club program would be enticing for older girls as well?
- What about a special Mother's Day girls' club program?
- What about a three-generation girls' club event—grandmother, daughter, and granddaughter?

Supplemental Material

Girls' Club Flyer

Birthday Parties

Description

Nearly every club can add birthday parties to its programming calendar. I recommend parties for all sorts of reasons, as you know, but I think children's birthday parties are very appealing. Birthday parties can be large, small, simple, or extravagant, but with a few decorations, a cake (of course), some fun activities, and the right personnel, every birthday party can be a success and can be a profit center for your club.

Kids' birthday parties can be a good source of income for your club. Providing kids' birthday parties is an added service to your members and a terrific way to introduce your club to nonmembers as well. Kids' birthday parties often introduce children to activities that will inspire further participation, and they will also encourage a greater family commitment to your club.

1. Parties should be available for children of all ages, with an age-appropriate activity selected to be the theme of the party.
2. Parties usually last approximately two hours.
3. Birthday parties can include
    - invitations;
    - table decorations;
    - plates, cups, silverware, and napkins;
    - club personnel for organization, setup, administration, and cleanup; and
    - club personnel to run activities.
4. Here are ideas for birthday party themes:
    - Arts and crafts, for the younger children. Children will make a special arts and crafts item to take home.
    - Fun and games, for younger children. Games include parachutes, relays, obstacle courses, and dodgeball.
    - Pool parties, for older children. These will require volunteer adult supervision.
    - Hip-hop dance parties.
    - Tennis, racquetball, volleyball, wallyball, or basketball parties.
    - Flag football, soccer, or floor hockey parties.
    - Gymnastics parties.
    - Cheerleading parties.
    - Spa parties—manicures and pedicures.

Tips for Success and Points to Consider

- The cost of parties will vary with individual clubs, but if you would open your club to nonmember children's parties, the fee would obviously be more than for a member.
- The parent can supply the birthday cake, or if your club works with a caterer or bakery, the cake can be included in the cost of the party.
- More extravagant decorations such as balloon bouquets can be added to the cost of the party.
- A juggler, clown, or balloon maker can be an added attraction to the party.
- Taking pictures of the parties and displaying them in a section of your club will be the best marketing tool (at little cost) that your club can have.

Variations

- Theme parties for kids do not have to stop with birthdays. New Year's Eve or New Year's Day parties can provide a couple hours of fun, noise-making celebrating for members' kids and guests. This is great way to promote your club to families in the community.

- At Halloween, have pumpkin carving parties or organize a ghost house. Be sure to add a physical activity to the day.

- Make Valentines for mom, dad, grandma and grandpa, aunts, uncles, cousins, and friends. Be sure to add a physical activity to the day.

- Plant flowers and seeds in little pots for the beginning of spring. Be sure to add a physical activity to the day.

Summer Camp Programs

Summer camp programs engage children in healthy, active, social activities every day, for a full week, at your club. When the children are happy at your club, the entire family will be more likely to be active and retained members. Children's camps tend to bond a family together and encourage kids and adults alike (parents) to find lasting friendships in a healthy environment.

Summer camp programs provide fun, games, crafts, swimming, hiking, climbing, and all sorts of sports for a full week of fitness, friends, and activities for children of all ages. Kids also learn how to socialize and appreciate making new and lasting friendships.

1. Children's camps will run for one week at a time. Some camps may be for full days (9 a.m. to 4 p.m.) or for half days (9 a.m. to noon).

2. Some children's camps will be designed for specific age groups, and others will be designed for all ages but will concentrate on or emphasize one particular activity or sport.

3. Summer camps can be designed for separate age groups.

Variety is the object. For example, the week's activities may include swimming, crafts, gymnastics, taekwondo, and tennis—all at an entry level. Children will discover different experiences and will probably find an area or activity that they would like to pursue in depth. Offering instruction and participation on a consistent basis is sure to develop healthy habits as well as potential athletes and untapped talents.

© Human Kinetics

Examples of summer camps divided by age groups would include these:

- Camp Discovery (ages 4-7)
- Camp Exploration (ages 8-10)
- Camp Adventure (ages 11-14)

Ultimate Outdoor Summer Camp

Description

Summer sports camps are popular for kids who want to concentrate on one activity. The following activities would be great for the 11- to 15-year-olds in your club. A summer sports camp could offer two to three weeks of learning and training in any of the following activities:

- Bike riding
- Skating (rollerblading)
- Hiking
- Golf

Sports camps can also offer a complete week of instruction and play featuring one sport such as soccer, basketball, swimming, or tennis. All ages can attend any camp and be divided among age groups within the camp.

- Soccer camps can provide soccer drill sessions concentrating on skill building and team play, controlled scrimmages, campwide sessions, and free swim to relax.
- Basketball camps can be designed for all levels; participants will be divided into groups by skill and age. Daily activities can include basketball skill building, offensive and defensive skills, team play, shooting, games, and free swim to relax.
- Swim and tennis camps can include daily activities in tennis skills and drills, sessions on the rules and etiquette of the game, and tennis games and competitions throughout the week. Swimming lessons, based on ability, will focus on stroke refinement and water safety. Other activities may include free swim and group games like capture the flag or Frisbee to relax.

Specialty Programs

Specialty programs are programs that are run annually, seasonally, or as one-time special events. Specialty programs can be run with many different formats and can focus on many different niches. They usually will involve several activity areas and departments in the club and almost always will require support and participation by the entire staff. Specialty programs will almost always serve all four groups of members—new members, existing members, inactive members, and potential members.

Here are some specialty programs that you should certainly include in your programming calendar of events. Be creative. All the programs can be adapted to any type of facility or fitness setting and can use whatever equipment you have. Most of the specialty programs feature lots of variations, and you will find that the variations create additional programs within the original framework of the specialty program.

Open House

Description

An open house is certainly one of the most special programs you can run. An open house can be held for many reasons other than a grand opening of a new facility, and effective clubs will hold an open house at least annually. The purpose of an open house is to expose your club or business to the community. The event must make people very interested and excited about attending, and then the event has to meet and exceed their expectations. An open house is primarily run for the benefit of the potential member, and it is expected to grow your business, but it is great for the inactive member as well. An invitation to your inactive members will more than likely be received as an opportunity for a new beginning. A well-run open house must take advantage of the fact that 60 to 80 percent of your new business will come from word of mouth and referrals. The open house will stir up lots of conversation—first from the members, who will be asked to bring guests to the open house, and second from people in the community who attend your open house. Without an exciting, fun event, you will fail to attract new business and in fact will drive your customers away. The open house can surely be your most productive program of the year.

1. The first people to inform about your open house are your members. You should solicit their help in bringing their relatives, friends, and coworkers to your open house. Announce the open house in your newsletter, if you have one; if not, send out an announcement or a special one-time newsletter.

2. In the announcement state that you'll be sending out an invitation to all your members. The invitation will include tickets to the event for your members and also for their guests. (Make the members' tickets one color and the guests' tickets another. You will need to identify guests for follow-up after the event.)

3. An easy yet effective promotional tool is to make promotional buttons for your staff to wear for at least three weeks before the event.

4. Conduct telephone campaigns in addition to sending the newsletter and the invitations. Most effective are the calls made by the salespeople to all the members who joined within the previous 90 days. A personal follow-up phone call from the salespeople is sure to result in referrals.

5. One good marketing strategy is to offer prizes to the members who bring in the most new members from the time the promotion begins to the time of the open house—or even extended to two weeks following the event.

6. The open house must be decorated to create a party atmosphere. Put balloons everywhere and display a list of door prizes or the prizes themselves.

7. Your staff will need to make a good impression. They should wear crisp uniforms and neat name tags as they receive the guests and use their professional greetings.

8. Everyone attending will receive a tour card (see the CD-ROM) for several activity areas in the club that must be visited: for example, the fitness center, the pool, the group exercise studio, the child care room, and the pro shop. As the guests visit the various activity areas, a staff person punches their tour card. When completed, the tour card is turned in for a prize drawing. Use of the tour card has three objectives:

- It's a fun group activity and gives the participant a sense of belonging.
- The tour card is tangible and is perceived as an activity in itself. It's a reason to give a prize and showcase your club at the same time.
- The tour card is used as a tracking tool for follow-up.

9. An open house event must have food and beverages (beer and wine if possible) and music. A DJ works best because he will verbally promote your club throughout the event and do a great professional job of announcing door prizes too.

10. Take pictures of the members and their guests to put on the bulletin board. Most important, take pictures of any new members who join during the event. Recognizing people who join at an open house gives credibility to the next one.

11. To give a sense of urgency and an incentive to join during the open house, offer special membership pricing, free items with the club logo, and discounted personal training sessions or group programs.

12. Every open house event should include a group activity such as the Grand Prix or the Cardio Circuit.

Tips for Success and Points to Consider

- Programs should be available for sign-up in all activity areas. Time some of the programs to begin approximately one to two weeks after the event.
- An open house is usually big enough to warrant sponsorship:

  - Ask local businesses for door prizes—car washes, pizza, restaurant coupons, movie tickets.

  - Ask club vendors, such as equipment manufacturers or contractors, to sponsor the event with money in exchange for promotions. Local restaurants may donate the food too.

  - This is a party! Do not run out of food or skimp on beverages.

Variations

- Open house events can be run with many different themes and for several different occasions. The grandeur of the program will produce the results.
- If run quarterly, for example, an open house can be offered to new members and their guests only.
- An open house can be an ideal program offered specifically to several corporations in your community.
- An obvious reason for an open house is the grand opening of a facility.
- A new addition to your facility, a renovation, a substantial redecorating, or even the addition of a full new line of equipment can be a terrific opportunity to offer a grand reopening.
- A holiday can be celebrated as an open house just as you would offer an open house party at your home. Christmas or New Year's, for example, could be an excellent time for an annual open house at your club.
- A member appreciation party is a popular annual or semiannual event that is very similar to an open house.

- Your members and your community will be very responsive to a health fair. The format of an open house is a very creative way to develop enthusiasm for health-related booths and educational programs.
- Special populations will arrive in droves when invited to a program such as an open house that is presented exclusively for them:
    - Seniors
    - Kids (juniors)
    - Teachers
    - Families
    - Hairdressers
- Charity events will draw the support you need when you say, "Thanks for your donation!" by inviting the attendees to participate in an open house.

Supplemental Material

- Open House Invitation
- Open House Tour Card

Grand Prix

Description

The Grand Prix provides a fun group experience that offers a variety of exercises and uses several different activity areas of the club. The program offers diversification and introduces the cross-training concept. The program moves quickly and covers a lot of ground in the allotted time. It involves lots of exercise, lots of experience, lots of fun, and very little competition.

1. The Grand Prix program is 100 minutes of total activity.
2. The number of participants will vary according to individual clubs, but the program can accommodate 10 to 100 participants.
3. The 100 minutes of total activity can be broken down as follows:
    - 20 minutes—warm-up exercises and aerobics
    - 20 minutes—court sports (racquetball, tennis, squash, wallyball)
    - 20 minutes—fitness center (cardio or other circuit equipment)
    - 20 minutes—walking or jogging
    - 20 minutes—cool-down and stretches

Tips for Success and Points to Consider

- If the group is small—10 participants or fewer—the whole group stays together in each activity. With a larger group—30+ participants—you can divide the group into three groups of 10. The whole group (30) can begin together in the group exercise studio for the warm-up exercises, and then you can divide each group of ten among the next three activities. Each group will rotate until everyone experiences all of the activities. Conclude with the entire group (30) back in the exercise studio for the cool-down and stretches.
- An added feature or the final 20-minute segment can be a clinic or workshop for educational purposes or a question-and-answer segment.

- You could end the program with a swimming event. It could be an addition rather than a part of the 100 minutes.
- The instructors and trainers must be on the ball, keeping the groups together, moving through the activities quickly, and maintaining a high energy level throughout the program.
- Using props like bells, whistles, tambourines, and gongs to start and stop the 20-minute sessions adds a fun flavor to the program.

Variations

- The Grand Prix can be a one-day event.
- It can be a monthly or bimonthly program offered for new members only. It's a wonderful way to integrate a new member into the club.
- The Grand Prix is a terrific format for any party such as a victory party, end-of-league party, or holiday party.
- The Grand Prix can be tailored for special populations—kids, seniors.
- The Grand Prix is a great format for running private parties or special corporate group events.
- The Grand Prix can be an ongoing program, ideally suited for the summer season. For example, it could be a women-only summer program that is offered one or two times per week for six to eight weeks during the summer. The activities can be varied each week, and the final segment can be nutrition information and a weigh-in for a weight loss program.
- The Grand Prix can be marketed to parents and grandparents, who could put their children and grandchildren in the child care room for the first four activities and end by sharing a group swim with the children. The ideas are endless!

Four Star Program

Description

The Four Star Program was originally created for and is presented here for the group exercise department. The best and most effective programs in your club will be created for the purpose of attaining retention. To be successful, a program must include a tracking system and a means to recognize performance. The Four Star Program is designed to do all of that and more!

- Identification—the Four Star Program identifies who comes to class, when they come to class, how often, how seldom, or not at all.
- It is an ongoing program that is easy, fast, accurate, and versatile.
- Any member can join at any time.
- Everyone can win.
- It can be used for the entire group exercise program or for specific classes, niches, or times.
- It is a program for gaining new members, retaining existing members, and reactivating inactive members.

1. Each participant receives a registration card (see the CD-ROM). The member registers her name, phone numbers, e-mail address, starting date, and the class day, time, and type. Using the card, the member only has to sign in one time—at registration.

2. The registration cards include a generic calendar—months to be labeled as needed.

3. The cards are filed alphabetically.

4. The members pull their cards when they arrive for class.

5. At the end of class, the instructor gathers the cards, punches or marks the date on each card to note attendance, and refiles the cards.

6. The instructor or program director checks the cards periodically and can instantly check who has been in class and when they have attended class.

7. When a member has received 25 dates marked on his card, his name is placed prominently on the Four Star Wall of Fame with one beautiful star beside it.

8. After a second 25 dates are marked, a second star is placed beside the member's name—then a third star after another 25 dates and fourth star after the fourth set of 25 dates.

9. Four stars beside the member's name represent 100 classes attended, and the member is awarded a Four Star T-shirt in recognition of performance and attendance in group exercise classes. (See the CD-ROM for a Four Star Program T-shirt logo.)

10. If a member comes to class twice a week for 50 weeks (nearly one year), she will have completed the Four Star Program and will have become a retained member of your club.

Tips for Success and Points to Consider

- The registration card should be heavier than regular paper so it will last for a full year.

- Cards must be checked every two or three weeks to determine who has not been attending the classes.

- Members get credit for attending any group exercise class. Members should name the class day, time, and type, which indicates which class attracted them to your group exercise program.

- If a member has not registered for a class in two or three weeks, she must be called and invited back.

- The Four Star Program is a great program to get inactive members back into the club. Call them and invite them to get registered.

- Seeing their names on a board with one or more stars next to it is a great incentive for members to continue participating.

- Although the Four Star Program is nearly a year long, the stars give recognition along the way. Small prizes can be awarded for one, two, or three stars.

- A party for all Four Star participants at least once a year is a great follow-up promotion for the Four Star Program.

- Taking the program beyond four stars is not necessary or recommended. After a member has been using your club for a full year, the member is more than likely going to remain a retained member and become involved in other programs in your club.

- A member may only register one class per day on the card. This is not a race! The idea is to keep members participating on a regular basis.

- Whenever a member joins the Four Star Club, that month (January to December) is the first month that is filled in on the card. Members may join at any time. This is a great program to get new members involved immediately.

- You may want to require that the program be completed in one year; however, I believe that is opening up a chance for failure rather than for success. The responsibility for tracking participation and ensuring success should be on the instructors and the program director, and of course the quality of the group exercise classes will in part determine success.

- Much of the success will be determined by the promotion and marketing of the program, but the real success will be in the follow-up. The staff must be held accountable for keeping the Four Star Program current, exciting, and filled with participants.

Variations

- The Four Star Program can be offered only to non-prime-time classes.
- The Four Star Program can be offered only to seniors.
- The Four Star Program can be offered only to yoga, Pilates, and tai chi participants.
- The Four Star Program can be a terrific tracking, recognition, and retention program for many other activity departments in your club.

Supplemental Material

- Four Star Program Registration Card
- Four Star Program Logo

New Year's Resolutions

Description

It's a fact! Every year members make New Year's resolutions to start exercising regularly and to get in shape—and then they break them. The New Year's Resolutions program can combat breaking both commitments. The purpose of the New Year's Resolutions program is to get new members, inactive members, and existing members to use the club twice a week for six weeks beginning January 1 and ending (around) February 14 (Valentine's Day). A second goal of the program is to involve the fitness staff and hold them accountable for the success of the program.

1. Contact all new members who have joined the club since October 1 and ask them to choose a New Year's resolution (from your list) that they would like to accomplish. Then ask them to join the New Year's Resolutions program.

2. Contact all members who have been sporadic or inactive since October 1 and ask them to do the same.

3. Have eight (or more) New Year's resolutions to choose from. You may get an excellent list from the suggestions the members give you:

   - To lose weight
   - To get in shape
   - To get back in shape
   - To quit smoking and exercise regularly
   - To exercise regularly
   - To increase my endurance and get more energy
   - To increase my strength and tone my body
   - To improve my flexibility
   - To lower my percentage of body fat
   - To lower my cholesterol
   - To lower my blood pressure

4. The New Year's Resolutions program can be broken into teams, each of which must have a staff person responsible and accountable for recruiting 15 new members and 5 inactive members. Note: 8 staff members $\times$ 20 members = 160 people using your club.

5. Hold a party with recognition and prizes for all members who completed the 12 exercise visits to the club and accomplished their resolution.

6. Give a bonus, award, or prize to the staff person whose entire team completed the 12 visits and accomplished their resolution. This is a great incentive for the staff captain to follow up with each of her members.

Tips for Success and Points to Consider

- You can run the program for longer than six weeks, but taking the program to Valentine's Day gives you an opportunity to sign everyone up for a follow-up program. (Always use one program to promote another.)

- You can require use of the club three times per week instead of two, but you want to make sure the participants will be successful. Perhaps you can require 15 workouts in six weeks, or, if there is an extra week available, use the time for makeups. Everyone should complete the program and win!

- Photos of the New Year's Resolutions team captains and their team members should be prominently displayed on a bulletin board. Specific measurements or results should not be displayed.

- Attendance in the program should be tracked.

Supplemental Material

New Year's Resolution Form

12 Days of Fitness

Description

The 12 Days of Fitness is obviously a play on the words of the Christmas carol, "The Twelve Days of Christmas." More important is the line in the song "On the twelfth day of Christmas, my true love gave to me . . ." And in the spirit of the season, this program encourages giving a gift—what better gift than the gift of fitness! This program will grow your business with new members, but the marketing strategies will be specific to existing active members, new members, inactive members, and potential members. The 12 Days of Fitness is a popular, productive, favorite program of clubs throughout the world. Although originally produced by Sales Makers, a marketing and management consultant firm, to increase membership sales, the program is a wonderful opportunity to involve all members in a special annual or semiannual event at your club. There are many innovative ways to make this program unique to your club and fun for the members.

1. Holiday greeting cards are sent to all members along with two 12 Days of Fitness membership certificates. Members give the certificates to their friends, relatives, or coworkers.

2. Recipients of the certificate are entitled to 12 consecutive days of free membership at the club—provided that they begin their free trial membership on or before December 31.

3. This program could pull a response equal to approximately 25 percent of your total membership. If your club has 1,000 members you should expect your members to refer about 250 trial members. You should convert at least 35 percent of the trial members if you get them into fun programs during their 12 days.

4. You must mail the certificates by the first Monday in December.

5. You must follow up the direct mail piece with a phone call or e-mail, in which you ask the following:
   - "Did you receive the certificates?"
   - "Do you require any additional certificates?"
   - "Whom are you planning to give the certificates to?"

6. The certificates are temporary membership cards during the 12 days that the recipients use them, beginning on their first visit.

7. The guests must all be called and invited to specific programs of their choice during that time.

8. Follow up! Follow up! Follow up!

Tips for Success and Points to Consider

- The 12 Days of Fitness program can be run on a semiannual basis. In July, run the 12 Days of Fitness program to increase sales and participation in the usual downtime of the year. You can either send a holiday greeting card promoting the program as "Christmas in July" or simply send a letter with the certificate to the same groups of people as in the December program. For example:

  - Send a 12 Days of Fitness letter to your existing members, asking them to give the free certificate to their friends.

  - Send a letter to your new members (those who joined during the last three months), welcoming them to the club and encouraging them to give the certificates to their friends, relatives, or coworkers. Note: New members are the most anxious to share the club experience with others like themselves.

  - Send a letter to your inactive members. Acknowledge that you have missed them and that this is a perfect opportunity to get reactivated. If there is any time they will become active it will be now—and will bring a friend as well.

- Send a letter to past guests or missed tours, people who toured your facility but didn't join. Thank them for visiting your club, and give them this second opportunity to make good on their New Year's resolutions and become valued members.

- Send a letter to former members, giving them an opportunity to come back. Not only would they get the complimentary passes for their friends, but if the former members rejoin, they could do so without a joining fee.

Variation

What a wonderful corporate opportunity program. Make this a special program for the corporations in your community.

Supplemental Material

- 12 Days of Fitness Greeting Card 1
- 12 Days of Fitness Greeting Card 2
- 12 Days of Fitness Certificate
- 12 Days of Fitness Letter

Courtesy of Sales Makers. www.sales-makers.com or 800.428.3334

Ladies' Luncheon

Description

There are many types of women-only programs in your club, and a Ladies' Luncheon, although a program in itself, should be part of all of them. Every club should have a Ladies' Luncheon. Here are some examples of Ladies' Luncheons. The purpose may be to grow a program, to retain the members, to recognize a particular niche, to bring socialization to a program, or to increase program participation within a certain time period.

1. The Ladies' Luncheon must be promoted well in advance and have a sign-up system.
2. The Ladies' Luncheon must include an activity event as well as a social luncheon.
   - A core cardio program—(treadmills, bikes, climbers)
   - A court sports round-robin
   - A circuit class
   - A sampling of group exercise programs
   - The Grand Prix
3. The Ladies' Luncheon should include some kind of a recognition program for program performance or attendance at the event (door prizes or awards).
4. Pictures of all the participants of a Ladies' Luncheon must be taken and displayed on a bulletin board for at least one month after the event. The Ladies' Luncheon is an event that every woman should want to attend. The members should feel as committed to the next party as they are to their next league match or group exercise class.

5. Involve all the women in the success of the program. Everyone attending should make a contribution to the luncheon, such as bringing food to a potluck luncheon. See the variations below for specific themes.

Tips for Success and Points to Consider

* The Ladies' Luncheon should be attended by as many staff people as possible. Your members want to get to know the staff personally and professionally. It is a great opportunity for the staff of other activity departments to promote other programs in the club.

* Managers and owners should make an appearance at every Ladies' Luncheon. It's a very easy way of forming a bond with the membership.

* If there is a theme involved with the Ladies' Luncheon, have staff wear costumes and definitely decorate the club. The ladies love it!

* Don't forget to take pictures. Display them visibly for at least one month and save them for promotion of the next Ladies' Luncheon.

Variations

* The Ladies' Luncheon may be given for a specific club program, but the year's calendar will provide you themes and dates to run the event almost any time during the year—St. Patrick's Day, Valentine's Day, Halloween, Easter, or Mother's Day. A theme will give everyone a good reason to attend. It will also spark conversation and excitement. If a holiday is the theme, the promotion is a cinch.

    - Halloween: The staff should definitely be in costume for the whole week of Halloween, as well as at the party.

    - Valentine's Day: Everyone wears something red, and little Valentine candies are inexpensive and fun.

    - St. Patrick's Day: Everyone wears something green, and the party is promoted with shamrocks that adorn the club.

    - Mother's Day: All the women get a carnation.

* The luncheon itself should involve the women. A potluck luncheon is an easy way out, but there are better, more fun ways of presenting the luncheon that also add to the commitment to the program.

    - A salad bar. The club provides the lettuce, and during the sign-up all the women sign their name next to a specific salad ingredient such as tomatoes, ham, turkey, onions, cheese, or olives. Add to the list rolls, butter, and desserts, and the luncheon is sure to be a huge success.

    - A taco party. The club provides the hamburger and taco shells, and all the participants sign their name next to a specific taco ingredient such as tomatoes, taco sauces, onions, olives, sour cream, or cheese. Add to the list rice, beans, and desserts, and the luncheon is sure to be a huge success.

* The Ladies' Luncheon can involve many programs within the program. The grand finale is the Ladies' Luncheon cookbook.

    - Keep all the recipes that are contributed to the luncheons throughout the year (or two years).

    - Take a snapshot of each of the contributors to place with each of the recipes (see page 182).

CRAB SNACKS ON ENGLISH MUFFINS

Mix all ingredients together and spread evenly over muffins. Cut into quarters. Place on cookie sheet and freeze. After frozen, remove and place in baggies and keep frozen.

When ready to use, broil frozen for about 10 minutes or until browned.

CRAB SOUFFLE
Sandy Coffman
The Racquet Ball Clubs

In a bowl combine:
6 eggs
1 can crab
1 stick butter, diced
1 cup shredded cheddar cheese
1 lb. carton cottage cheese
6 tblsp. flour stirred into cottage cheese
1 pkg. spinach souffle (thawed)

Mix thoroughly. Bake at 350° in a 9 x 13 pan for 1 hour.

FOR THE BEST IN UNDERGROUND LAWN SPRINKLING

COFFMAN'S RAINJET LAWN SPRINKLER SERVICE
2365 North Calhoun Road
Anytown, USA 12345

M. R. COFFMAN, PRESIDENT

CALL DAY OR EVE.
(555) 123-4567

- Take snapshots of the luncheon itself and include them in the cookbook.

- Sell advertising space to the members of the club or community. An ad can simply be a copy of a business card printed in the cookbook, as shown above. For example, 20 business cards sold at $50 each will give you $1,000 to cover or defray the cost of printing the cookbook.

- Sell your club cookbook through the club by October 1, just in time for Christmas presents!

• Ladies' Luncheons are wonderful opportunities for end-of-league parties such as for women's racquetball or tennis leagues.

• A *daytime* Ladies' Luncheon is a terrific event to have quarterly for all the women who participate in any part of the club during daytime (non-prime-time) hours. Depending on the size of your facility, a daytime Ladies' Luncheon will honor those who use your facility between 9 a.m. and 3 p.m.

• Invite all women from group exercise, the fitness center, court sports, and the pool to join in for a social celebration. Encouraging daytime participation will always be beneficial for your club. The evening or prime-time classes can be invited as well, even if it is a luncheon, because it is a one-day event.

• Invite all group exercise classes to enjoy a Ladies' Luncheon. It is a tremendous opportunity for all the instructors to socialize with the members and to promote their classes.

• Ladies' Luncheons help lap swimmers and aquatic exercisers to come together, meet one another, and celebrate their love for the water.

Supplemental Material

Ladies' Luncheon Flyer

Get Your Act Together

The purpose of Get Your Act Together is to provide a fun, social program that will encourage your members to come to the club to socialize and make new friends. Get Your Act Together provides the ultimate club environment for your members.

1. Get Your Act Together is basically a social program that is promoted as a contest night.
2. The contest night runs for four weeks every Thursday evening (or whatever evening you choose). Here is an example:
   - Hula hoops—"*You Provide the Hula, We'll Provide the Hoops!*" Hula hoops will be available during the week for practice, on request. Prizes can be given for the longest hula hooper or the one with the most intricate moves.
   - Limbo contest—Always a winner! "*How Low Can You Go? Get those abdominals and quadriceps in shape now!*"
   - Polka contest—A very aerobic dance indeed! The tango, salsa, and disco are some other possibilities. Make it fun!
   - Puttin' on the Hits! The Art of Karaoke!

Ladies' Affair

Description

The Ladies' Affair is a special one-day event—best run on a Saturday—that is obviously for women only but does not have to be specific to women-only clubs. It is a program that will generate activity from all four groups of members—new, existing, inactive, and potential. It is an excellent event that if offered annually will generate growth year after year. The program combines a club activity, a luncheon, and a "fair" setting, with tables or booths set up throughout the club. It's an event that can generate much interest from your members as well as your surrounding community. It can definitely be a marketing program for your club.

1. The Ladies' Affair is best centered around a court sports activity such as a racquetball or tennis tournament, which is set up as a one-day event and welcomes all skill levels and ages—each with their own division of play.
2. Women from other clubs should be invited to attend. The day not only is fun for the participants but also showcases your club.
3. The Ladies' Affair will take up the majority of the space in your club for approximately six to eight hours depending on the number of participants. The program will run from about 9 a.m. to 3 p.m.
4. The fair consists of various booths that are set up like a shopping bazaar and are open to members, participants, and guests continuously throughout the day. The booths contain crafts, retail products, and educational materials—much like a rummage sale or a flea market—which are displayed and sold during the Ladies' Affair. A booth is an eight-foot banquet table.
5. The booth space is sold to people displaying their products for a set amount of money (e.g., $30). The person purchasing each booth must donate a

door prize to be given at a drawing during the luncheon. Some (only a few) examples for booths are these:

- Arts and crafts
- Food (e.g., baked goods)
- Housewares
- Cosmetics
- Photography
- Artwork

6. The women will play in their event (tennis, racquetball) and be able to shop and socialize all day.

7. A luncheon is served for participants only.

8. An entry fee is charged for each participant and includes the tournament, the luncheon, door prizes, and trophies.

Tips for Success and Points to Consider

- Depending on the size of your club, 20 or more booths can be scattered throughout the club to showcase your club.
- Your pro shop can run special offers for your own booth space, and you can include an in-house fashion show during the luncheon.
- The nonmember entry fee should be larger than the member fee.

Variations

- The fair can be a health fair instead of a shopping bazaar. If your club is big enough to accommodate enough booths, you can combine the two.
- If you don't have a court sports program at your club, you could run the activities through your group exercise studio and the fitness center. Special 30-minute group exercise classes can be run throughout the day:
  - Yoga
  - Pilates
  - Tai chi
  - Taekwondo
  - Self-defense
  - Step
  - Balls
  - Salsa
- The fitness center can run demonstrations as well:
  - Short versions of the WOW! program
  - Circuit classes on the equipment
  - Fifteen-minute core cardio classes—treadmill, bike, climbers

Cruisin' Campaign

Description

The Cruisin' Campaign is a summer retention program designed to keep your members active from June through August. These are the months that clubs generally experience their greatest attrition. The program is easy and fun and requires a minimum of commitment. The object is to keep your members interested in your club! The incentive is the chance to win a four-day cruise.

1. This is a full-club program, so all the activity areas will have participation opportunities. Use all the activities in your club. Some large multipurpose facilities will have eight or more options, whereas others may have only a few areas for fitness available. For those, you may have to double up on required activities or get creative with various types of exercises or workouts.

2. This campaign should be open to members only. It is specifically important to get new members active and to keep existing members active. The Cruisin' Campaign can also be used to bring back the many members who joined in the winter months with good intentions but dropped out for one reason or another. Special marketing efforts will be needed to invite those members to join this program, but it could work very nicely for them and perhaps be instrumental in saving many members.

3. The drawing for the winner of the cruise will be done at a party at the end of the program. Participants' names are put in a box for the drawing each time they work out at the club in one of the designated activities.
   - Only one eligible workout per day is allowed.
   - Optional (fun) activities will be additional opportunities for putting names in the drawing to increase members' chances of winning.
   - Bonus opportunities for putting names in the drawing can be given for completing five eligible workouts in the fitness area, five in the group exercise program, or five in the court sports area.

4. Here are some examples of eligible workouts:
   - A fitness introductory class (e.g., core cardio class)
   - A circuit training class
   - Any workout with a personal trainer
   - Any group exercise class listed on the schedule
   - An introductory racquetball or tennis lesson
   - A round-robin event or tournament

5. Here are some examples of fun miscellaneous activities that will earn participants the opportunity of putting their name in for the drawing:
   - Juggle three tennis or racquetballs for a full minute (or 30 seconds)
   - Wear a club T-shirt (with logo) during a workout
   - Jump rope briskly for two minutes
   - Make five baskets on the basketball court
   - Yell out in a group exercise class, "Hey, Cancun, I'll be there soon!"

6. Each participant should have a Cruisin' Campaign sheet or card that is filed alphabetically at the club for tracking purposes. Participants get the card and the workout initialed by a staff person each time they come in.

Tips for Success and Points to Consider

- Get a cruise donated by a local travel agency or at the very least negotiate a trade for one.

- Sixty to eighty percent of the members who joined your club up to 90 days before the start of the program should be in the Cruisin' Campaign. Any member who joins the club within the first couple weeks of the program should join the Cruisin' Campaign as well. This will require a program director to set goals and divide responsibilities among the staff to market and promote the program. The staff will have to be held accountable for achieving this, so the promotions and marketing efforts must start no less than three weeks before the beginning of the program.

- Door prizes other than the grand prize (cruise) should be included in the party.

- If you charge an entry fee for the program, have Cruisin' Campaign T-shirts made up for the participants. Have the staff wear the shirts for the three weeks before the start of the program.

- If the program is run successfully, the Cruisin' Campaign will be an annual event that members will talk about and look forward to year after year.

Deck the Halls

Description

The holiday season is a busy time of year for your members, and December is often a slow month in the business. Deck the Halls is a fun program to keep your members active without a huge commitment or stressful goal. Keeping your members active makes Deck the Halls a great seasonal retention program. Of course, the program will end with a holiday party!

1. Deck the Halls will run between the holidays of Thanksgiving and Christmas . . . three to four weeks.

2. You can keep the program confined to the fitness center or any other specific exercise area, but it will be a more fun, productive program if it is run as a total club event.

3. The basic concept is that a member must use the club two times per week for the duration of the program.

4. A huge Christmas tree made of paper or poster board is put up on a wall. An ornament made of construction paper is placed on the tree for each member who joins the program.

5. Every time a member uses the club during the program, a foil star is put on his ornament. Anyone with six stars or more on their ornament is eligible for a prize at the club Christmas party.

Tips for Success and Points to Consider

- The promotion must be visible, memorable, and exaggerated.
- Each participant who completes the goal can get a prize such as an ornament with the club logo on it.
- Each participant who completes the goal can be eligible for a drawing for a prize given at the party.
- Several trees can be placed throughout the club. Each tree can be "owned" by a staff member who will be held accountable for the members who are on that tree. The staff member's picture can be put at the top of the tree. A specific color ornament can designate that a member is a new member, anyone who has joined the club since September 1. Each staff member will be responsible for getting a specific (goal) number of new members on his or her tree in addition to a specific (goal) number of total members.
- An active, aggressive marketing campaign including phone calls from all staff to the members will be necessary to make this program good for the club as well as the member.
- The "Name the Christmas Carols" game can be played just for fun, in the spirit of the season, and all completed entries can go into a drawing for prizes at your holiday party.
- You can also use the "Name the Christmas Carol" handout as an added part of any other program you are running in the season. Most important, use it in the spirit of adding fun to your program!

Variations

- You can deck the halls of your club with strings of paper Christmas lights or ornaments. Participants in the program get their names put on the lights or ornaments when they join Deck the Halls. Each time a member uses the club during the program, he puts his name in a drawing at the front of the club at the Countdown to Christmas table.
- Members may only get credit for one workout a day.
- Drawings for prizes can be done every day for the final week, with a grand prize drawing at the Christmas party, or all drawings can be done at the party. It is possible to have hundreds of participants in this valuable and fun retention program.
- Prizes given to the staff member who got the most members or new members to join the program make this an excellent employee retention program as well.

Supplemental Material

Name the Christmas Carols

20/20 Women's Life-Changing Club

Description

Weight loss is not easy! The 20/20 program incorporates moderate group exercise and sound nutritional counseling. Every club in the fitness industry today should offer a nutritional or weight loss program to their members. The 20/20 weight loss program is presented here for women only, but it could easily be marketed to men as well. It may even be offered as a Gentlemen's Club Weight Loss Program. As with all the programs in this book, innovation is key and your creativity may be the key to making the programs successful for your facility.

The purpose of the 20/20 Life-Changing Club is to offer a weight loss program that incorporates regular exercise, group support, leadership, and accountability along with a diet plan.

The 20/20 Women's Life-Changing Club is about losing 20 pounds in 20 weeks. Participants will sign up and commit to two 10-week sessions. By offering two separate 10-week sessions, a club is able to add beginning participants twice. The club is also able to reward participants for achievement midway through the 20 weeks or give struggling participants an opportunity for a new beginning after an initial 10-week session.

Four workouts per week are strongly recommended to achieve a successful result. The workouts must be interesting and fun so participants will remain active. The 20/20 is a group program, so the workouts must be done in a scheduled group format to cultivate the sociability of the program and the enjoyment of exercising. The workout, therefore, must be scheduled at various times during the week to accommodate all schedules—early morning, daytime hours, and late afternoon or prime time.

The workouts must change each week to incorporate cardio, weight resistance, and flexibility exercises. The workout sessions can also be used for weigh-ins, counseling, and meal planning.

Tips for Success and Points to Consider

- The 20/20 Women's Life-Changing Club will require constant follow-up. Weekly phone calls to the participants will be needed to ensure adherence to the program and participation in the workouts.
- Attendance awards will be as important as weight loss awards.
- You may want to limit the number of participants to 20 per session, to make the program exclusive (and more desirable).
- If you are running the program for the first time, you may want to offer a $100 reward to the first 20 participants who achieve the 20-pound goal.
- You may want to offer a 20/20 Life-Changing Club program to women only and one to men only during the same period. You could keep a fun challenge going between the two groups.

Supplemental Material

20/20 Weight Loss Flyer

Courtesy of 7 Flags Fitness & Racquet Club.

Heartthrobs Programs

The purpose of the Heartthrobs programs is to encourage participation and increase club use and retention. The Heartthrobs programs are designed around Valentine's Day—February 14. The general program is adaptable to many different activity areas of the club, and although several programs evolve from the Heartthrobs concept, capitalizing on the title "Heartthrobs," and the "heart" concept with Valentine's Day makes these programs fun and successful.

The Heartthrobs programs are promoted to all members of the club including existing members looking for a special fun program or diversification in their routines. It is an excellent program for all the new members who joined the club in December and January, especially those who did not get involved in a program. The Heartthrobs programs are also terrific as a tool to bring back all the inactive members who have not used the club in December or January. The Heartthrobs programs are incredibly important to your business.

- December is notorious for members not using the club. People are busy over the holidays—traveling, entertaining, shopping, and decorating.
- January is always a great month for selling memberships. Unfortunately, most people who join clubs in January are filled with great intentions and often either fail to get started or drop out by February or March.
- The majority of people need special programs and incentives to help them exercise regularly. Joining a club is the first step to success. Joining a program is the second step.
- Clubs tend to rest on their laurels in February, reveling in the fact that they have sold so many memberships, but experience has proven that without special programs and promotions, many members will quit.
- The Heartthrobs programs get them in and keep them coming in.

The Heartthrobs programs can take on many formats. The title, Heartthrobs, can be the name of one specific program or the title of the programming theme that will be promoted throughout your club and throughout your activity areas.

Keep in mind that programs must be promoted at least three weeks in advance of start-up time. Your promotions—fliers and bulletin boards—must be out by the middle of January, in the heart of your busy season, and an all-out marketing effort must be underway even while you are selling the memberships.

Invite all your senior members who are couples—married or with significant others—to come in and get their pictures taken for your wall of Heartthrobs. This invitation alone will bring your senior members into the club and give you an opportunity to promote an exercise program. Your senior members will enjoy a Heartthrobs Ball. Valentine's Day is a fantastic day for an Old-Fashioned Sweetheart Dance. Your group exercise studio can be turned into a Heartthrobs ballroom. You can be sure that everyone whose picture is on the wall of Heartthrobs will be there.

Here are some programs that will be part of your February (Valentine's) Heartthrobs theme. Your promotions throughout the club and the variety of programs available convey the message that everyone should be involved in one of the Heartthrobs programs in the club.

Heartthrobs in the Fitness Center

Description

The Heartthrobs fitness program is a general fitness program that will encourage people to exercise and use the club regularly. All workouts are to be done in the fitness center. Your catchphrase can be *"Exercise is good for your heart!"*

1. The program runs for six weeks—January 1 through February 14.
2. A huge heart is placed on the wall in the fitness center. Every member who joins the six-week Heartthrobs program gets a small paper heart put on the huge heart. Put the name of the member on his or her heart.
3. Each time a member works out in the fitness center during the six-week period, a foil heart or star is placed on his paper heart.
4. A member must have 12 stars on her paper heart to receive a prize at the Heartthrobs party.
5. A star must be placed on a member's paper heart by a staff person.

Tips for Success and Points to Consider

- Each fitness instructor can be the Heartthrob of a huge heart and all the members on his heart are his Heartthrobs. The members will ask each other, *"Who is your Heartthrob?"* That staff person will be held accountable for seeing that all his Heartthrobs complete 12 workouts and attend the Heartthrobs party.

• Charge an entry fee to cover the cost of the Heartthrobs party and for a T-shirt with a big heart on it, the club logo, and the word *Heartthrob.*

Heartthrobs Personal Training Package

The purpose of this program is to promote the personal training program in your club. Offer a special Heartthrobs price for a four- or six-week package of personal training sessions for couples only. You are encouraging people to sign up as couples, to get in shape together. It's a great promotion!

1. The Heartthrobs Personal Training Package can be sold to one couple or to two individuals. This will give an even better price to your members and will get people into the habit of working out together.

2. The Heartthrobs Personal Training Package can be sold to members joining in January and finishing the package during the week of February 14 or to members joining your club the week of February 14 and using the package for the six weeks following Valentine's Day. It's a great opportunity to grow your personal training program and introduce personal training to members who may not buy it on their own.

3. Be sure to put pictures of your personal training Heartthrobs on the wall. These pictures do not necessarily have to be "before and after" shots. The pictures are wonderful promotional tools for your personal training program as well as the Heartthrobs program. Asking for testimonials is a good idea too!

Courtesy of Sandy Coffman

Heartthrobs Mixed-Doubles Events

Description

What a wonderful excuse for a mixed-doubles round-robin or tournament in your court sports program! The Heartthrobs mixed-doubles racquetball round-robin will include divisions for all levels of play. Be sure to check out the court sport round robins presented in chapter 6. It's a good program to introduce doubles play to many members and especially as mixed doubles. Because this is a special fun event, an instructional hour before the round-robin may be included. A Heartthrobs mixed doubles tennis tournament is sure to become an annual event. If you are fortunate to have both racquetball and tennis available in your club, the two events can run simultaneously and everyone—racquetball participants and tennis participants—can join the party. Make it an annual event that members will all want to become part of year after year. By the way, all players must wear something red! Make it fun!

1. The Heartthrobs round-robin can be run as a special one-day event either on the weekend before Valentine's Day or on the day itself.

2. An entry fee will help pay for the party afterward and for Heartthrobs T-shirts for all the players.

Supplemental Material

Heartthrobs Word Search

Nutrition and Weight Loss

A sound nutrition and weight loss program should be part of every club or health facility. However, very few clubs have any organized program at all, and those that do are seldom touting any huge success stories (outside of a few individuals). Given the obesity problem in the United States and indeed the world, the nutrition and weight loss programming efforts will have to escalate in our clubs and our industry as a whole. I do know that the majority of people will find success in fitness if it is fun and that group programs are more fun than individual programs. I know, too, that nutrition itself is not what we would call a fun topic, but if you apply the group concept to a nutrition and weight loss program and organize the program as outlined in the first half of this book, you will undoubtedly create a whole new programming department in your club that will grow your business and help people along the way.

The first thing is the title of the program: It may be the one thing that stops your marketing strategy in its tracks. I'm sure you can come up with many ways to give a new twist to a nutrition and weight loss program; here are a few ideas to think about:

- Pinch an Inch
- Don't Say "Nuts" to Nutrition—They're Good for You!
- We're All in This Together
- Let's Do Lunch
- Diets Don't Work
- Dump the Diet, my personal favorite

Dump the Diet

Description

The purpose of Dump the Diet is to create a healthy lifestyle that works and is workable. Dump the Diet covers every phase of healthy living and eating but incorporates group activities along the way. It emphasizes a "lifestyle forever" approach to weight loss rather than a quick project. Most important, this nutrition and weight loss program continually promotes and involves all the other programming areas of your club while educating and entertaining you on a weekly basis. It can truly be a club within your club.

1. Dump the Diet is generally for anyone interested in losing 10 to 25 pounds. Those pounds may be the same ones they've been trying to lose all their lives, or they may be brand-new. Everyone will understand.

2. The group meets one time a week for conversation and education. Continually explore the pros and cons of the latest diet craze and books on the bestseller list. Solicit outside speakers if possible:
   - The Atkins Diet—Dr. Robert Atkins
   - The South Beach Diet—Arthur Agatston, MD
   - Eating for Life—Bill Phillips
   - Younger Next Year—Chris Crowley and Henry S. Lodge
   - The Three Hour Diet—Jorge Cruise
   - Eat Right 4 Your Type—Dr. Peter J. D'Adamo
   - 8 Weeks to Optimum Health—Dr. Andrew Weil

3. You can include cooking classes for group sessions.

4. Have members bring in 100-calorie snacks.

5. Hold fitness assessments before and after an 8- or 10-week program.

6. Have a group weigh-in before and after an 8- or 10-week program.

7. Hold two exercise sessions each week—one cardiorespiratory, one strength training.

Tips for Success and Points to Consider

- Have a pharmacist or doctor talk about supplements and drugs for weight loss.
- Have short (two-minute) progress reports from each of the group participants.
- Give prizes for attendance.
- Make a confirmation call to each participant before every meeting.
- Gather menus from around your community and discuss how to order and make substitutions.
- Have a restaurant experience.
- If more than one group is meeting at your club, make the percentage of the group weigh-in loss be a friendly competition.
- Periodic demonstrations are a must! Get a table, a chef's apron and hat, a blender and a hot plate, and you are ready to go. This promotion will be produc-

tive not only for your weight loss and nutrition programs but also for selling your cookbook as well. What to demo?

- 100-calorie snacks

- Smoothie samples

- No-fat treats

- Yummy vegetables with low-cal, no-fat dips

- Baked instead of fried anything

- No-salt bites of anything

Variation

Make it a family affair! Teach the kids about nutrition with mom and dad.

Afterword

The programs presented in this book are not to be considered complete and unabridged. They are presented in part to get your creative juices flowing. They are a sampling of the many opportunities you have to create joy, entertainment, and success in marketing health and fitness in your facility. The programs are presented in a manner for you to build on, improve on, and transform into new and innovative success stories. The systems, if followed, are proven and guaranteed. No program needs to fail!

We will continue to improve our product, but we are on a journey toward something bigger and more encompassing than just providing the product that can provide a fit body. The fun experience—the mind, body, and uplifted spirit of fitness—far outweighs the technical aspect of fitness. The members themselves must make the commitment to fitness, and we can help them by creating an environment that helps make it happen. New clubs, big clubs, small clubs, and upgraded and updated facilities will continue to get people through the doors, but changing what they do inside the building—programming—is the way to keep them there. Fitness is the destination, programming is the journey, and for all our members and for all our professionals, the joy is in the journey.

Club programming success—guaranteed!

1. The perfect leader—This person must be knowledgeable, certified, happy, and energetic, with a sincere understanding of the industry and the needs of its members. The perfect leader is a professional communicator.

2. A personal invitation—Every member must believe that you have turned her membership number into a name. Your programs must be personalized with invitations to participate, not merely run on expectations.

3. Specific schedules—Every program must have a beginning and an end to provide room for new members, comeback players, and potential members. Every ending offers opportunities for growth and new beginnings.

4. Group participation—The "club" environment suggests that people come together for common interests and goals. In our industry, that goal is a happy, healthy lifestyle. We must provide the club experience.

5. Fun!—Attrition is our only enemy. No one quits your club because they are having too much fun. People come for fitness, and they stay for fun.

6. Sociability—People need and respond to other people. Sociability and camaraderie will create a fun club environment and must be part of successful programs.

7. Recognition—Everyone needs recognition of performance or achievement. Recognition is best when done by the leader in front of peers.

8. Exclusivity—Club members and all people have various interests and represent all ages, all making up different niches. Niche marketing is putting similar people together, and it will surely contribute to successful programming.

9. Exciting promotions—Promotions tell your story. Exciting promotions create enthusiasm for your programs.

10. Follow-up programs—The goal of programming is retention, so always use one program to promote the next.

11. Tracking system—It is impossible to recognize achievement without tracking performance.

12. Accountability of staff—Every program must have a responsible leader who tracks the performance of the participants and follows the necessary steps and systems to achieve program success.

13. Sense of urgency—Programs must be timely. Allowing enough time for exciting promotions is important, and a member must be encouraged to react to the promotions within a certain time period.

14. Incentive—Giving incentives to join a program in a timely manner is a good marketing

tool, and providing incentives to maintain participation is a good retention strategy.

15. Easy entry—Getting active and involved in programs should not be complicated or intimidating. Programs should be available for any member to participate in immediately.

16. Purpose—Every program should be able to define its purpose. Whom is it for? What will it accomplish?

17. Goal—Certain goals are necessary to set: How many members are needed? What percentage of growth is needed? How many participants join a follow-up program? The goal of programming is retention.

18. Marketing plan—Identify your target market and use effective promotional strategies and communication skills to reach it.

19. Budget—Every program, like every business, must have a budget that meets its financial needs to achieve success.

20. Results—Fun, fitness, and financial success.

To love what you do and know that it matters—can anything be more fun?

Index

Note: The italicized *f* following page numbers refers to figures.

About the Author

Sandy Coffman is president and owner of Programming for Profit in Bradenton, Florida. She has more than 30 years' experience in professional programming and staff training for health clubs and recreational facilities. Coffman was part owner, program director, and staff trainer for three multipurpose facilities in Milwaukee, Wisconsin, for 11 years. She now consults, trains, and gives motivational and educational presentations for businesses and corporations worldwide.

Coffman is a contributing writer to many trade publications and a guest lecturer at several state universities. She is a provider of continuing education credits for the American Council on Exercise, the Aerobics and Fitness Association of America, and the Senior Fitness Association. She is on the faculty of the International Council on Active Aging and works extensively to promote fitness among older adults.

Specializing in customer service, communication skills, retention, programming, niche marketing, and staff evaluations, Coffman's client list—in addition

Courtesy of Sandy Coffman

to for-profit fitness clubs—includes the United States Tennis Association (USTA), where she serves as a consultant for the Welcome Back to Tennis program, a multitude of YMCAs and YWCAs, and several city park and recreational departments.

Coffman is a featured national and international speaker and was voted the International Health, Racquet and Sportsclub Association's Top Convention Speaker in content and presentation. She has received awards for her presentations at the European Bodylife Conference, the Canadian Can-Fit-Pro Conference, and the Italian Fitness Federation.

CD-ROM Installation Instructions

System Requirements

You can use this CD-ROM on either a Windows®-based PC or a Macintosh computer.

Windows

- IBM PC compatible with Pentium® processor
- Windows® 98/NT 4.0/2000 or XP recommended
- Adobe Reader® 8.0
- Microsoft® PowerPoint® Viewer 97 (included)
- 4x CD-ROM drive

Macintosh

- Power Mac® recommended
- System 10.4
- Adobe Reader® 8.0
- 16 MB RAM (32 MB recommended)
- Microsoft® PowerPoint® Viewer OS9 or OS10 (included)
- 4x CD-ROM drive

User Instructions

Windows

1. Insert the *Successful Programs for Health and Fitness Clubs* CD-ROM. (Note: The CD-ROM must be present in the drive at all times.)
2. Select the "My Computer" icon from the desktop.
3. Select the CD-ROM drive.
4. Open the "Contents.pdf" file.

Macintosh

1. Insert the *Successful Programs for Health and Fitness Clubs* CD-ROM. (Note: The CD-ROM must be present in the drive at all times.)
2. Double-click the CD icon located on the desktop.
3. Open the "Contents.pdf" file.

For customer support, contact Technical Support:

Phone: 217-351-5076
Monday through Friday
(excluding holidays)
between 7:00 a.m. and 7:00 p.m. (CST)

Fax: 217-351-2674

E-mail: support@hkusa.com